Pre-Reformation Wills

from Rickmansworth Parish

(1409 to 1539)

edited by Heather Falvey

Rickmansworth Historical Society

First published 2021

ISBN: 978-0-9544583-5-5

British Library Cataloguing-in-Publication Data
A catalogue record for this book is available form the British Library.

Rickmansworth Historical Society

Printed & bound by Print2Demand
1 Newlands Road, Westoning, Beds, MK45 5LD

To Dr Margaret Aston

Her detailed study of the arson attack on St Mary's in 1522 is the inspiration for this edition of the pre-Reformation parishioners' wills.

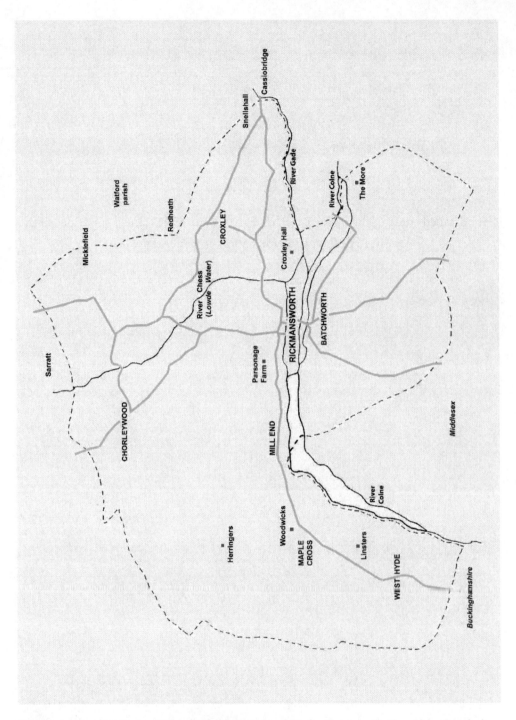

Figure 1: Sketch map of the original parish of Rickmansworth (by Alan Crosby)

Contents

Illustrations, Figures & Tables

Cover

Figures — Page

Tables

Preface

Over the years I have been involved in several projects to transcribe and publish medieval wills, including the second part of the Baldwyne probate register from the archdeaconry of Sudbury (Suffolk) for the Suffolk Records Society, and two registers from the Prerogative Court of Canterbury and a series of wills in English registered in the Prerogative Court of York for the Richard III Society. During that time I had looked at some medieval wills from Rickmansworth parish; in 2019 I decided it was time to look at all of them. Fortunately I went to the Hertfordshire Archives and Local Studies in February 2020 to obtain copies of those documents that I had not already got; during the following months of lockdown I transcribed and, where necessary, translated them and wrote the Introduction.

I had studied many sixteenth century Rickmansworth wills for my dissertation entitled 'Rickmansworth and Croxley: a community in south-west Hertfordshire during the mid-sixteenth century' for an Advanced Certificate in Local History at the Institute of Continuing Education at the University of Cambridge (UCICE), completed in 1996. My interest in the local history of the area, however, had begun with the medieval manor house, or palace, of the More, on the site of what is now Northwood Prep School, researching not only its former residents but also the actual building. I moved on to other areas of study but retained an interest in the medieval parish and manors of Rickmansworth. Parts of the Introduction began as talks given to the Rickmansworth Historical Society and to participants in the Richard III Society's Milles Wills Project.

This book adds to the growing number of published medieval wills, but, as my analysis towards the end of the Introduction demonstrates, this collection is significant due to the sheer number of medieval wills and other probate documents surviving from the original extensive parish of Rickmansworth preserved in the probate registers of the archdeaconry of St Albans. As much as one would like to claim that this is because parishioners of medieval Rickmansworth were special in some way, it is, of course, due to the administrative methods used by the archdeaconry at the time and to the subsequent preservation of the archive that it generated.

Acknowledgements

Thanks are due to Professor Mark Bailey for writing the foreword to this book. Back in 1993 he was my first local history tutor: the UCICE Certificate in English Local History (1993–95) was the beginning of 14 years of part-time academic study culminating in a PhD at the University of Warwick. Thanks to Chris Bennett and his excellent team at Hertfordshire Archives and Local Studies for allowing me to look at, and photograph, wills in the original probate registers as well as download microfilmed images, and for permission to reproduce H. W. Bursch's painting on the cover. Thanks to the Marquess of Zetland for permission to reproduce Richard Wilson's 'View from Moor Park towards Rickmansworth' and to Andrew Macnair for providing a map of the Rickmansworth area from his digitized version of the *Map of Hartfordshire* by Dury and Andrews. Thanks to the British Library Board for permission to reproduce Thomas Baskerfeild's picture of Rickmansworth church. Thanks to Alan Crosby who drew the sketch map of the old parish and to Anita Pond who designed the lovely cover. My medieval Latin is not brilliant, so special thanks are due to Anne Drewery for translating the more obscure Latin sections that defeated me in several of the documents.

And finally credit must be given to the late Dr Margaret Aston: her magnificent study of the arson attack on St Mary's church in 1522 inspired my own research on the pre-Reformation parish. This book is dedicated to her memory.

Foreword

Wills are a very important source for historians of late medieval and early modern England. They provide various insights into the lives of ordinary people: their religious convictions and piety, their family and social networks, their wealth, their personal and domestic possessions, and the tools of their trade. It is no surprise, then, that scholarly editions of wills – translated and edited by a reputable editor, and published by a county or learned society – are popular (and well thumbed) additions to institutional and personal libraries. Yet this publication of extant wills from the parish of Rickmansworth between 1409 and 1539 is no ordinary edition of wills for many reasons.

First, the sheer number of wills and other probate material to have survived from this far corner of Hertfordshire is unusually large, and some unusually early survivals, too. In total, 213 wills are published in this edition, with an additional 35 probate documents of various kinds. One reason for the large survival of material is the enormous size of the late medieval parish of St Mary's Rickmansworth, which covered 10,000 acres and contained a number of discrete settlements within its almost 26-mile boundary.

Second, the medieval fabric of the parish church of Rickmansworth has not survived, so the wills provide rare snippets of information that enable us to reconstruct a sense of its layout and furnishings: its chapels, images, and side altars.

Third, in 1522 this church was the target of an arson attack that destroyed the chancel and the vestry. The identity of the attackers is not definitely known, but they were almost certainly Lollards from nearby parishes seeking revenge for recent local persecutions. The wills provide evidence of the conformist parochial community donating funds over the next few years to effect the necessary repairs. The whole episode is carefully reconstructed to complement Margaret Aston's earlier work on the subject. Very few medieval parish churches were the target of arson attacks.

Fourth, the Introduction ranges widely across a variety of topics, which partly illustrate the rich seam of information contained within wills but also display the editor's exceptional knowledge of late medieval and early modern Rickmansworth.

Heather Falvey lives locally and has been researching its history for many years, and her knowledge, expertise and passion are apparent on every page of the book. The Introduction includes, inter alia, tables documenting references to saints' images within the church, a reconstruction of its layout, biographical details of the men serving as parish clergy, population levels, local peaks of mortality (notably a local plague outbreak in 1471–2 and a national epidemic in 1479), agriculture, occupations and local topography. We are provided with a colourful and expertly-crafted picture of a working community, and some of the leading personalities within it.

Finally, Heather is a top class editor as well as an incomparably well-informed local historian. Consequently, the Introduction concludes with an accessible and accurate background to the contemporary probate system and the compilation of wills, which will be highly valuable to any student or local historian seeking to understand the system.

There is, then, a great deal in this volume to attract the interest and to reward the attention of local residents and the membership of the Rickmansworth Historical Society. It will be read widely and widely admired.

Mark Bailey
Professor of Later Medieval History
University of East Anglia
July 2021

Abbreviations

Aston, 'Troubles of churchwardens'	M. Aston, 'Iconoclasm at Rickmansworth, 1522: Troubles of churchwardens', *Journal of Ecclesiastical History*, 40 (1989), pp.524–552
BL	British Library
Duffy, *Stripping of the Altars*	E. Duffy, *The Stripping of the Altars: Traditional Religion in England 1400–1580* (New Haven and London, 1992)
HALS	Hertfordshire Archives and Local Studies, Hertford
HRS	Hertfordshire Record Society
TNA	The National Archives, Kew
OED	*Oxford English Dictionary* (online version)
VCH Herts	W. Page ed., *The Victoria History of the Counties of England, A History of Hertfordshire*, 4 vols (London, 1902–1914)
Wills at Hertford	B. Crawley, ed., *Wills at Hertford, 1415–1858* (British Record Society, London, 2007)

The name of Rickmansworth

The spelling of the name of the parish had numerous variants, frequently based on Rykmersworth. In the Introduction, except when quoting from an original document, the standard modern spelling has been used. In the main text the spelling is given as in the original document, including abbreviated forms. The 'er' was often abbreviated by a hook between the 'm' and the 's': this is shown as [er]. The probate clerks frequently abbreviated this long name simply to Ryk, partly, I suspect, to save precious space in the register.

The name of the parish

Within the wills parishioners usually referred to their parish church (or its churchyard) as being of St Mary or of the Blessed Mary; only William Gybbys (79) referred to the churchyard of the Blessed Virgin Mary and John Rydale (130) to the parish church of the Glorious Virgin Mary. In the Introduction it is referred to as St Mary's; the the main text the name is reproduced as written in the will.

Notes on the documents

Numbering

Each document has been allocated a number in the main text. In the Introduction and footnotes the number given in brackets after a testator's name is the number of their will (or other probate document). The documents have been published here in chronological order of writing; in many other editions of wills they are published in order of probate date. Although the latter method indicates the order in which parishioners died, I decided to present these wills in order of writing because it gives a chronology of life (and perhaps illness) in the parish. Most of the wills were written not long before death, but in some cases although the testator recovered from their current illness they did not make another will.

Old and new style dating

Prior to 1752 the new year began on 25 March, rather than 1 January. This can be seen in wills that were written in, say, November and granted probate in the following January. For example, the will of Robert Randolf (220) was written on 22 November 1525 and granted probate on 23 January 1525, which in modern dating would be 23 January 1526. To avoid confusion, in the wills and probate clauses such dates have been indicated by 'double dating', so the probate date of Randolf''s will is given as 23 January 1525/6. In the text of the Introduction such dates have been modernised.

Contemporaries were aware of the 'old style' dating. In some wills (none here) the year in a date between 1 January and 24 March was said to be 'according to the computation of England'. Occasionally here the date is given in the 'new style'. For example, the will of John Rolffe the elder (135) is given as being made 23 March 1485; it was granted probate on 24 May 1485.

Date of probate

In the probate clause the year in which probate was granted may be described as 'the year abovesaid'. This is referring to the year in the previous probate clause or the year written at the top of that page in the register; it was not necessarily year in which the relevant will was written and which was given above in that will.

Money, Weights and Measures

Money:
1 shilling (s) contained 12 pennies (d)
1 pound (£) contained 20 shillings (s) or 240 pennies (d)
1 noble was 6s 8d (a coin equal to 1/3 of £1)
1 mark was 13s 4d (a sum of money, not a coin; equal to 2/3 of £1)

Weight:
1 pound (lb) contained 16 ounces, approximately 0.45 kg
1 stone contained 14 pounds

Length:
1 foot contained 12 inches, approximately 30 cm
1 yard contained 3 feet, approximately 0.9 m
(See the Glossary other specific lengths.)

Liquid measure:
1 quart contained 2 pints, approximately 1.14 litres
1 gallon contained 8 pints, approximately 4.55 litres

Corn measure:
1 bushel contained 4 pecks, approximately 27 kg
1 quarter contained 8 bushels, approximately 217 kg

Land area:
1 acre contained 4 roods, approximately 0.4 hectare

Pre-Reformation wills from Rickmansworth parish (1409 to 1539)

On 27 November 1436, John Deye (28) of 'Rykmersworth', being of sound mind, made his will. After bequeathing his soul to God and requesting burial in St Mary's churchyard, he made various religious bequests, including 8d to the light (or candle) of the Blessed Trinity, 12d each to the lights of the Holy Cross (the rood) and St Katherine, 6d to the light of St Edmund, and 3s 4d to the church's fabric. Medieval wills such as Deye's reveal details of life in the pre-Reformation parish and also of the parish church itself. The terminal date used here for the 'pre-Reformation' period is December 1539. Although, in general terms, in England the officially sanctioned Reformation began either with the opening of the 'Reformation Parliament' in 1529, or when the Act of Supremacy was passed by Parliament in 1534, or when the Ten Articles were issued by Convocation in 1536,[1] arguably in south-west Hertfordshire a more significant event was the surrender, on 5 December 1539,[2] of St Albans Abbey, which not only owned all of the manors in Rickmansworth but also had the right to appoint the vicar. The last will recorded here, therefore, is that of the wealthy baker, Thomas Spenser (248), which was made on 22 August 1539.

In the case of St Mary's at Rickmansworth the fact that medieval wills may provide information about the medieval parish church is particularly relevant because nothing remains of that medieval building: the existing tower was built in 1630; church itself was demolished in 1825 and rebuilt soon after; that building was demolished in 1888 and replaced by the present church, which was dedicated in 1890.[3] That building probably has much the same footprint as the medieval church. A plan of the latter, drawn in 1825, shows its layout at that time. (Figure 2). From the plan it is clear that there had been some changes since the medieval period. For example, the font had probably been moved: the plan shows it by the pulpit, but usually it would be near the north door.

---

[1] S. Doran and C. Durston, *Princes, Pastors and People: The Church and Religion in England, 1500-1700* (2nd edition, London, 2003), p.206.

[2] E. Roberts, *The Hill of the Martyr: An Architectural History of St Albans Abbey* (Dunstable, 1993), p.153.

[3] See, for example, G. Cornwall, 'In parenthesis', *The Rickmansworth Historian*, 34 (Spring 1978), pp.843–847.

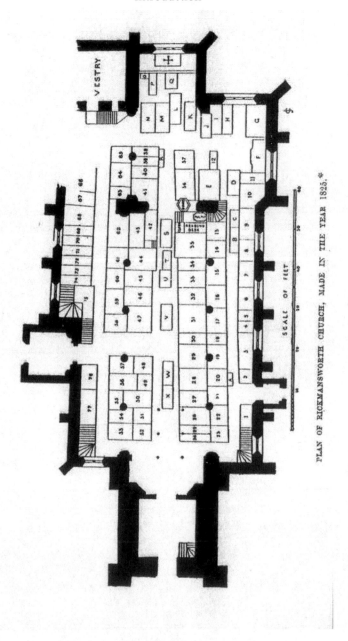

Figure 2: Plan of St Mary's drawn in 1825. The high altar at the east end of the chancel is denoted by ✚ (at the top of the page).

From: J. E. Cussans, *The History of Hertfordshire*, vol. III, *The Hundred of Cashio* (London, 1881), p.150.

Figure 3: St Mary's church and Mr Whitfield's house (the Bury) (c.1787-1806) by Thomas Baskerfeild

A drawing by Thomas Baskerfeild of the old church in the late eighteenth or early nineteenth century shows the north side and the seventeenth century tower. (Figure 3.) There are two other drawings by him, one showing the west face of the tower and the other the tower and lychgate from Church Street.[4] There are two pictures of the old church in a collection at HALS, but they too are of the north side and the tower.[5] (One has been reproduced on the front cover.) None of the surviving drawings show the chancel at the east end, which the plan suggests was quite small.

This Introduction discusses both medieval wills and medieval Rickmansworth. Having outlined the physical extent of the parish, extracts from wills demonstrate features of the medieval church's interior and how parishioners contributed to its fabric. Some significant events in the 1430s, 1520s and 1530s that impacted on parish life are summarised. The size of the parish's population is estimated using taxation returns from 1307 and 1524. There is a discussion of many local place names recorded in the wills, of the development of the name 'Rickmansworth', and of evidence for parishioners' connections with other places. The number of probate documents surviving from pre-Reformation Rickmansworth is analysed and, by comparison with survivals from elsewhere, it is clear that this is a significant collection. The English medieval probate process is explained, and also what these particular wills reveal about the probate process in the archdeaconry of St Albans, in which Rickmansworth was situated. Finally the contents of a will are explained.

Throughout the Introduction the word 'will' is used as a generic term. In theory the will (Latin: *ultima voluntas*) dealt with the disposal of landed property and the testament (Latin: *testamentum*) covered religious bequests and the disposal of personal property.[6] Technically most of the documents referred to here were testaments, but as will is the more familiar term, it is used in the following discussion. For the sake of simplicity 'testator(s)' has been used throughout; the female equivalent is testatrix (testatrices).

---

[4] BL, Additional MS. 9063, f. 216r, 'Rickmansworth from Mr Whitfield' (the tower); f. 217r, 'The Exterior to Rickmansworth Church' (the tower & lychgate and Church Street).
[5] HALS, DZ/119/2/202A, Rickmansworth church, by H. W. Bursch (dated 1835 but of the old church) and 202E, 'Rickmersworth church', drawn by Thomas Hearne, engraved by John Pye, c.1815.
[6] In the transcripts *testamentum* (and the variations in its Latin case endings) has always been translated as 'testament'.

The pre-Reformation parish

The original parish of Rickmansworth, adjoining both the Buckinghamshire and Middlesex borders with Hertfordshire, covered approximately 10,000 acres.[7] The parish boundary measured nearly 26 miles and encompassed the settlements at Batchworth, Chorleywood, Croxley, Maple Cross, Mill End and West Hyde as well as Rickmansworth itself, where the church of St Mary was situated.[8] The church belonged to the abbey of St Albans, and had been confirmed to the abbey by Pope Honorius III in 1219.[9] The abbey was therefore the rector and held the advowson of the vicarage, that is, had the right to appoint the vicar. It was only in the nineteenth century that the various settlements gained their own parish churches: in 1845 the chapel of Christ Church was built at Chorleywood; in 1846 part of the parish was formed into the district chapelry of West Hyde; parts were assigned to the chapelries of Northwood (Middx) in 1854, of Croxley Green in 1872, and of Mill End in 1875.[10] Prior to these new churches being built, inhabitants were expected to worship at St Mary's regardless of the distance from their home. Marriages were to take place there, children were to be baptized there and parishioners were buried in the churchyard, or occasionally inside the church. St Mary's was the centre of parish life. Thus, unintentionally, the title *Pre-Reformation wills from Rickmansworth parish* is a little misleading: they are wills from all over the old parish, not simply from Rickmansworth itself. Parishioners' wills might reveal details about the church building and something of places within the parish, but very rarely did testators state in which settlement they lived, so although all parts of the parish are represented in the wills, it is almost impossible to pinpoint in which particular settlement the testator resided. It does seem likely, however, that those testators who made bequests to other parish churches lived in that general direction, so a bequest to Sarratt parish church might indicate an inhabitant of Chorleywood, to Chalfont St Peter (Bucks) an inhabitant of Maple Cross, to Watford an inhabitant of Croxley.

---

[7] *VCH Herts*, vol. 2, p.371. When, in 1898, the ecclesiastical parish was divided into three civil parishes, the area of Rickmansworth Urban was 574 acres, that of Rickmansworth Rural 7,463 acres, and that of Chorleywood 1,986 acres.

[8] See B. Thomson, 'Rickmansworth parish – beating the bounds (a bluffer's guide)', (in 3 parts) *Rickmansworth Historical Review*, 9 (June 2016), pp.10–16; 10 (October 2016), pp.11–17; 11 (February 2017), pp.11–17.

[9] *VCH Herts*, vol. 2, p.385.

[10] *VCH Herts*, vol. 2, p.371.

St Mary's church

The plan of the original church (Figure 2) indicates that medieval St Mary's had a 'traditional' layout. At the east end of the church was the chancel with the high altar situated against the east wall, beneath the east window. However, some of this would have been obscured from parishioners' view because dividing the chancel from the nave would have been a rood screen. The (usually wooden) screen, which Eamon Duffy describes as framing the liturgical drama at the altar,[11] was, in effect, a row of unglazed windows on a dado, which was solid only to waist height. The dado would be decorated, perhaps with pictures of saints. There was also a doorway through which the ministers and choir would pass. Above, or on top of the screen, would be the rood, one of the main features of the church: Christ on the cross with the Virgin Mary and St John the Evangelist kneeling either side. The form of the rood itself varied: it might be a large carved wooden image, or a painting on a panel.[12] From an early sixteenth century document we know that there was a roodloft at St Mary's, access to which was probably via stairs, so that candles could be placed on the beam and lit to burn before the image of Christ crucified.[13] Such images were removed during the Reformation so few medieval roods have survived, but some new ones were erected during the 'Gothic Revival' of the nineteenth century. Indeed, given its name, it is perhaps not surprising that the Roman Catholic church of the Holy Rood in Market Street, Watford, has a very fine rood and roodloft.[14] Several of the Rickmansworth wills reveal features in the church because wealthy parishioners asked to be buried inside the church in a particular

---

[11] Duffy, *Stripping of the Altars*, p.112.

[12] For a detailed discussion of surviving rood screens, see the contributions in S. Bucklow, R. Marks and L. Wrapson, eds., *The Art and Science of the Church Screen in Medieval Europe: Making, Meaning, Preserving* (Woodbridge, 2017).

[13] R. C. T. Dade, *The Church of St Mary the Virgin, Rickmansworth* (Gloucester, c.1941), p.14, states that 'As early as 1456 there is a bequest left "to the new solar of the crucifix called the Rodeloft"'. This particular bequest, however, was not made to Rickmansworth church. It is in the will of Hugh Langford of Chipping Barnet, which follows the will of Margaret Slynger (63) in the register. The bequest of the '*novo solario crucifixi voc* 'le Rodeloft" is to the chapel of St John the Baptist in Chipping Barnet. The early sixteenth century document that mentions the Rickmansworth roodloft, is the 1522 indulgence (see Appendix 3).

[14] Although it has a rood and loft, it has no screen. The church was designed by John Bentley and paid for by Mr Stephen Taprell Holland of Otterspool (Aldenham). See R. Bennet and J. E. Wright, *Church of the Holy Rood, Watford: A History and Description of the Church* (Watford, 1989). The church opened in 1890.

location. Two requested burial in the nave in front of the rood: William Sebyn (188) and William Spone (247).

From John Deye's will (28) quoted above, we know that there were many images of saints in St Mary's. As Eamon Duffy observed, 'images filled the churches, gazing down in polychrome glory from altar-piece and bracket, from windows and niches'.[15] Many candles, often called lights, usually of costly beeswax, burned before the various images of saints and holy beings and on side-altars as well as on the high altar and on the candlebeam on the rood.[16] The cost of these candles had to be met out of church funds and many wills included bequests to 'lights'. Indeed, the first registered Rickmansworth will mentions several lights in the church, and this, in turn, reveals images that were definitely present in the church then, and there may have been more. On 8 March 1417 John atte Well (4) made bequests to the lights of the Trinity, of the crucifix (i.e. the rood), St Mary, St Edmund and St Katherine. Nearly 100 years later, in 1511, John Durrant alias Estbury (203) made bequests to the lights of the Trinity, St Mary the mother of our Lord, St Katherine, St Anthony and St Mary Magdalene. These two wills are quite detailed regarding images or lights: both mentioned 5 lights, including those of particular saints, not all the same.

Other wills reveal the presence of different images. (See Table 1.) The time when a particular image is first mentioned in a will may indicate a new acquisition, so perhaps, for example, the image of St George was only set up in the church in the 1520s. There is, however, no way of knowing, since no testator actually bequeathed an image or money toward the purchase of one, nor, unlike the parish of Bassingbourn (Cambs) where an image of St George was purchased and installed, are there any records of the parish raising money for this purpose.[17] At Rickmansworth there were at least three statues of the Virgin Mary (the church's patronal saint): one in the nave, one in the chancel and a statue of Our Lady of Pity, or the Piéta. Many testators, however, simply bequeathed an amount of money to 'all the lights' in the church.

---

[15] Duffy, *Stripping of the Altars*, p.155

[16] A. Sapoznik, 'Bees in the medieval economy: Religious observance and the production, trade, and consumption of wax in England, c.1300–1555', *Economic History Review*, 72 (2019), pp.1152–1174.

[17] For the Bassingbourn image of St George, see, for example, D. Dymond, ed., *The Churchwardens' Book of Bassingbourn, Cambridgeshire, 1496–c.1540* (Cambridgeshire Records Society, vol. 17, 2004), pp. xl, lx–lxviii.

Table 1: Images/lights in St Mary's, with the year when first mentioned

Image/light	Testator	Will	Year
St Mary (the Virgin) (location unspecified)	John Canoun	2	1409
Rood; Crucifix; Holy Cross	John atte Well	4	1417
Holy Trinity	John atte Well	4	1417
St Katherine (virgin & martyr)[a]	John atte Well	4	1417
St Edmund (the martyr)[b]	John atte Well	4	1417
Sepulchre[c]	John Elverede	16	1430
St Mary (in nave)	Richard Robard	38	1442
St Mary (in chancel)	John atte Hyde	51	1452
St Nicholas (bishop & confessor)	Katherine Turnour	69	1459
St Christopher	Katherine Turnour	69	1459
St Mary the Piéta	John Boterfeld	107	1476
St Clement	Roger Belche	110	1476
St Mary Magdalene	John Durrant	203	1511
St Anthony	John Durrant	203	1511
St George	William Belche	223	1526

Sources: Rickmansworth wills; column 3 gives the will numbers.

a. as Thomas Wodeward (52) specifically mentioned the lights of St Edmund and St Katherine the martyrs, it is likely that the image was of St Katherine of Alexandria.

b. St Edmund was an East Anglian saint, so the presence of his image in St Mary's might suggest early links with East Anglia

c. the Easter sepulchre, used for Holy Week and Easter ceremonies

Funds were collected to maintain the lights in Rickmansworth church: lights were kept burning before images so that the saint would intercede for the particular testator's soul and the souls of departed parishioners. Some of the bequests to lights were of animals, for example, Richard Slynger (57) bequeathed two sheep to the lights of St Edmund and St Katherine. These would probably be sold by the churchwardens to raise money to purchase wax. Such funds might be liable to tax, if the crown were desperate for money. The 1524 returns for the 1523 lay subsidy indicate that the sums of money in the various collecting boxes in St Mary's were taxed at 4d. Indeed the returns tell us how much was in each box: in the box of the Trinity 30s 4d, of St Katherine 20s and of St Anthony 20s 6d.[18]

---

[18] TNA, E179/120/114, returns of the 1523 Lay Subsidy made in 1524. See Appendix 2.

The saints' images in the church might have stood in a niche with a stone canopy or they may have stood on a side altar dedicated to that saint. In his will, written in March 1449, Thomas Gybbes (47) mentioned the altar of St Katherine, the altar of St Edmund and the candlebeam of the Blessed Virgin. Some wealthy parishioners asked to be buried in front of a particular image in the church. For example, in 1507 Edward Metcalfe (197) requested burial in front of the image of St Christopher, and in January 1526 Thomas Goldstone (222) asked to be buried before the altar of St Nicholas. In 1491 George Danyell esquire (153) requested burial in the aisle of St Edmund suggesting that there was more than simply an image on an altar dedicated to that saint.

Several wills provide details of the chapel of St Katherine within the church. From the will of Joan Stokker (204), dated 16 January 1513, it is clear that the chapel of St Katherine had recently had a new window. She requested that her executors 'with thadvyse of the discrete of the parissh, see that the new wyndowe that now is unglasid in saint Kateryn chapel be honestly glasid as hastely as it may be conveniently at my charge'. She then asked to be buried in that chapel and that 'a stone of marbill be bowte by myn executours tobe leyde on my husband John Stokker & me with a knowlage on the same who they ar that ar buryed ther under.[19] In fact, it seems that this chapel was a new addition to the church. In his will, which is undated but was granted probate on 1 July 1499, John Assheby (175b) asked to be buried in the new aisle of Rickmansworth church, between John Rolff (118) and the entry to the chapel.[20] Fourteen years later his widow Anne Asshby (209) asked for her body to be buried within the parish church of Rickmansworth 'afore the ymage of Saint Kateryn in the new Ile of the said chirch', presumably next to him, although she did not say so specifically. In 1631 the memorial recording her burial place was noted by John Weever in his book of *Ancient Funeral Monuments*: it is the only pre-Reformation Rickmansworth burial monument that he recorded.[21]

There was also another chapel relating to Rickmansworth church: the chapel of Our Lady of the Island. It has been suggested that this was the Lady Chapel within the parish church but several early sixteenth century wills explain that this was in fact a free-standing chapel in the churchyard. In February 1519 Edward Gybbys (214) asked to be 'buryed within the chapel of our lady of the Ilond being within the

---

[19] Indicating that she had had her husband buried in the place where she also wished to be buried – he had requested burial in the churchyard (John Stokker, 181).

[20] Rolff's will is heavily abbreviated in the register and his burial request is not recorded.

[21] J. Weever, *Ancient Funeral Monuments* (London, 1631), pp.590–591.

chirchyard of the parissh chirch of Rykmersworth'. He also left 3s 4d to the upkeep of the chapel. Several other parishioners left money for repairs to chapel of Our Lady of the Island, including John Stokker (181) 4d in 1502; Edward Metcalfe (197) 8d in 1507; Walter Barre (207) 8d in 1513; and Anne Asshby (209) 6s 8d in 1514.

Regarding the church building itself, many parishioners gave money to the fabric or repair (sometimes the 'reparation') of the church. In the early years of the sixteenth century a new vestry, where clerical vestments were kept, was being built. On 30 June 1506, John Frere (194) left 7s 'toward the making of a new vestyary'; in 1507 Edward Metcalfe (197) left 6s 8d towards 'the makyng of a new store house'; on 16 December 1509 John Gybbys (202) left 3s 4d to the construction of the new vestry; in March 1511 John Durrant (203) gave 6s 8d 'To the edification of the said church being done in this year'; and in January 1513 Joan Stokker (204) bequeathed 6s 8d 'to the fynysshyng of the new werk in the chyrch of Rykmersworth'. To put these bequests in context, in 1540 the daily wage rate for a carpenter was 7d to 8d, and for a labourer 4d to 5d.[22]

As already noted, several parishioners requested burial inside the church or the chapel in the churchyard: these would have been wealthy individuals. Within these wills there are 22 requests for burial in church and 6 for burial in chapel of Our Lady of the Island. The majority of burials, however, were in the churchyard next to friends and relatives. In 1462 William at Welle (74) asked to be buried in churchyard between his wives Margery and Rose. In 1505 Joan Baldewen (191) asked to be buried beside her first husband Thomas Reed in churchyard. On the other hand, in 1448 Thomas Edred (46) requested a specific burial spot in the churchyard: between the chapel of the Blessed Mary and the wall of the church.

As well as community in death, there was also a lively community of living parishioners. For example, there was a brotherhood or fraternity of Our Lady and St Katherine. Such religious guilds were popular in the medieval period. They were sources of sociability within the parish for the living and of remembrance of the dead. In return for a small annual subscription, members, both men and women, would receive a kind of funeral insurance because the guild would provide for their funeral, which would be attended by the brothers and sisters of the guild. Members prayed for the souls of departed brothers and sisters throughout the year and also

---

[22] D. Woodward, 'The determination of wage rates in the early modern north of England', *Economic History Review*, 2nd ser. XLVII (1994), pp.22–43, p.30.

enjoyed an annual dinner.[23] According to George Belche, one of the wardens in 1525-6, he had spent 'upon the dynar as he thynkyth abought five pownd[es]'.[24]

Parishioners might also donate money to the fraternity in their will, as did William Belche (223), who, in February 1526, bequeathed 6s 8d to 'the fraternity of the brotherhood of Our Lady & St Kateryn … to the intent that the brethern & sustren therof do pray for my soule'. It is possible that the guild held masses in the chapel of our Lady of the Island. In 1455 the will of Joan Edelyn (60) indicates that there was also a fraternity of the Holy Trinity in the parish. She made a practical bequest to the fraternities of the Holy Trinity and St Katherine of one large spit and an andiron, both part of the equipment used for cooking over a fire: two items to be used when the guild had its annual dinner. The guilds' dinners, and other parish social events, were held in the building known as the church house. It is very likely that the church house was the house known today as 'The Priory', which is adjacent to the churchyard (part of it is visible on the right of the cover picture). In 1473 Thomas Audytor (or Andytor) (100) bequeathed two sheep to the house called 'the Chyrchehowse'; again most likely the sheep would be sold and the money donated to the church house's funds. And in 1494 Katherine Rydale (163) gave a little brass pot to the church house. According to the 1524 returns of the lay subsidy, at that time there was £10 in the box of Our Lady's Fraternity: this was taxed at 5s.[25]

We know something about the workings of the Rickmansworth guild because of a dispute over the guild's funds was taken to the archdeacon's court in the autumn of 1532.[26] The wardens of the guild in the year 1525-6, George Belche and John Haydon, were accused of insufficient accounting. The onus fell on Belche to make their case since Haydon had died in 1531.[27] Several parishioners made depositions (statements) concerning the running of the guild and of the conduct and accounting of Heydon and Belche. For example, on 18 January 1533 Thomas A Dene, a 30-year-old smith, stated that:

> upon a sonday or an other holyday sex yeres past as he remembreth, which day he can not otherwyse specifye, between hygh masse & evynsong this deponent cam into the church hous of Rykmersworth when & where he

---

[23] Duffy, *Stripping of the Altars*, pp.142–54.

[24] HALS, ASA/7/2 fol. 78r, statement by George Belche, recorded 17 May 1533.

[25] See Appendix 2.

[26] Discussed in detail by Aston, 'Troubles of churchwardens', pp.530–33.

[27] George Belche was one of the witnesses to Haydon's will (236).

founde George Belch, John Heydon, William Creke, Robert Rowlles, Roger Gonner, John Mylward, Thomas Spenser & diverse other men rekonyng & cowntyng for the said Fraternyte. They had among theim upon a tabull a boke and certeyn paper billes with a box & money, but hough moch this deponent can not say, nor who recevid it but he hard Robert Rolles say the Wardeyns have lost vj li [£6].[28]

Interestingly Thomas Spenser indicated that the guild's income included money given by women when they were churched, that is, when they were received back into the parish community after childbirth.[29] Religious guilds were suppressed in the reign of Edward VI.

Some of the most important items of church 'furnishing' were the bells, which summoned parishioners to services and indicated the approximate time of day. Churchwardens' accounts from other parishes indicate that bells were also rung in celebration, or as a warning, on particular occasions. For example at Baldock in 1540 the wardens paid ringers on Corpus Christi day.[30] As we shall see, there were five bells in St Mary's steeple. In 1442 John Dyer (37) bequeathed 12d to the new bell being made and in May 1444 Henry Panter (39) left 12d to the bell 'newly set up'. Bells were rung frequently and their ropes often needed replacing or repairing: in June 1472 Joan Buttervyle (95) bequeathed 8 pounds of hemp for the repair of the bell ropes.

Other parishioners gave items to be used during the mass. In 1455 Joan Edelyn (60) bequeathed a silver cup – a chalice – costing up to 4 marks (£2 13s 4d). In 1502 John Stokker (181) donated 'a good & a sufficient masse boke well written & well notyd aftir the discretion of the vicar …, and other such as can skill of such things'. In 1503 John Tredeway (186) donated 'a good and an honest surples for the vicar … to doo God service in, to the honour of the parissh'. In 1513 Joan Stokker (204) donated silver cross valued at 20 marks (£13 6s 8d) and in 1514 Anne Asshby (209) donated a pyx of silver and gilt for the sacrament to be put in, valued at £5, and a pair of silver cruets, valued at 40s. These items would probably have been stored in the vestry but in the late fifteenth there was also room in the church known as the 'jewel house'. In 1495 Stephen Holtyng (166) asked to be buried 'in the church, near

---

[28] HALS ASA/8/1, f.56r, examination of Thomas A Dene, dated 18 January 1533.

[29] HALS ASA/8/1, f.54v, deposition of Thomas Spenser of the parish of Rykmersworth where he has lived for 24 years, baker, examined 29 November 1532.

[30] A. Palmer, ed., *Tudor Churchwardens' Accounts* (HRS, vol. I, 1985), p.55.

the font, facing the door of the jewel house'. This was before the new vestry had been built. It is possible that the 'jewel house' was in the original tower since the font would usually be at the west end of the church near the north door.

In 1552 the government of Edward VI ordered inventories to be made of the 'church goods' of every parish. An inventory of St Mary's church goods was drawn up on 1 November 1552: the items were in the safe keeping of John Foxe of Rickmansworth, probably one of the churchwardens.[31] The church goods at that time, which most likely had been in the parish for years, were: five bells in the steeple and a sanctus bell,[32] a silver and gilt cross weighing 58 ounces, four silver and gilt chalices weighing 29, 24, 18 and 15 ounces respectively, a silver and gilt pyx weighing 18½ ounces, a pair of cruets of silver parcel gilt weighing 8 ounces, a silver censer weighing 32 ounces, a silver pax weighing 2½ ounces, a cope of white 'bawdkynne',[33] a blue silk vestment and a hand bell. Some of these items may well have been the bequests mentioned above.

Many, but by no means all, wills were made not long before death. It could be argued that the reason for certain religious bequests in wills is that the scribe – frequently the vicar or one of the parish clerks – either prompted or heavily influenced the testator. While it is tempting to make this the explanation for the generous bequests of silverware, mass book and surplice mentioned earlier – those wills were all witnessed by the vicar, Thomas Coton – there is also much evidence of independent thought in the bequests. It is clear from the wills that many parishioners of Rickmansworth actively supported their parish church: by contributing to new building work, paying for glazing of widows, supplying books and vestments, maintaining lights. But one night in early 1522 there was a serious arson attack on the church and many of these items were destroyed. We know about this from two different but related sources.

Firstly: what happened that night.[34] In the church of Rickmansworth persons unknown 'cruelly & wilfully' set fire to all the images and to the canopy inside which

---

[31] TNA, E315/497, fol.7. See G. D. Martin's two articles on the church plate: 'St. Mary the Virgin, Rickmansworth: the Church Plate', part 1 & part 2, *Rickmansworth Historical Review*, 18 (June 2019), pp.22–32 and 19 (October 2019), pp.8–17.

[32] See Glossary.

[33] See Glossary.

[34] Taken from British Library C.18.e.2 (96), The Rickmansworth Indulgence (1522) (reprinted in Aston, 'Troubles of churchwardens', p.552). See Appendix 3.

was the blessed sacrament. To make sure of the blaze, the incendiaries put tow (fibres of flax or hemp) and banner staves (poles to hold religious banners) 'bytwene the spares & brases of the chaunsell' (perhaps the rood screen). These acted as firelighters and as a result the chancel was burned and the pyx melted. They also broke into the vestry and set fire to all the ornaments and jewels, i.e. plate, burning the vestry and everything in it. In the roodloft they wrapped tow about the rood and about a pair of organs:[35] this melted all the wax in the loft, which weighed about 280 pounds. They broke open the font (presumably took the cover off) and scattered the holy water all over the church floor, showing complete disregard for the sacrament of baptism.

Something had to be done. Money had to be raised to repair the terrible damage. No doubt parishioners rallied round; perhaps the churchwardens, Henry Wedon, Henry Evelyn and Richard Fotherley, raised a parish rate to help pay for the repairs but as there are no surviving churchwardens' accounts we cannot know. We do know, however, that they decided to set in motion a scheme to raise money for the church through the generosity of people elsewhere.

The doctrine of purgatory was important to medieval Christians (and indeed is to Catholics today): it was the place where souls went to be purged of their sins so that they could then enter heaven. Time in purgatory could be reduced by having prayers said for one's soul or by doing good works. Indulgences sold by pardoners made it possible to reduce time in purgatory.[36] They became increasingly popular in the Middle Ages as a reward for displaying piety and doing good deeds. Good deeds included charitable donations of money for a good cause, and money thus raised was used for many righteous causes, both religious and civil. So it was that the churchwardens of Rickmansworth apparently approached Cardinal Wolsey, who, as Abbot of St Albans, was lord of the manors in Rickmansworth and head of the Liberty of St Albans, to sanction an indulgence that could be sold on behalf of the church to raise money for the much needed repairs. Subsequently an indulgence was issued by Wolsey and John Longland, bishop of Lincoln, described as Wolsey's friend.[37] Spatially Rickmansworth lay in Longland's diocese, but as it was part of exempt Liberty of St Albans it was outside the bishop's jurisdiction. To everyone who gave anything towards the restoration of Rickmansworth church the Cardinal granted 100 days of pardon from their penance in purgatory and the bishop of

---

[35] The organ in a church was often referred to as 'a pair of organs'.

[36] See, for example, Duffy, *Stripping of the Altars*, pp.288–9.

[37] Aston, 'Troubles of churchwardens', p.525.

Lincoln granted 40 days. Anyone who gave money would receive a copy as proof of their soul's release from those days of penance: just one of these copies of the indulgence has survived. It is now in the British Library.[38]

So, what happened next? An arrangement was made with professional collectors to sell the indulgence over a period of three years. They collected money but refused to hand it over and so the Rickmansworth churchwardens, Henry Wedon, Henry Evelyn and Richard Fotherley, commenced a law suit in Chancery to try to recover the £10 13s 4d that had been collected.[39] The churchwardens claimed that the collectors/sellers of their indulgence had agreed to collect for three years ending on feast of All Saints in the 17th year of the reign of Henry VIII, that is, on 1 November 1525; so the fire had happened sometime in 1522, probably earlier rather than later in the year. The date of lawsuit is unknown except that it was brought during Wolsey's chancellorship, which ended on 18 October 1529. The wardens claimed that although Thomas Carter, Jerome Richardson and John Wryght had agreed to render their account, they never paid over the money and refused to provide any record of their collection.[40] The lawsuit hangs on legal niceties but the main point is that although money was apparently collected it had never been handed over. The collection had been made over a wide area during the three years: within the dioceses of Salisbury, Winchester, Chichester, Bath and Wells, Exeter and all the dioceses in Wales.

Who were the arsonists? Short answer is that we do not know. They were described in the indulgence as 'wretched & cursed people'. They were never identified but one can have a pretty shrewd guess as to their background. It is more than likely that they were Lollards, or were Lollard sympathisers. Lollards were heretics in pre-Reformation England. Typically they thought that prayers for the dead were worthless and criticised as superstitious the veneration of images, the use of crucifixes and the cult of saints. There is no way of telling how many there were in England in the early sixteenth century: they were statistically insignificant at the national level but in a few areas they amounted to a sizeable presence within the community, even if never a numerical majority. One of the areas in which they were concentrated was the Chilterns: Rickmansworth is on the edge of the Chilterns.

---

[38] J. E. Cussans reported that this copy of the indulgence was found pasted inside the cover of a book bought by the British Museum in January 1868. (*History of Hertfordshire*, vol. III, *The Hundred of Cashio*, p.149)

[39] TNA, C1/593/49–50.

[40] The collectors were from St Albans. (Aston, 'Troubles of churchwardens', p.529)

Amersham, only 10 miles away, was a noted centre of Lollardy. Much of what is known of Lollardy in this area is based on the writings of (another) John Foxe, in what became known as Foxe's *Book of Martyrs*, first published 1563.[41] In Foxe's work there is some specific evidence pointing to the possible spread of Lollard opinion in Rickmansworth itself. He had access to a now lost register of the bishop of Lincoln that recorded Longland's proceedings against heretics in the diocese of Lincoln in 1521. Those who gave evidence, or 'detected' heretics, were former heretics who had 'abjured' or confessed; if they refused to give evidence they were likely to be burned as heretics. Furthermore, on 28 January 1522 two Amersham men, Thomas Barnard and James Morden, had been burnt at the stake at Amersham. Margaret Aston found links between Morden's family and the Tredway family, four of whom were assessed in the 1524 subsidy at Rickmansworth: two in West Hyde and two in Chorleywood.[42]

Perhaps the arson attack was an act of revenge for Longland's prosecutions. There were certainly connections between Rickmansworth and the parishes to the west that featured so strongly in bishop's enquiries. Indeed Wolsey and Longland tried to make (conservative) religious mileage out of the arson attack. The indulgence reported two miracles that occurred during the fire. Firstly, despite the severe damage to, or even destruction of, the chancel and the vestry of the church, although the pyx melted, 'the blessyd body of our lorde Jhesu cryst in forme of brede was founde upon the hyghe awter & nothynge perysshed'.[43] Furthermore, 'where as the flambynge fyre was in the sayd lofte about the blessyd ymage of Jhesu cryst nother the sayd ymage nor the towe about it was nothynge hurte thrughe the myght & power of our savyour Jhesu cryst'. Nevertheless, despite these claims by Wolsey and Longland in the indulgence, this was a time when news of Lutheran reform – particularly the condemnation of the sale of indulgences – was spreading. As Aston comments, 'Lollard iconoclasts, who had long nurtured ideas of image-burning, are not known ever to have brought off before so spectacular a bonfire as that at Rickmansworth'.[44] It is not possible to prove any direct Lollard connection but the fact of the attack, and its timing, is highly suggestive.

---

[41] J. Foxe, *Actes and monuments of these latter and perillous dayes touching matters of the Church, wherein ar described the great persecutions ... practised by the Romishe prelates* (1st edition, London, 1563); enlarged and reissued in 1570, 1583 and 1587.

[42] Aston, 'Troubles of churchwardens', p.547; and see Appendix 2.

[43] This and the next quotation come from the indulgence. See Appendix 3.

[44] Aston, 'Troubles of churchwardens', p.549.

However, it seems that the people of Rickmansworth did not simply wait around for the indulgence money to come in, which, under the circumstances, was just as well. In the surviving wills parishioners were making provision for the repairs to the church. Previously this had been a standard bequest but perhaps it was more meaningful now? For example, William Dolte (219) died in the summer of 1524: he left 3s 4d to the reparations of the church. Also lights were still being supported, despite 280 pounds of wax literally going up in smoke and, perhaps, images being damaged. In 1526 William Belche (223) left 8d to the rood light, 4d to the Trinity light, and 2d each to the lights of St Katherine, St Edmund, St Anthony, St Nicholas, the Piéta, St George and St Clement. It seems that in May 1529 the repair work was nearing completion, for in that month the blacksmith John A Dene (233) bequeathed 6s 8d 'to the reysyng of the organs'. In 1530 John Hede (234) bequeathed £20 for books for the church. And in 1536, Henry Wedon (244), one of the churchwardens at the time of the arson attack, bequeathed 6s 8d 'to the gyldyng of the rood'. Of course, what parishioners did not know was that in just a few years' time the images and the rood would be attacked again, this time 'officially' during the course of the Reformation.

Clerical personnel at St Mary's

The wills reveal the names of various men directly associated with St Mary's church, not only vicars but also parish clerks and priests. A parish clerk, usually a layman, assisted the incumbent during services and was usually educated.[45] Clerks at Rickmansworth included John Bramanger (whose name is spelled in various ways), Thomas Stretman, James Kelly, Thomas Ward and John White. Sometimes they were given bequests, sometimes they witnessed wills. It is likely that in many of the latter cases they also wrote the will. Some of the priests mentioned in the wills were, or later became, vicar. The first priest to be named was Thomas Mees, who witnessed William Smyth's will (44) in 1447; he may also have been 'master Thomas, chaplain', who had received a bequest from Thomas Godthank (29) in 1437

The probate register records that the vicar Henry Bornwash (49) had died intestate on 10 March 1451, indicating that he had not made a will. The point of the record is that his goods which had been left in the parish had been inventoried, that is listed and valued, by John Wymond and John Bramanger. However, the inventory was not lodged in the records of the archdeaconry court because 'his goods were set

---

[45] J. S. Purvis, *Dictionary of Ecclesiastical Terms* (London, 1962), p.49.

aside by the collector of the Lord Pope because the vicar was chaplain to the Lord Pope by [papal] bull'. This tantalising entry suggests that Bornwash had high connections. He had arrived at Rickmansworth in 1430 under something of a cloud. The St Albans Abbey chronicler recorded that in that year, Henry 'Borwwasche', vicar of St Peter's in St Albans, had upset his parishioners, who had been murmuring against payments due to the vicar. To solve this, the abbey had arranged for the then vicar of Rickmansworth to exchange parishes with Bornwash.[46] However, it seems that he was subsequently embroiled in disagreements with Rickmansworth parishioners, since the abbey chronicler records that in 1433 he was involved in a suit in the archdeacon's court regarding the suspension and excommunication of Richard and Margaret Whitman of Rickmansworth.[47] John Spygone, Roger Bourynge, Henry Sewhard and Richard Gybbe, as well as John Wynkebourne, had also been suspended from the communion of the church at the request of the vicar.[48] Bornwash himself was subsequently excommunicated by the Dean of the Court of Arches, but after direct supplication to the Pope, Bornwash was absolved from excommunication in 1435.[49] Although vicar for some 20 years, perhaps significantly, of the 32 wills made during that period he was mentioned by name as a legatee in only one of them: John Tyler 'maltman' (25) left 6s 8d to 'Henry Bergwasch my vicar and curate'. Furthermore, he only witnessed (or wrote) one, that of Petronilla Dier (32).[50]

In 1451 Bornwash was succeeded by master John Wynton, perpetual vicar. In contrast to Bornwash, during Wynton's nearly 30-year incumbency he was mentioned by name in 10 of the 70 wills. In 1454 Joan Wodeward (55) bequeathed 12d to 'master John the vicar'. He was one of the executors of William Creke in November 1452 (53), of Rose Gybbes in 1462 (73), of John Mertok in 1479 (120), and of John Gardyner in 1479 (124); supervisor of Andrew Ragon in 1454 (54), of Thomas Gybbes in 1462 (72), and of Stephen Stalon in 1475 (105); witness of Thomas Trot in 1458 (66), and of John Tymberlake in about 1466 (78).

---

[46] H. T. Riley, ed., *Annales Monasterii S. Albani, (A.D. 1421–1440)*, vol. 1, p.46.

[47] The matter of the Whitmans' excommunication is chronicled in great detail in Riley, ed., *Annales Monasterii S. Albani*, vols 1 and 2; see below, p. xlvi.

[48] Riley, ed., *Annales Monasterii S. Albani*, vol. 2, p.28.

[49] Riley, ed., *Annales Monasterii S. Albani*, vol. 2, pp.74–79.

[50] The vicar is mentioned but not named by Thomas Daye (27a & b), Henry Panter (39) and Roger Bryan (48).

Wynton died in 1480 and was succeeded as vicar by Thomas Hemingford, who was instituted on 14 November,[51] but Hemingford was known to parishioners long before that. He was an Austin (Augustinian) friar. In 1462 Thomas Gybbes (72) of Herynghers (Heronsgate) had asked that Brother Thomas 'Hamyngford' celebrate mass for half a year for the souls of his father and his friends.[52] Just 10 days later his wife Rose (73) made John Wynton, vicar, and Thomas Hemingford, chaplain, two of her executors. By 1473 the latter was vicar of Sarratt and was asked to say prayers for the soul of Guy Stokker (99).

In January 1481 Thomas Coton was nominated as the next vicar by George Danyell and John Assheby, but not actually appointed as he was described as 'chaplain, not yet master'.[53] However it seems likely that he was appointed to the vicarage in May 1485, when Hemingford was deprived of the living at Sarratt on the grounds of apostacy; however the latter was still in Rickmansworth in 1491 when James Foderley (155) appointed him one of the supervisors of his will and requested him to pray for his soul for half a year. Coton was vicar until at least August 1525. He is mentioned by name in 28 wills as legatee, witness, executor or supervisor, and was one of the administrators of the estate of Hugh Damport (157). In 1495 the contents of Stephen Holtyng's will (166) was contested in the archdeacon's court. The statements of three witnesses are recorded in the probate register together with the text of the will. One of the witnesses was sir Thomas Coton, who had been appointed one of Holtyng's executors.[54] In his statement he gave his age as '30 years and more'. As he was a chaplain in the parish in 1481, it seems likely that he was nearer 40 than 30 in 1495. From time to time in the 1520s Cardinal Wolsey resided at his house, the More, just outside Rickmansworth.[55] On 30 August 1525 the Treaty of the More, a peace treaty between England and France was signed there.

---

[51] HALS, D/EX976/17/126, List of Rickmansworth incumbents compiled (before 1911) by H. R. Wilton Hall, sub librarian of St Albans Cathedral Library.

[52] Hemingford's name is spelled in a variety of ways. It has been standardised here.

[53] H. T. Riley, ed., *Registra quorundam abbatum monasterii S. Albani: qui saeculo XVmo floruere*, vol II, *Registra Johannis Whethamstede, Willelmi Albon et Willelmi Walingforde*, p.227; Aston, 'Troubles of churchwardens', p.535.

[54] The 'sir' denotes a cleric without a university degree.

[55] Records of Wolsey's movements suggest that between 21 September 1523 and 26 September 1529 he may have spent as few as 76 days at the More, and a maximum of 155 days; so at most less than half a year in 6 years. (Based on 'The itinerary of Cardinal Wolsey', in N. Samman, 'The Henrician Court during Cardinal Wolsey's ascendancy, c.1514-1529' (unpub. PhD thesis, University of Wales, 1989), pp.393–437.)

Archbishop William Warham was one of the signatories. In a letter to Wolsey he explained that rather than stay at the More, he would stay with the vicar, Thomas Coton, whom he described as Wolsey's chaplain: 'I wold bee well contented to bee with my folk at my old host the vicar of Rigmansworth, your gracis chapellaine, being in myne opinion a very honest and loving man'.[56]

In 1517 there was a priest in the parish called sir Herry Taylour and from 1527 onwards one named sir Richard Porter. The vicar after Coton was William Man and he too appears as the first witness to four of the wills, suggesting that he had written them.[57] He served the parish for about 25 years, dying in early March 1559.[58]

Population size of the old parish of Rickmansworth

While the inhabitants resided within this one large parish, their homes were situated in one of a number of manors. Tenants' rent for their dwelling (and any associated land) was payable to the lord of the manor. It is said that when St Albans Abbey was founded most of the land in south-west Hertfordshire was granted to the abbey by king Offa to provide it with income.[59] By whatever means the area came into the hands of the abbey, by the time that the 'Domesday' survey was taken in 1086, Rickmansworth (Prichemareworde) was recorded as being held by the Abbot of St Albans.[60] The rivers in the area already played a part in the local economy: there was a mill, a large area of meadow and income for the abbot from fish. The manor was heavily wooded, sufficient to support 1,200 pigs: perhaps the largest area of woodland in what is now Hertfordshire.[61] However, from slightly later records, it is clear that there was not simply one large manor that was coterminous with the parish: within the large pre-Reformation parish were twelve manors, all of which belonged to St Albans Abbey, and the boundaries of some of them extended into

---

[56] Quoted in Aston, 'Troubles of churchwardens', p.534, citing Register Warham (Lambeth Palace), ii, fol. 385v.

[57] Wills 240, 241, 242 and 244.

[58] HALS, 1AW75, will of William Man, vicar of Rickmansworth, 2 March 1559; HALS, A25/326, inventory of William Man, vicar of Rickmansworth, 9 March 1559.

[59] *VCH Herts*, vol. 2, p.373.

[60] J. Morris, ed., *Domesday Book: Hertfordshire* (Chichester, 1976), 136a, entry 15.

[61] Not that there were necessarily 1,200 pigs in the area, but there was enough woodland to support that number.

neighbouring parishes.[62] The manors were: the main manor of Rickmansworth, the More,[63] Croxley,[64] Snellshall,[65] Pinchfield/Pinesfield, Bigging, Ashleys, Batchworth, Britwell,[66] Micklefield,[67] Langleys or Linsters,[68] and Woodwicks.[69] A handful of details relating to these some manors are provided by the wills here. For example, in 1452 William Crek(e), esquire, (53) held the manor of 'Mykelfeld', and bequeathed sums of money from its profits to various individuals. Richard Hammond (133) refers to Thomas Creke, esquire, bailiff, in connection with the surrender of Hammond's cottage in Rickmansworth, so Thomas Creke was probably the bailiff of the main manor. Similarly Joan Stokker (204) had made a formal surrender of her property to John a Dene, 'Bayly to my lord of Saint Albons of his lordship of Rik". Since the land and church belonged to the abbey of St Albans, as already noted, the terminal date for this study of pre-Reformation Rickmansworth is 1539. Not only did the way in which religion was practised change dramatically by parliamentary statutes and orders from the bishops in Convocation, but also the abbey was dissolved and the manors passed into new ownership.[70] The extent to which life changed for the average tenant or parishioner, however, is a moot point – they were still expected to pay their rent to the lord of the manor and to attend St Mary's – but nominally things were very different.

---

[62] For example, the manor of the More extended into Watford and into Northwood (Middx). Information about all of the manors is in *VCH Herts*, vol. 2, pp.373–384.

[63] See, for example, H. Falvey, 'The More: Archbishop George Neville's palace in Rickmansworth, Hertfordshire', *The Ricardian*, vol. IX, no. 118 (September 1992), pp.290–302; H. Falvey, 'The More: Rickmansworth's lost palace', *Hertfordshire's Past*, 34 (Spring 1993), pp.2–16; H. Falvey, 'William Flete: More than just a castle builder', *The Ricardian*, vol. X, no. 124 (March 1994), pp.2–15; H. Falvey, 'The More revisited', *The Ricardian*, vol. XVIII (2008), pp. 92–99.

[64] Croxley Hall is the original manor house; the medieval barn close by belonged to it.

[65] Its site was north-west of Croxley, on the border with Watford. See, B. Thomson, *The Lost Manor of Snells Hall and Cassiobridge House and its People* (Rickmansworth, 2018).

[66] From 1430s ownership descended with the More; the site is marked by Brightwells Farm in Watford parish, near to Hamper Mills.

[67] The manor house is Micklefield Hall; by the 1550s part of the manor of Croxley.

[68] Now one farm north of West Hyde.

[69] The site is Woodoaks Farm, at Maple Cross. See A. Jacques, 'Woodwick – a knight's fee manor', *Rickmansworth Historical Society Newsletter*, 90 (December 2010), pp.3–15.

[70] After the dissolution manor of the Rectory of Rickmansworth was formed; this became Parsonage Farm.

It is useful to have a rough idea of the size of the local population but it is notoriously difficult to calculate the size of the medieval population because, of course, there were no censuses. The historian is reliant on calculations based on taxation records, which were made for entirely different reasons than to aid population calculations. Such records only list those who were assessed for taxation: there were always inhabitants too poor to be assessed who were missing from such records and probably others who were sufficiently wealthy but evaded paying. One therefore has to make allowance for such omissions by using statistical multipliers. Furthermore taxation returns only list taxpayers, not people within their household, so allowance has to be made for them as well. Another issue to bear in mind is that taxation turns were compiled by township or vill, and such areas were not necessarily coterminous with the ecclesiastical parish or, with the manor(s), so one is not necessarily comparing like with like. To calculate the approximate population at the beginning of the period covered by these wills, it would be best to use returns of the poll taxes levied in 1377, 1379 or 1380; however, no poll tax returns have survived for this part of Hertfordshire. The only suitable medieval tax returns are those of the 1307 lay subsidy. For the end of the period there are the lay subsidy returns of 1524.[71] Using the 1307 returns is not without its difficulties, since they relate to the population prior to the Black Death of 1348/9, which, it is estimated, more or less halved the population.[72]

In 1307 66 men and one woman (Amice Bithewod) were assessed for taxation. The returns for 'Rikemersworth' give some indication of where the taxpayers lived (Crokesl' and Mikelfeld are mentioned) but this does not seem to be reported fully. It has been suggested that only about one third of the population was assessed for tax at this time, the other two thirds being insufficiently wealthy.[73] So, there were 67 tax paying households and about 134 non-taxpaying, suggesting about 201 households in 1307. Therefore, following the depredations of the Black Death, in the 1350s there were probably only about 100 households in the area covered by 'Rikmersworth' in the 1307 lay subsidy. Although this is only a rough guess, it is known that three different chaplains were instituted at St Mary's in quick succession in the summer of 1349: William de Lepham on 16 May, Roger Wood, or de Orel, on

---

[71] See Appendix 1 and 2 for the full listings of these two lay subsidies.

[72] See, for example, M. Bailey, *After the Black Death: Economy, Society and the Law in Fourteenth-Century England* (Oxford, 2021), pp.135–137.

[73] M. Bailey, 'Introduction', in J. Brooker and S. Flood, eds., *Hertfordshire Lay Subsidy Rolls, 1307 and 1334* (HRS, vol. XIV, 1998), p.xxii.

6 June, and Robert Monant, or Mendance, on 16 August.[74] So whether William and Roger had died, or they had had to move on rapidly to other parishes, there was disease around in mid 1349.

In early 1524 inhabitants in the Rickmansworth area were assessed for the first payment of the 1523 lay subsidy. The returns list taxpayers by five settlements: Rickmansworth, West Hyde, Chorleywood, Croxley and Batchworth. In all 147 individual were assessed for tax. Of these 31 were servants who were assessed on wages; three were heiresses; five were assessed on wages but were not servants; and 108 were assessed on their land or goods. (See Table 2.) It would seem reasonable to suggest that these two latter groups, 113 people in all, were heads of tax-paying households, so an increase of 46 taxable households on 1307.

Table 2: Taxpayers in the various settlements in 1524

place	A. Servant, paid wages	B. Heiress	C. Taxed on goods or land	D. Paid wages, not servant	E. Total taxed	F. Taxable households (C + D)
Rickmansworth	19		50	3	72	53
West Hyde	3		18	0	21	18
Chorleywood	3		13	1	17	14
Croxley	2		15	0	17	15
Batchworth	4	3	12	1	20	13
Totals	31	3	108	5	147	113

Source: TNA, E179/120/114; see Appendix 2.

It has been suggested that for the lay subsidy granted by parliament in 1523 about 30% of households were either too poor to be assessed or evaded assessment, so there were probably about 147 households in 1524.[75] This is fewer households than the admittedly tenuous figure of 201 for 1307 but it known that in general the population in early sixteenth century England was much lower than at the beginning of the fourteenth century. As already noted, the ravages of the Black

---

[74] HALS, D/EX976/17/126, List of Rickmansworth incumbents.

[75] 113 + (30% of 113). N. Goose and A. Hinde, 'Estimating local population sizes at fixed points in time: Part II – specific sources', *Local Population Studies*, 78 (2007) pp.74–88, p.79. (This figure just happens to coincide with the number of people taxed; the heiresses and servants were not householders.)

Death in 1348-9 are estimated to have halved the population, and for various reasons the population did not recover its pre-Black Death size, let alone surpass it, until the mid-sixteenth century.[76] Allowing for an average of 4.75 people in each household, the figure of 147 households, or 699 people, although not precise, indicates that the parish as a whole was relatively sparsely populated.[77] In 1524 Rickmansworth itself, although by far the largest settlement, and where the parish church was situated, was a village rather than a town; indeed there was no formal market until 1542, when Henry VIII granted a market by charter.[78]

Table 3: Documents by decade of probate, i.e. recorded deaths per decade

decade	probates
1400-09	2
1410-19	2
1420-29	10
1430-39	19
1440-49	14
1450-59	21
1460-69	13
1470-79	44
1480-89	21
1490-99	31
1500-09	25
1510-19	13
1520-29	18
1530-39	16
Total	249

In the absence of parish registers, which, although instituted in 1538, do not survive from Rickmansworth until the seventeenth century, the annual number of deaths in the parish is impossible to know. However, the number of wills proved and administrations granted in a particular year, or decade, provides a crude indicator of variations in the death rate. Table 3 shows the number of Rickmansworth probate

[76] K. Wrightson, *Earthly Necessities: Economic Lives in Early Modern Britain* (New Haven and London, 2000), p.99.

[77] Goose and Hinde, 'Estimating local population sizes', p.79.

[78] *VCH Herts*, vol. 2, p. 372.

documents per decade. The documents in the main text are numbered 1 to 248 but in Table 3 the total of recorded deaths is 249: Elizabeth and John Newell, who were named together in one grant of administration (162), have been counted as individuals. The 1470s stand out as a crisis decade, with 44 probates granted; these are broken down by year in Table 4.

Table 4: Deaths in the 1470s

Year	Deaths
1470	2
1471	1
1472	11
1473	7
1474	1
1475	2
1476	4
1477	5
1478	2
1479	9
(1480)	(3)

In 1472 two wills were granted probate on 25 May and one administration and two wills on 27 May, suggesting an outbreak of some sort of illness, but the will preambles give no clue. There were two connected pairs of deaths in this year. The two wills granted probate on 27 May were those of the brothers John Wyllyes (86) and Thomas Wyllyes (87), both young, apparently unmarried men who had appointed their father, Henry (Willeys), as sole executor. Perhaps the family lived in the Chorleywood area as both Thomas and Henry (111) left bequests to the church at Sarratt. Two men had died at the More earlier in the year: Peter Arstock (89) on 30 January and Thomas Shorthouse (90) on 8 February.

In 1479 the Gardyner family experienced five deaths in quick succession. Probate of the will of William (112) was granted on 22 March 1477 to his executors, his wife Joan and sons Roger and John. On 7 October 1479 probate of Roger Gardyner's will (121) was granted to his executors, his wife Alice, mother Joan and brother John. However, Alice (122) had made her will two days earlier and had died before 23 October, when her father Thomas Russell of Chalfont St Giles (Bucks) was granted probate of her will. Her mother-in-law Joan (123) made her will on 13 October;

probate was granted on 11 November to her son John; who in turn made his will on 16 November (124), probate being granted to his wife Joan and the vicar, John Wynton, on 27 November.

Clusters of family deaths also occur at other times: Simon Canoun (1) and John Canoun (2) appear to be father and son: both wills were recorded in the Croxley court book on 23 May 1409. Similarly John atte Hyde (23) and William atte Hyde (24) whose wills were both proved on 13 February 1434 seem to have been been father and son. Husband and wife Thomas (72) and Rose Gybbes (73) of Herynghers (Heronsgate) died within a few days of each other: his will was proved on 19 May 1462, hers was written on 20 May and proved the following day.

Making a living in the parish

It is difficult to know exactly what was happening with regard to agriculture in and around medieval Rickmansworth, both because it was in a 'transitional zone', neither part of London nor deep in the heart of the countryside, and because there is little direct evidence of the nature of agriculture and animal husbandry in the parish. More is known about farming practices in the parish the second half of the sixteenth century because there about 145 probate inventories dating from 1545 to 1599: these value the crops, whether on the ground or in the barn, and also animals, as well as farming equipment and household goods. Since it is unlikely that practices would have changed much in the intervening years, the following is a summary of findings based on 20 wills with accompanying probate inventories from the years 1546 to 1588.[79]

In the later sixteenth century Rickmansworth inhabitants were not dependent on one particular crop or type of animal for their livelihood. They were engaged in mixed husbandry: the fertile crop-growing land was surrounded by meadows and woods, both of which provided the means to support the rearing of animals, for sale or for their own use. Wheat and oats were grown in similar quantities, barley slightly less. Wheat was used primarily for bread-making and was sometimes grown together with rye, this mixture being known as maslin, which was also ground into flour. Most of the barley grown would have been used in the production of ale as

---

[79] Based on the analysis in H. Falvey, 'Rickmansworth and Croxley: a community in south-west Hertfordshire during the mid-sixteenth century' (unpublished dissertation, UCICE, Advanced Certificate in English Local History, 1996), chapter 3, 'The community at work'.

harvested barley would be converted to malt. Oats, and peas, were used as fodder crops. The large quantity of oats produced by Rickmansworth inhabitants in the sixteenth century reflects the importance of horses and stabling to the local economy. Many roads linked Hertfordshire and London so there was much demand for stabling in the county. The sporadic use of the More by its wealthy owners – Archbishop Neville from about 1460 to 1472, Cardinal Wolsey in the 1520s and Henry VIII in both the 1520s and 1530s – would have resulted in many people requiring temporary local stabling facilities, and fodder, for their horses.[80]

A handful of the wills published here give some hints about farming activities. That of Richard Belche (228), drawn up in 1528, is very informative. Although Belche does not give his status, he seems to have been farming on a reasonable scale, having both livestock and crops to bequeath.

> To Johan my wyff all my houshold stuff, oon fylde of whete called long fylde, five acres of ~~wh~~ wootes [oats], half of all my barley that is or shalbe sowyn this yere, oon horse, four kyen, ten yowys with ten lambys, four hogges. To my moder a cowe, a hog, a busshell of whete & a busshell of malt. To my broder George all my horssys not before bequethyd and my carte with the pertenances to the same.

Several testators bequeathed malt, such as John Elverede (16) and Thomas Daye (27a&b). The presence of two 'maltmen' – John Tyler (25) and Thomas Botervylde[81] – indicates that malt was produced in quite large quantities. All but one of the testators who bequeathed quantities of grain specified whether it was wheat, barley (or malt) or oats; only William Crek (53) bequeathed unspecified grain.

Several wills mention sheep and/or cows. That of William Gybbys (79) has many bequests of sheep: six to each of his nine children, 32 to three named servants and nine to godchildren, that is, 95 sheep in total. He also bequeathed three cows, including one cow of 'brendyld' colour. Since he also bequeathed five bushels of wheat to specified recipients, one bushel to the rood and one bushel to each of the

---

[80] Wolsey's visits to the More are discussed above. Regarding Henry VIII, for example, between 28 July 1522 and 23 September 1530, Henry VIII visited the More on 10 occasions (1 visit before Wolsey took it over and 2 after Wolsey's last visit but before his death). Calculated from 'The itinerary of Henry VIII', in N. Samman, 'The Henrician Court', pp.333-392.

[81] See below. Botervylde (spelled various ways) was mentioned in 4 wills (25, 46, 51, 71.)

lights in the church (number not specified), it is clear that he had been farming on a large scale.

Much of the large area of woodland mentioned in Domesday was still in existence and it would have been important to the inhabitants for pasturing pigs. The trees belonged to the lord of the manor(s), the abbot of St Albans, and provided two products to sell: timber, from the trunks of timber trees, for making beams and planks, and wood, produced by coppicing and pollarding and the branches of felled timber trees, for fencing, wattle-work and, most importantly, fuel. Manorial tenants may have had the right to gather fallen wood and, by the sixteenth century at least, tenants were renting some of the woodland.[82] Richard Over's will (149), which is a combined testament and will, is one of the few that provides details of landholding and the rights and responsibilities that went with it:

> I will that Letice my wife shall have my tenement in which I dwell called Selmyns, with all the lands, meadows, pastures and feedings, with all the appurtenances of the tenement for the term of five years after my death peacefully, without interruption or impediment by anyone, & my aforesaid wife shall pay, or cause to be paid, annually to the lord the rents & services that ought to be paid for the tenement & its appurtenances, and to do no waste in the woods or underwoods, namely, in 'le heggerowes', and that she will mow [*damaged*] of the tenement, & I will that she have sufficient, that is, 'fierbote hechebote & stakebote'[83] to support [*damaged*] hers [&] mine & to sufficiently repair & maintain the aforesaid tenement [*damaged*] & after the aforesaid term of five years is complete, I will that my son William have [the aforesaid tenement and its appurtenances] called Selmyns, holding to him & his heirs forever.

The rivers in the area contributed to the local economy in many ways. They provided fish, power to mills, and water for crops and animals and for such processes as dyeing and tanning. In 1407 Simon Canoun, the first testator, had been granted a section of the river called 'Pyghtellesburne' to make a sluice for catching fish, probably part of the river Gade as it flowed through Croxley moor.[84]

At the beginning of a few of the probate documents the person's occupation is clearly stated, for example, John Tyler 'maltman' (25), William at Welle 'Wolman'

---

[82] Falvey, 'Rickmansworth and Croxley', p.28.
[83] See the Glossary for these terms.
[84] BL, Add MS 6057, fol. 25r.

(74) and Robert Marchand (93) 'bocher'. In another set of wills that I have co-edited occupations only seem to be given to distinguish men of the same name,[85] so, frustratingly for local historians, it was not usually necessary to give the testator's occupation. Nevertheless, some information about occupations and trades is available for Rickmansworth parishioners. While it is possible that the 'maltmen' John Tyler and Thomas Botervylde were maltsters, that is, they made malt from barley for the brewing of ale, it is more likely that they were traders in malt because supplying malt to the medieval London market was a specialism of Hertfordshire.[86] As a 'woolman', at Welle would have bought wool from graziers and sold it to a cloth-maker or cloth merchant.[87] As a butcher Marchand would have dealt with both the slaughter of livestock and the preparation of animal flesh for food.[88] Richard Yan (7) described himself as 'farmer (*firmarius*) of Crokeslee', meaning that he was the lessee of the manor of Croxley, paying rent for it to the abbey of St Albans; he was therefore the tenant of what is now Croxley Hall Farm.

Also from the text of their wills we know a little about other people with specific occupations. In 1441, Thomas Roos (35), who lived in Batchworth, indicated that he was a weaver: he left 'all his equipment pertaining to the art of weaving' to his son Henry. In 1463 Richard Vale (75) left to his servant John Quyntyn[89] all his instruments, or tools, pertaining to the craft of milling; perhaps he was the miller at Mill End. In 1530 John Hede (234) rented land called 'Stockers' and a mill at Batchworth. Roger Adam (81a & b) had 'Merceryware' in his shop. In its broadest sense 'mercery' was 'all merchandise except the weighty or bulky commodities such as victuals, corn, wine, metals, wool and wood'.[90] In the fifteenth century the Mercers' Company of London supervised, amongst other commodities, the trade in the luxury cloths of silk and linen, and the cloth of mixed linen and cotton called

---

[85] H. Falvey and P. Northeast, eds., *Wills of the Archdeaconry of Sudbury, 1439–1474: Wills from the Register 'Baldwyne', Part II: 1461-1474* (Suffolk Records Society, vol. 53, 2010), p.li.

[86] B. Campbell et al., *A Medieval Capital and its Grain Supply: Agrarian production and distribution in the London region c.1300* (London, 1993), p.30. Thanks to Prof Mark Bailey for this information and reference.

[87] See N. Amor, *From Wool to Cloth: The triumph of the Suffolk clothier* (Bungay, 2016), chapter 3, 'Wool and the wool trade'.

[88] Definition 1a of 'butcher' in the *OED*.

[89] The word used here is '*fa[mu]lo*', from *famulus*; slightly different in meaning from *serviens*.

[90] A. Sutton, 'Mercery through four centuries 1130s-c.1500', *Nottingham Medieval Studies*, 41 (1997), pp.100–125, p.100.

'fustian', but mercers dealt in all manner of goods. Provincial mercers stocked the cheaper goods – only a few dealt in silk – mostly fustian and linen and sometimes the poorer substitute hemp cloth. Linen and its substitutes were a very important part of their stock, especially bedding and furnishing items.[91] Presumably Adam did stock some high-end goods since he was owed money by Archbishop Neville, probably for purchases for the More. Rarely for Rickmansworth wills, Adam's will also mentions particular items of bedding. The last will published here is that of Thomas Spenser (248), who described himself as a baker, and had a bakehouse and a shop of some kind.[92] After the death of Spenser's wife Anne, his son Charles was to have

> all the Implements of my bakhowse, that is to saye, Troves, bordes, brake and a furnyshe (furnace) sett with a panne, the coborde, the table and forme in the hall, A cownter in the Ware shoppe, a brasen morter.

People of higher social status

Among the testators and people named in the wills are several people of some standing either inside or outside the parish, some, but not all, connected with the manor of the More. The manor house was situated within the parish of Rickmansworth but the manor itself extended into the parish of Watford. In 1416 William Flete became the tenant of the manor. He was a member of parliament for Hertfordshire in the parliaments of April 1414, November 1414, 1423 and 1433.[93] He is referred to in one of the wills, but only because his 'tenement' was mentioned in relation to a stretch of the king's highway that was to be repaired.[94] His successor at the More was Sir Ralph Butler, Baron Sudeley.[95] None of the wills here refer specifically to Butler but on 15 October 1451 William Kneth 'servaunt of my lord of Suydeley' made his will. Kneth's religious bequests were to the church of Our Lady of Watford, suggesting that he lived in Watford parish.[96] Sudeley was followed by George Neville, bishop of Exeter and later archbishop of York, whose debts to Roger

---

[91] Sutton, 'Mercery', p.125.

[92] A 'shop' was frequently a workshop but here it seems to be retail premises.

[93] Falvey, 'William Flete: More than just a castle builder'.

[94] Thomas Daye (27a & b)

[95] Falvey, 'The More revisited', p.93.

[96] HALS, 1AR64r, will of William Kneth. There are no personal bequests other than to his wife, so Kneth's will gives no details of others then employed at the More.

Adam have been noted above. Two of his household had died while at the More in 1472: Peter Arstock (89) in late January and Thomas Shorthouse (90) in February. They were not local men but may have been clerics and were certainly part of Neville's household.[97] A few months later the More was confiscated by Edward IV and it became part of the Duchy of Lancaster. Bailiff's accounts from the manor of 'Moor' for 1474-76 survive in the Duchy's archive, but they are in very poor condition and are virtually illegible.[98] One of the Duchy's local officials was Nicholas Leventhorp, esquire (134), who requested burial in the chapel of Our Lady of the Island. On 23 July 1484 Leventhorp was instructed to pay various people for food stuffs, including William Robyns for 'hay and horsbrede' 52s 3d.[99]

In August 1479 John Mertok (120) referred to John Wynkburn of Rykmersworth as 'yeoman of the king's chamber'. Wynkburn's own will (132) sheds no light on this, although he made some quite substantial cash bequests and requested burial inside the church. The duties of the four yeomen of the chamber during the reign of Edward IV have been recorded in detail; they were paid 3d per day.[100] Perhaps Wynkburn's role related to Edward IV being at the More.

Robert Bytterley (128), said to be 'late of the parish of Rykmersworth', died intestate in January 1480. He was probably related to Alice Bytterley of Sarratt, who had died in late October or early November 1479. She too left no will; her administrators were Philip Bytterley, gentleman, and Master John Botley, bachelor of common law.[101] It is clear that the Bytterely family were well-connected. Aside from his wife, Isabel, Robert's administrators were Master Richard Lessy, William Robyns esquire, James Cawode gentleman & sir Thomas Hemmyngforth, vicar of Sarratt. Master Richard Lessy was a graduate of both Oxford and Cambridge, with a music degree from the latter. He had close connections with Cecily Neville, mother of Edward IV and Richard III, being a member of her chapel at Berkhamsted castle as a child, and subsequently a member of her household and dean of her chapel. In 1481 he was

---

[97] See H. Falvey, 'Some members of the household of George Neville, Archbishop of York', *The Ricardian*, vol. XXII (2012), pp.55–58.

[98] TNA, DL29/53/1018, manor of Moor, Rickmansworth, bailiff's accounts, 1474–1476.

[99] R. Horrox and P. W. Hammond, eds., *British Library Harleian Manuscript 433*, 3 vols (Stroud, 1979–82), vol. 2, p.151.

[100] A. R. Myers, *The Household of Edward IV* (Manchester, 1959), p.117; wages, p.226.

[101] HALS, 2AR36r, the administration of the goods of Alice Bytterley of Sarratt, granted 16 November 1479.

described as one of her counsellors.[102] William Robyns may have been the William Robyn who held the manor of The Lea in Watford in the late fifteenth century.[103] As has already been noted he also had connections with Nicholas Leventhorp, esquire, and with the Duchy of Lancaster. James Cawode, gentleman, is less easy to identify: all that has been found is a lawsuit involving his executor in the 1490s.[104]

John Assheby (175a & b) held the non-manorial estate of Breakspears in neighbouring Harefield (Middx). It had been acquired by his father, George, in about 1447. George, who was clerk of the signet to Margaret of Anjou, wife of Henry VI, died in 1474. John's son, also George, was a clerk of the signet to Henry VII and Henry VIII.[105] It appears that John was an assistant clerk, or assistant to the clerk of the signet, from 1457 to 1459, but the nature of his subsequent career is unknown.[106] Whatever it was, he was designated 'gentleman' in the grant of administration issued by the archdeacon's court, and must have had property in more than one diocese since his will was proved in the Prerogative Court of Canterbury; although this might only be referring to property in Rickmansworth as well as Harefield since the latter was in the diocese of London. Both his will and his wife's are only testaments and so do not mention any landed property. Both requested burial in the new aisle of St Mary's church.

Outside the parish

Of course, Rickmansworth parishioners had connections with people and places elsewhere, either through business or family, and these are discussed in the next section. But there were also two (alleged) incidents that ultimately attracted the attention of the Pope, which are mentioned briefly: the circumstances are too complicated to cover in detail here.

---

[102] Information from Dr Joanna Laynesmith. See J. L. Laynesmith, *Cecily Duchess of York* (London, 2017); and also various references to Richard Lessy in the *Calendar of Papal Registers* via British History Online.

[103] *VCH Herts*, vol. 2, p.462.

[104] TNA, C1/222/70 and C1/233/71.

[105] 'Harefield: Manors', in *A History of the County of Middlesex*, Vol. 3, ed. Susan Reynolds (London, 1962), pp. 240-246. http://www.british-history.ac.uk/vch/middx/vol3/pp240-246 [accessed 30 August 2020].

[106] J. Otway-Ruthven, *The King's Secretary and the Signet Office in the XV century* (Cambridge, 1939), p.158. The career of George senior is given on p.185.

During the 1430s there was a dispute between William Creke, who held the manor of Micklefield, and Richard and Margaret Whitman, who lived in the parish, possibly not too far from Creke. The *St Albans Abbey Chronicle* records at very great length how in 1433 the Whitmans were excommunicated following a complaint by Creke that they had defamed, that is, publicly slandered, him.[107] Creke appears to have had the support of the vicar Henry Bornwash in all of this. Richard Whitman eventually appealed to the Court of Rome to have the excommunication quashed; in the meantime in early 1435 he was imprisoned in the abbot's gaol in St Albans but was released in July. It was probably not long after his release that he brought a suit in the court of Chancery against Creke alleging that Creke had forcibly entered his property and removed some of his belongings. He also stated that Creke's wife was the abbot's sister's daughter and thus the abbot had previously taken Creke's part against Whitman and had imprisoned him.[108] The result of the Chancery suit is unknown but in his will (53), made twenty years later, Creke made a provision for the substantial sum of 6s 8d to be paid annually to widow Margaret Whitman; perhaps a sign of remorse, or at least of concern regarding how his earlier actions might affect his soul's progress through purgatory.

On 4 May 1481 the Pope sent a letter to three bishops residing in London, directing them to hear both sides of a defamation suit brought by Anne Avelyne, widow of Richard Avelyne of Thorpe (Surrey), and Anne Osborne against Thomas Yong of Thorpe, and Elizabeth his wife, and Maud Bullok of 'Rigmannsworth'.[109] Both women named Anne were daughters of Robert Osborne of London. The Pope's letter does not give the name of their mother but they seem to have been full sisters even though they both had the same Christian name. Anne and Anne had petitioned the Pope because, although they were born of a lawful marriage (so they said), nevertheless Thomas, Elizabeth and Maud had alleged that they were illegitimate and had 'evilly defamed them'. These three had gone so far as to approach the archbishop of Canterbury, Thomas Bourgchier, about this matter. The archbishop, who was also a papal legate in England, had taken the matter up and, together with William Pikkenham, auditor-general of the archbishop's court, had, according to the two Annes, 'unjustly threatened to declare the said Anne Avelyne

---

[107] Riley, ed., *Annales monasterii S. Albani*, vol. 1, pp.369–408 & vol 2, pp.1–88.

[108] TNA, C1/44/235, Richard Whitman *versus* William Creke, undated but sometime between 1433 and 1443.

[109] *Calendar of Entries in the Papal Registers relating to Great Britain and Ireland, Papal Letters, 1471–1484*, vol. XIII, part II, (London, 1955), p.777.

and Anne Osborne to be illegitimate'. The two women had therefore petitioned the archbishop's immediate superior, the Pope. In response to their petition, the Pope sent the above-mentioned letter to John, bishop of Beirut, John, bishop of Ross and William, bishop of Sidon, all residing in the city of London. In this matter suits were also brought in the court of Chancery by various people; it appears that the issue was the identity of the rightful heirs to certain lands in Surrey (including Thorpe), Berkshire, Wiltshire and Buckinghamshire, and hence the two Annes' need to establish their legitimacy.[110] Again the outcomes the various suits are unknown, and since both Maud's will (193) and her husband William's (113) are testaments, there is no mention of any land in either of them.

Places mentioned in the wills

The wills provide a few pieces of information about buildings and land in the parish but not in any great detail. Property was usually transferred through the manor court and so only very cursory details of landholdings are given in wills (if at all). As already noted, it is usually impossible to tell from a will in which area of the parish a particular individual lived; although if they were alive in 1524 and mentioned in that year's tax listing that does indicate where they dwelled. Occasionally we may know where they lived because they made a bequest for repairs to the king's highway between their house and the church, or to other local roads.

In early 1435 Thomas Daye (27a & b) made a bequest to the repair of the king's highway between the tenement of William Flete and the barn of Ellen/Helen Bayly. Flete held several properties in Rickmansworth, including the four manors of Britwell, Batchworth, Ashleys and the More, from the Abbot of St Albans,[111] so which section of road Daye meant is not clear but it was likely to be in Batchworth. Thomas Audytor (100) may have lived in Maple Cross: he left 3s 4d for the repair of the king's highway between 'Bottis pyghtyll & Mapilcrosse' and also made a bequest to St Peter's church at Chalfont. Thomas Gybbes (101) made a bequest for repairing the king's highway called Ryggeweylane and also to his son his great table in his house called Kendale.[112] Stephen Stalon (105) left 13s 4d to the repair of the king's highway which lead from 'redeheth' to the bridge called 'Caysebrigge'; perhaps from what is now Sarratt Lane, across the green at Croxley and down what is now

---

[110] TNA, C1/15/344, C1/28/511, C1/41/268, C1/44/70.

[111] Falvey, 'William Flete: More than just a castle builder'.

[112] This was not the modern Ridge Way that is between Hill Rise and Shepherds Way.

Baldwins Lane.[113] William Hammond (172) had two houses in Mill End: one called 'Tokys' and the other called 'Hichemany'. John Tredeway (186) may have been the tenant of the manor of Linsters, which by 1460 consisted of a house and perhaps 100 acres of arable land: he bequeathed 3s 4d for mending the higway between 'lynsters & mapill crosse'.[114] Both John Hereward (42) and William Smyth (44) hinted at roads in need of cleaning up: Hereward left 20d to the way adjacent to the place called 'Fowle slowgh' and Smyth made a bequest for the repair of a way called 'Pyssyng daill'.

Some of the wills identify field names, but as there are very few detailed maps the location of these fields cannot be ascertained.[115] John Wellys (115) made his will at St Albans when he was ill. He refers to various houses and lands that he owned which seem to have been in Rickmansworth: his house called Bowrynges, his meadow called Hermytage, and the lands and tenements called Shepartes and Groves. On the other hand, Thomas Sywarde (174) simply stated that he had surrendered his copyhold lands into the hands of Thomas Coton, vicar, and John A Dene to the use of his wife.

Rickmansworth parishioners also had connections with other places, some probably where relatives lived or where they had business associates. The woolman William atte Welle (74), for example, had a daughter, Agnes, married to John Seybroke of Harpenden; he made bequests to the parish churches of Tring and Aylesbury; and appointed as one of his executors John Walloxton of Isnamstede Cheyne (Chenies). John Mertok (120), although he requested burial inside St Mary's near the grave of his son, also John, owned the manor of Warehache in Ware, which was to pass to his wife, Margaret.[116] His feoffees came from various places: William Staneley,

---

[113] The road following this route is not on the earliest maps of the area but is on that by Dury & Andrew, published in 1766.

[114] *VCH Herts*, vol 2, p.383: in 1460 Linsters comprised 'one messuage and a carucate and half of land'. (See Glossary.)

[115] The only detailed maps are of the 'Freehold Estate called Woodwick', dated 30 April 1760 (HALS, DZ/120/7/4/44213); Croxley manor in 1766, owned by Gonville & Caius College, Cambridge; and the parish tithe map of 1839 (HALS, DSA4/80/2; the tithe award giving details of landholders is HALS, DSA4/80/1).

[116] According to the *VCH Herts* there was a manor in Ware called 'Waters alias Martocks, now Mardocks'. John Mertok is not mentioned in this entry but 'Margaret Martock' is. (*VCH Herts*, vol. 3, p.390)

esquire, of Burleigh (Rutland), and Robert Forthe, yeoman, of Aylesbury (Bucks), as well as John Wynkburn of Rickmansworth, yeoman of the king's chamber.

Some of the place names given in the wills are earlier than the dates cited in *The Place Names of Hertfordshire* (*PNH*) as their first mention. 'Herynghers' (Heronsgate) is given in the will of Thomas Gybbes (72), written in May 1462; the earliest date in *PNH* is 1599. 'Mapilcrosse' is given in the will of Thomas Audytor (100), written in 1473; the earliest date in *PNH* is in the reign of Henry VII, which began in 1485.[117]

And then there is the name of Rickmansworth itself. In many of the wills it takes the form Rykmersworth, or variations on this spelling. Quite often the clerk of the probate court abbreviated it to Ryk' – why take up valuable space with such a long name when there was nowhere in the county similarly named, let alone in the archdeaconry? The settlement started life in the Saxon period as a single farmstead. *PNH* suggested that, as 'worth' means 'farm' in old English and that 'Ricmaer' was a Continental personal name, the whole name meant 'Ricmaer's farm'.[118] However, more recently it has been suggested that the farm was named after its physical situation. The Old English word for ridge is 'hrycg' and for mere is 'maere', which together describe perfectly the location, as it was both on a ridge and at the confluence of three rivers.[119] Interestingly the 'modern' form first appears as 'Rykmansworth' in the will of William Smyth (44), made in December 1447 and then in that of Henry Willeys (111), made in December 1476. In June 1485, in Joan Wynkeburn's will the form 'Rikmansworth' is used. There is no way of knowing whether the form of the name was used independently by the scribe or stated by the testator; by contrast, in the wills of Joan's husband John (132) and Henry's sons John (86) and Thomas (87) the name 'Rykmersworth' is used. We will now consider the process of making a will.

The probate process in medieval England and the records that it generated

A will was often made when a testator was on their deathbed, although occasionally during an illness from which they later recovered. A will might be made before an

---

[117] J. E. B. Gover, A. Mawer and F. M. Stenton, eds., *The Place-Names of Hertfordshire* (Cambridge, 1938), pp.82–3.

[118] Gover, Mawer & Stenton, *Place-Names of Hertfordshire*, p.81.

[119] A. and C. Jacques, *Rickmansworth: A Pictorial History* (Chichester, 1996), p.xii.

undertaking that might involve personal risk, such as travelling on a long journey, perhaps overseas, or going off to war. In general, there were three main groups of testators: men with family commitments struck down in the prime of life; wealthy men whose affairs were abnormally complex; and single women (widows or spinsters) who had no obvious heir and wished to distribute a large number of small legacies amongst family and friends. None of these three groups is typical of the population as a whole and so will making was not a 'majority' activity. Most men did not need to make a will, either because they did not have much to leave, or because the inheritance process that applied to them was quite simple – most land was passed on according to manorial custom. It is not possible to estimate the proportion of the medieval population that left a will. Given the identities of those most likely to make a will, as outlined above, the proportion was very low. Even in the early modern period when burial registers were (supposed to be) kept, estimates of the proportion of testators in the population can only be found in studies of individual parishes. These figures vary greatly due to local circumstances: the range is about 8 per cent to about 25 per cent of adult males.[120] And, unlike southern Europe, in England married women were not allowed to make a will unless they held landed property in their own right.[121]

Usually a will was written down: it was 'dictated' by the testator very often, as already noted, to their parish priest.[122] The priest was involved because he might be the only person who could write in a rural parish; but sometimes there might be a local scribe. In towns notaries public might write wills, but again more usually priests. The will was signed or marked by the testator and by witnesses. Where witnesses' names have been recorded they provide glimpses of friendship or occupational networks within a community. Occasionally a will was spoken on the deathbed in front of witnesses. These witnesses subsequently reported the content to an officer of the probate court, who wrote it down. '[A] written version of this

---

[120] Some of these estimates are given in N. Goose and N. Evans, 'Wills as an historical source', in T. Arkell, N. Evans and N. Goose, eds., *When Death Do Us Part: Understanding and interpreting the probate records of early modern England* (Oxford, 2000), pp.38–71, pp.44–45.

[121] K. L. Reyerson, 'Wills of spouses in Montpellier before 1350: a case study of gender in testamentary practice', in J. Rollo-Koster and K. L Reyerson, eds., *"For the salvation of my soul": Women and wills in medieval and early modern France* (St Andrews, 2012), pp.44-60.

[122] Michael Sheehan has described the process of making a will in M. M. Sheehan, 'English wills and the records of ecclesiastical and civil jurisdictions', *Journal of Medieval History*, 14 (1988), pp.3–12.

nuncupative will was prepared and authenticated with the seal of the officer' and marked or signed by the witnesses.[123] Within in this collection there is only one nuncupative will, that of John Tymberlake (78). Further copies of an original will or a nuncupative will were 'prepared and sealed to be used during the implementation of the will'.[124] Hardly any original medieval wills, or their probate copies, have survived.[125]

The probate process in England was dealt with by the church courts and so, after the death of the testator, executors presented the will/testament to the relevant ecclesiastical authority for probate.[126] It was the responsibility of the executors named in the will to obtain probate. They had to decide to which court the will should be taken and determine where the appropriate official was to be found. Some courts met in different locations, especially if the archdeaconry (or other relevant jurisdiction) was large. Some were proved very soon after they were made, not only indicating that the testator had indeed been on their death bed, but also that the executors knew what they were supposed to do. Perhaps prior discussion and planning had taken place.

The ecclesiastical probate courts

In general there were three tiers of probate jurisdiction. The majority of testators had their wills proved in the archdeacon's court. Originally the archdeacon had deputised for the bishop, but over time he came to act in his own right.[127] All but four of the wills published here were proved in the archdeacon's court. In general, right of appeal was to the bishop's court but this would not apply to parishes within

---

[123] See also, A. E. B. Owen, 'A scrivener's notebook from Bury St Edmunds', *Archives*, xiv, (1979), pp.16–22.

[124] Sheehan, 'English wills', p.4.

[125] The first original Rickmansworth will is that of Henry Soonner[*sic*], proved in 1545. (HALS, 295AW4)

[126] Sheehan, 'English wills', p.5. Sometimes the will was enrolled in borough records, for example, the earliest London wills were enrolled in the Hustings Roll in 1258, but note only wills not testaments.

[127] J. Cox and N. Cox, 'Probate 1500-1800: a system in transition', in Arkell, Evans and Goose, eds., *When Death Do Us Part*, pp.14–37, p.15, n.3: 'Not all dioceses were divided into archdeaconries and in others the archdeaconries appear to have been subdivided for the purposes of probate. Particularly in the north – where archdeaconries were huge – there were lower rural deans' courts'.

the archdeaconry of St Albans since this was an 'exempt jurisdiction' outside the control of the bishop of Lincoln within whose diocese the archdeaconry lay physically. The archdeaconry was coterminous with the liberty of the abbey of St Albans. The archdeaconry of St Albans, with the abbot of St Albans at its head, 'stoutly maintained its freedom from episcopal control'.[128] Until the dissolution of the monastery the abbot appointed the archdeacon, who presided over the ecclesiastical court. Its duties included not only granting probate of wills, for which fees were charged, but also hearing cases concerning irregularities in faith and morals, that is, matters touching the spiritual welfare of both clergy and laity.

Records from St Albans indicate that in the period 1580–1625, on all but 26 occasions, ordinary sessions of the archdeacon's court were held in the 'parish church of St Albans'.[129] This would have been within the former abbey church, which had been purchased by the Corporation in 1553 to serve their parish of St Andrew.[130] In 1588 an extra session of the court was held 'in the Great Porch of St Albans Church'.[131] Perhaps the archdeacon's court always met in the 'Great Porch', and had done so before the dissolution of the monastery in 1539. Certainly, some medieval grants of probate were recorded as being given at the monastery, for example, those of Elizabeth and John Newell (both 162), Lettice Danyell (167) and William Cooke (169). The wills of Maud Horsman (9) and Maud Dyer (10) were granted probate at Rickmansworth, by William Alnewyke, archdeacon, on 5 May 1428: presumably Alnewyke was in the parish on other business. Otherwise, where stated, Rickmansworth wills were proved at St Albans.

In general knights, clergy and men with substantial possessions (usually valued over £10) had to have their wills proved in the bishop's court, or consistory. This court was presided over by his chancellor or an official known as the ordinary. He was competent to exercise all the bishop's jurisdiction but the bishop retained the right to act himself. Right of appeal was to the archbishops' court. Possession of goods of valued at more than £5 in more than one archdeaconry of the same diocese also

---

[128] S. Flood, 'Introduction' in B. Crawley ed., *Wills at Hertford, 1415–1858* (London, 2007), p.ix.

[129] R. Peters, *Oculus Episcopi: Administration in the Archdeaconry of St Albans, 1580–1625* (Manchester, 1963), p.54.

[130] Roberts, *The Hill of the Martyr*, p.154.

[131] Peters, *Oculus Episcopi*, p.55.

required wills to be proved in the consistory.[132] (Again having a will proved in the consistory did not apply if the deceased had died in the archdeaconry of St Albans.)

When property was held in more than one diocese, wills had to be proved in the archbishop's court: in southern England that of the archbishop of Canterbury, which later became known as the Prerogative Court of Canterbury (PCC); in northern England in court of archbishop of York (PCY). The will of John Assheby (175b) is the only pre-Reformation PCC Rickmansworth will.

Surviving wills

As already noted, very few original medieval wills have survived. What we have are copies of wills that were written into the register of the court that had granted probate. These registers survive from various ecclesiastical jurisdictions. One might think that each court that exercised jurisdiction over probate kept a register of probates granted but in fact it appears that they did not. Firstly, they have not survived in many places; secondly the survivals vary in nature and content; thirdly, we know that in some places they were never kept.[133] But in theory, for the full text of a medieval will we need to look in the registers of the various ecclesiastical jurisdictions.

The earliest will that Michael Sheehan has found recorded in a bishop's register is from 1269 in the register of the bishop of Worcester. Sheehan notes that 'quite large numbers of testaments survive in this way from the fourteenth century'. He goes on:

> with improvements of office procedure in the bishops' consistories and the courts of the archdeacons, probate registers were kept, beginning at York in 1316, increasingly after 1350, and attaining a daunting scale during the fifteenth century. The great series of prerogative-probate registers of the archbishops of Canterbury and York begin in 1383 and 1389 respectively.[134]

Frustratingly, apart from the archdeaconry of York, he does not specify *which* other courts had begun to keep probate registers but, for example, registers survive from

---

[132] Northeast and Falvey, eds., *Wills from the Register 'Baldwyne', Part II: 1461–1474*, p.xliv.

[133] For example Dr Andrew George, the former archivist of the record office of the diocese of Coventry and Lichfield, confirmed that no probate registers were kept by the consistory court there.

[134] Sheehan, 'English wills', p.5.

the commissary court of Bury St Edmunds (Suffolk) from 1354,[135] the archdeaconry of London from 1393,[136] and the archdeaconry of St Albans from 1413.[137]

Register entries (usually) comprise a transcript of the testament and/or will plus the probate sentence. The probate sentence was a certificate of approval added to the original will by the clerk of the proving officer. Ideally it comprised: the date when the will was presented for probate; by whom it was presented; before whom it was proved; which executors would act; by which date the executors should produce an inventory; and an order to produce an account. These last two documents rarely survive because they were on loose sheets.

Part of the probate sentence was the grant of administration in which the executors present in court were named and 'power reserved' to those not present. The whole probate sentence should have been copied by the registry clerk when he registered the will, but this did not always happen, and the Latin, because it was of a standard nature, was often highly abbreviated. Sometimes only the probate sentence was entered in the medieval probate register i.e. a note that administration had been granted to the executor(s). There are four Rickmansworth entries that are only probate sentences.[138] Some of the entries might only be records of grants of administration: usually in such instances the deceased had died intestate (without making a will) and the court granted power to named people to administer the goods of the estate, very often the widow and/or a son. In this collection 32 grants of administration are recorded in the archdeacon's register. One applies jointly to the goods of husband and wife John and Elizabeth Newell (162), and another applies to the goods of John Assheby (175a) being within the archdeaconry; his will (175b) was proved in the Prerogative Court of Canterbury because he held property elsewhere (actually in the diocese of London).

---

[135] S. Tymms, *Wills and Inventories from the Registers of the Commissary of Bury St Edmunds and the Archdeacon of Sudbury* (Camden Society, xlix, 1850), p.vii. A commissary court was a diocesan court empowered to handle probate matters falling entirely within the diocese. (J. Richardson, *The Local Historian's Encyclopedia*, (2nd edn, New Barnet, 1986), p.77.)

[136] 'Sources: Wills and inventories', in *A Survey of Documentary Sources for Property Holding in London before the Great Fire*, ed. D. Keene and V. Harding (London Record Society vol. 22, 1985), pp.219–221, entry 529d.

[137] Flood, 'Introduction', in Crawley ed., *Wills at Hertford, 1415–1858*, p.x. (A will from Hertfordshire written in 1413 was registered in 1430: the book title does not reflect this.

[138] Wills 33, 141, 149 and 150.

Often entries in a probate register were made in chronological order of the date when probate was granted, but not always. In the St Albans registers some entries are in order of probate date but others were not. It seems likely that the probate clerk(s) made notes of probates granted while the court was sitting in different places and then copied the wills and/or wrote their notes into the register later when they were in the place where the register was kept. The documents have been published here in order of date of writing rather than date of probate.

Generally probate clerks remain anonymous; however, the clerk does give his name on the first folio of the third St Albans register. Next to the very detailed probate sentence for the will of John Alen (242) is written (in Latin) '[by] Robert Garret, clerk, Registrar of testaments'. It is likely that Garret was a notary because his signature appears to be a 'sign manual': his name together with an intricate symbol.

Wills in the court book of the manor of Croxley

The first three wills published here were not proved in the archdeacon's court but were recorded in the Croxley court book. The deceased were unfree tenants of the manor of Croxley and their wills have survived because there is a sixteenth century copy of the manor court book in the British Library.[139] In legal theory villeins (unfree tenants, i.e. copyholders, customary tenants) held nothing that was not already the property of their lord; however it is clear that as a matter of privilege villeins were permitted to make wills.[140] The church taught that it was a man's duty to make a will 'at least upon his death-bed, with his last confession'. If he had nothing that was not his lord's he would be unable to make restitution for unpaid tithes, nor make any gift to the Church. Thus, Ada Levett says, 'it is common to find that ecclesiastical lords permitted their villeins to make wills'. The probate of such wills, however, took place in the manorial court, not before the archdeacon. On the St Albans estates the wills of freemen (i.e. tenants of freehold land) were proved by the archdeacon of the abbey (an exempt archdeaconry), the wills of villeins went for probate to the cellarer in the halimote (the manorial leet court). Some can be found in thirteenth century court rolls, but the practice was confirmed in 1350 and recorded in several of the abbey's courts' books. In 1350 it was said to be a custom

---

[139] BL, Add MS 6057, the court book of Croxley Manor. There is also a nineteenth century copy: BL, Add MS 5834.

[140] This paragraph is a summary of A. E. Levett, *Studies in Manorial History* (Oxford, 1938; reprinted 1963), pp.208–223.

since before the memory of man that testaments of unfree tenants should be proved before the cellarer and that all cellarers had done so, whereas any freeman who held a messuage freely ought to have his testament proved by the archdeacon of the monastery of St Albans. A few years after 1350 wills of villeins were more routinely enrolled in court books, but they are more common between 1377 and 1420 than later, indeed the custom of enrolling wills upon the court roll apparently did not last very long: it was likely to have been due to the interest of two or three particular cellarers.

The three wills granted probate in the Croxley court and recorded in the court book are those of Simon Canoun (1) and John Canoun (2) (possibly father and son) on 23 May 1409 and the will of John atte Forthe (3) on 24 September 1416.[141] There is, however, in the court book an oblique reference an earlier Croxley will. At the court held on the Thursday in Pentecost week 18 Richard II (11 June 1394), when Robert Chestan was cellarer, the jury presented that John Gile[sic] had died; the heriot for his holding was a horse priced 12d and his heir was his daughter Margaret, who was a minor aged 17. The court ordered to distrain Margot Gyles to prove her husband's testament.[142] Thus the earliest *mention* of a local will was in 1394.

The documents

Of the 213 wills published here, 153 were written in Latin. The first English will, that of John Gybbes (45), was made on 6 March 1448. The use of English in the wills increased gradually over time. The last Latin will is that of John Durrant alias Eastbury, made on 10 March 1511. It is worth noting that English words were used in some of the Latin wills to specify particular items, perhaps where there was no direct Latin equivalent. For example, William Gybbys' will (79), written in 1466, has the word 'brendyld' to describe the colour of a cow. Interestingly the *OED* has 'brinded' or 'brended' meaning 'of a tawny or brownish colour, marked with bars or streaks of a different hue' dating from 1430, but variants of 'brindled', in a separate entry, date only from 1678; Gybbys' will has the English word 'brendyld' nearly 250 years earlier. The English will of Alys Pygot (161), written in 1492, also has

---

[141] BL, Add MS 6057, fols. 26r and 28v. These three wills are also published in their original Latin in Levett, *Studies in Manorial History*, pp.224–225.

[142] BL, Add MS 6057, fol. 121r. See Glossary for 'distrain'.

'bryndlyd Bulloke'. In addition Alys's will mentions a 'garlyd bollok': this means 'spotted, speckled' and the *OED* gives 1506 as the earliest example.

Table 5: Rickmansworth probate material by year of writing

decade	wills	M	F	admin	M	F	probate	M	F
1400-09	2	2	0	0	0	0			
1410-19	2	2	0	0	0	0			
1420-29	10	7	3	0	0	0			
1430-39	18	12	6	1	1	0	1	1	0
1440-49	14	14	0	0	0	0			
1450-59	20	16	4	1	1	0			
1460-69	12	10	2	2	1	1			
1470-79	37	30	7	6	5	1			
1480-89	13	9	4	6	5	1	1	0	1
1490-99	22	18	4	7	[a]5.5	1.5	2	2	0
1500-09	22	20	2	4	4	0			
1510-19	9	6	3	3	3	0			
1520-29	18	16	2	1	1	0			
1530-39	14	13	1	0	0	0	1	0	1
Totals m/f		175	38		26.5	4.5		3	2
Totals	213			31			5		

[a] The 'half' male and 'half' female refer to the joint administration of Elizabeth and John Newell (162)

In all there are 248 numbered documents published here but the following analysis covers 249 documents because there is both an administration and a will for John Assheby. (Table 5 summarises the document types.) The first three are the wills recorded in Croxley court book. There are 213 are wills in total, of which three have two versions: Thomas Daye nos. 27a and 27b; Roger Adam 81a and 81b; John Ayleward 96a and 96b. One will was recorded twice in the register, with exactly the same wording and same date of probate: John Gray (212). It appears that the validity of the will of Stephen Holtyng (166) had been challenged: the entry in the register includes statements by two of the original witnesses and by the vicar, sir Thomas Coton (perhaps the writer of the will), confirming that its contents were authentic. There are 31 grants of administration. One of these is for the goods of husband and wife Elizabeth and John Newell (162), rather unusually it does not name the administrator. Another anomaly is the probate material relating to John Assheby, gentleman, whose main property was in Harefield (Middx) but who requested burial in 'the new Isle of the Churche of Rikmersworth betwixt John Rolfe and thentre [the entry] into the saide Chapell'. As noted, for Assheby there is a grant of administration from the archdeacon's court and a will that was proved in the Prerogative Court of Canterbury (175a and 175b). There are five documents that simply record that probate was granted: Peter atte Stirte (33), Ann Newton (141), Thomas Botterfeld (149), John Baker (150) and Margaret Eglestone (239).

Table 6: Surviving wills from nearby parishes (from published sources)

decade	Rick'	Sarratt	Bricket Wood *etc*	Kings Langley	St Albans urban
1400-09	2	0	0	0	
1410-19	2	0	1	0	
1420-29	10	0	4	0	
1430-39	18	3	7	0	
1440-49	14	0	3	0	
1450-59	20	6	5	0	
1460-69	12	2	4	0	
1470-79	37	2	2	0	128
1480-89	13	2	2	0	76
1490-99	22	1	1	1	89
1500-09	22	2	8	0	
1510-19	9	2	9	0	
1520-29	18	2	8	7	
1530-39	14	1	11	6	
Total	**213**	**23**	**65**	**14**	**293**

How does the number of surviving wills Rickmansworth compare with villages and towns elsewhere? Table 6 provides an analysis that has been carried out using published wills. Regarding Hertfordshire parishes, from the neighbouring parish of Sarratt there are 23 from the period 1435 to 1539;[143] from Bricket Wood and some other parts of St Stephen's parish there are 65 dating from 1418 to 1539.[144] There are

---

[143] P. and B. Buller, eds., *Pots, Platters & Ploughs: Sarratt Wills & Inventories 1435–1832* (Sarratt, 1982).

[144] L. Munby, M. Parker et al., eds., *All My Worldly Goods, I, An Insight into Family Life from Wills and Inventories 1447–1742* (Bricket Wood, 1991); M. Parker, ed., *All My*

14 from Kings Langley from 1498 to 1539.[145] The latter was in the archdeaconry of Huntingdon: the probate registers from that archdeaconry start much later than those of St Albans archdeaconry. The survival of wills from St Albans itself far exceeds even the Rickmansworth figure: there are 293 wills from the three urban parishes of St Andrew, St Peter and St Michael between 1471 and 1499.[146]

Table 7: Will numbers for Rickmansworth and further afield

decade	Rick'	Houghton Regis	Sudbury (to 1474)	Stratford-upon-Avon
pre-1400	0	0	0	1
1400-09	2	0	0	0
1410-19	2	0	0	0
1420-29	10	0	0	0
1430-39	18	0	0	0
1440-49	14	0	20	0
1450-59	20	0	22	0
1460-69	12	0	16	1
1470-79	37	0	11	1
1480-89	13	0		0
1490-99	22	0		2
1500-09	22	8		5
1510-19	9	1		1
1520-29	18	8		4
1530-39	14	13		11
Total	213	30	69	26

Looking further afield, some other comparisons are possible. (See Table 7.) In Bedfordshire the archdeacon's registers also start later: in the period 1500–1539 there are 30 wills from the parish of Houghton Regis.[147] From the market town of

---

Worldly Goods, II, Wills and Probate Inventories of St Stephen's Parish, St Albans, 1418–1700 (Bricket Wood, 2004).

[145] L. Munby, ed., *Life & Death in Kings Langley 1498–1659* (Kings Langley, 1981).

[146] S. Flood, ed., *St Albans Wills, 1471–1500* (HRS, vol. IX, 1993).

[147] Houghton Regis: A. F. Cirket, ed., *English Wills, 1498–1526* (Beds Hist Rec Soc, 37, 1957); P. Bell ed., *Bedfordshire Wills, 1480–1519* (Beds Hist Rec Soc, 45, 1966); M. McGregor, *Bedfordshire Wills proved in the PCC, 1383–1548* (Beds Hist Rec Soc, 58, 1979).

Sudbury (Suffolk), centre of the archdeaconry of Sudbury, there are 69 wills entered in the archdeacon's probate register between 1440 and 1474, *versus* 92 from Rickmansworth up to 1474.[148] From the town of Stratford-upon-Avon there are 26 wills dating between 1348 and 1539, although as the table shows there are none between 1348 and the 1460s, and very few until the 1530s.[149]

All of this indicates that Rickmansworth is somewhat precocious as far as will making is concerned; or rather, one should say that the survival of the registers from the archdeaconry of St Albans, and indeed the Croxley court book, makes Rickmansworth precocious as far as the *survival* of wills is concerned. Nevertheless, this indicates that the Rickmansworth wills are significant. Indeed, as we have already seen, they reveal much about the medieval church and its parishioners.

The form of a medieval will[150]

The components of a medieval testament

By the fifteenth century there was a fairly standard way of composing a testament. This pattern was not fixed, nor were all of the elements included in every one, but, in general, a pre-Reformation testament comprised the following.

Invocation: The majority began with the words, 'In the name of God, Amen'.

Date of writing: Usually expressed as day, month and year, but occasionally by liturgical feast-days, such as William Creke (5) on the feast of the exaltation of the Holy Cross (14 September) 1425. The regnal year was normally reserved for dating wills proper, but here it was used nine times from 1492 onwards.[151] The Roman calendar, based on the Kalends, Nones and Ides of the months, was used just twice: Walter Selwode (14) and John Elfred (17).

---

[148] P. Northcast ed , *Wills of the Archdeaconry of Sudbury, 1439–1474: Wills from the Register 'Baldwyne', Part I: 1439–1461* (Suffolk Records Society, vol. 44, 2001); Northeast and Falvey eds., *Wills from the Register 'Baldwyne', Part II: 1461–1474*.

[149] S. Appleton and M. Macdonald, eds., *Stratford-upon-Avon Wills 1348–1701: vol. 1, 1348–1647; vol. 2, 1648–1701* (Dugdale Society, vol 52, 2020).

[150] Based on the Introduction to Northeast and Falvey, eds., *Wills from the Register 'Baldwyne', Part II: 1461–1474*, pp.xlix–lxxv.

[151] Charts for converting regnal years can be found online and in such books as C. R. Cheney, *Handbook of Dates for Students of English History* (London, 1991), and Richardson, *Local Historian's Encyclopedia*.

The testator: After giving his/her name the testator usually stated in which parish they lived, but rarely their occupation. Where appropriate, descriptions of status and condition, such as esquire (four), gentleman (three) and widow (nineteen), were more likely to be given. Katherine Turnour (69) explicitly stated that she was 'late the wife of Richard Turnour'. Most men had common Christian names such as John, Thomas or William, although some unusual names do occur, such as Baldewin Rous (40) and Helias Stokker (59). Similarly, common female names such as Katherine, Ann and Maud (Matilda) occur, but also Idiota Colyer (11), Petronilla Dier (32) and Lettice Danyell (167).

State of mind: For legal reasons testators emphasised their mental competence and so declared themselves to be sound of mind and of good memory, but, they might add, being sick in body. If the testator was near to death the will could be nuncupative, that is, spoken, and written down later; here only John Tymberlake's (78) was, being made in the presence of John Wynton, vicar.

Commendation, i.e. religious preamble: Almost always the first 'bequest' of the testament was that of the testator's soul: 'I commend my soul unto Almighty God, the Blessed Virgin Mary and all the saints in heaven', or something very similar. Much has been made of the form that the commendation took in original wills. Some historians have suggested that is was the testator's own statement of religious conformity (or not); others have suggested it was in the form that the will-writer thought correct.[152] Most of the commendations in these registered wills follow the format given above, but there are a handful that do not, the most eloquent, perhaps not surprisingly, is in the one will that was proved in the Prerogative Court of Canterbury, that of John Assheby (175b). Apart from references at the end to the Virgin and all the saints, one might think that this was the preamble of the will of a late sixteenth century 'Puritan'. Indeed, Assheby's will reinforces Eamon Duffy's argument that such preambles were not simply a product of Protestantism. On the other hand there are 78 wills here that simply open with 'In &c.'; give the testator's name and other details about them; and the first bequest is to the high altar for tithes forgotten. But, despite the loose association of Lollardy with Rickmansworth, there are three reasons that indicate that these abbreviated preambles do not denote some sort of reaction against the Church. Firstly, testaments could only be granted probate in a religious court, so in the preamble it would not have been prudent to

---

[152] Much of the discussion has centred on post-Reformation preambles and whether they disclose the testator's religious convictions, but Eamon Duffy has also discussed this in regard to medieval wills. (Duffy, *Stripping of the Altars*, pp.354–76.)

ignore the Church's teaching. Secondly, these wills with highly abbreviated openings have been entered in the register with similarly worded wills from other parishes. Thirdly, from the layout on the pages, it is clear that all were shortened because the clerk in the probate court wanted to save precious space in the register: that part of the preamble takes up at least two or three lines on the page and the use of &c (in some cases several times) indicates that the usual formula had been followed in the original testament which the clerk had copied into the register.

Place of burial: Most testators requested burial in the parish churchyard. Powerful and wealthy parishioners could request burial inside the church, some specifying the actual place within the building.

Unpaid debts: A substantial portion of most testaments related directly, or indirectly, to the 'health of the soul', that is, its passing through purgatory. Money for forgotten tithes and offerings were always given to the 'high altar'. Duffy explains this apparent obsession with the possibility of unpaid tithes, arguing that it was no mere form of words. Four times a year the parish priest would solemnly pronounce to his parishioners the Greater Excommunication or General Sentence.[153] This formidable curse listed a comprehensive range of offences against the Church, its personnel and precepts. Anyone might, deliberately or by oversight, fail to pay their tithes: this offence incurred the rigour of the General Sentence, i.e. excommunication. 'Unpaid tithes, like other debts, hindered or cut off the benefits of prayer and almsdeeds, and left the soul longer in purgatory.'[154] In the shortened wills this phrase has not been abbreviated, perhaps because it involved a particular amount of money or the bequest of an item, such as a cloth, or even a sheep.

Some medieval testators bequeathed a 'mortuary', also called a 'principal'. This was a traditional burial payment due to the incumbent, usually the second-best animal, after the heriot had been claimed by the manorial lord. Three Rickmansworth parishioners made such bequests: Roger Bryan (48) bequeathed his best gown to the vicar for a mortuary; Alice Gardyner bequeathed the 'best animal' that she had for her 'mortuary and principal legacy'; and John Wynkburn (132) bequeathed to the vicar 'in the name of [his] mortuary one grey-coloured colt'.

The burial: One aspect of the doctrine of purgatory was the belief that the soul's progress could be helped by the prayers of the living. The burial was an opportunity for gathering together a number of people who would add their prayers in this way.

---

[153] Duffy, *Stripping of the Altars*, p.356.
[154] Duffy, *Stripping of the Altars*, p.357.

Examples from Suffolk show that refreshments might be provided, occasionally for the whole parish; priests and clerks were paid; money was given to the poor. In many cases this might be was repeated seven days later and again after a month. The Rickmansworth testators made fewer explicit provisions for the arrangements on their burial day, although William at Welle (74) mentions mass and his 'exequies' on the thirtieth day and William Revell (103) makes detailed provision for the anniversary of his death, and of various other people's, to be celebrated for ever.

Bequests to churches: As already noted there were various bequests to the 'reparation' of St Mary's, or to specific building projects, or to other churches.

Church interior: Similarly bequests were made to fittings and the decoration of churches. For example, Margaret A Dene (168) bequeathed an altar cloth to each altar within the church and the chapel of Our Lady of the Island.

Priests' services: Most testaments included bequests to members of the clergy specifically requesting their prayers. Priests were paid to celebrate mass for a stated number of years or fractions of a year. For example, Nicholas Turnour (61) wanted a priest to celebrate (mass) for him and his forebears for one year.

Charitable giving: Giving to the poor, sick and needy, to poor prisoners, to the repair of roads and bridges, etc., were believed to be for the 'health of the soul'.

Indulgences: Another means of shortening the soul's time in purgatory was to take advantage of some of the many indulgences, or pardons, which had been granted by bishops and popes. Many pilgrimage sites had been granted indulgences, and pilgrimage itself was regarded as beneficial to the soul. Only one Rickmansworth parishioner asked for a pilgrimage to be done for them: Agnes Grover (231) asked Edmund Twechyn and his wife to 'goo in pilgrimage' to Our Lady of Walsingham.

Household items: As real estate, houses should have been dealt with in the will proper, but household articles might be bequeathed in the testament. There are some bequests of pots and pans, and bedding, and also of clothing, by both men and women. Some testators possessed items made of precious metals, such as silver spoons. Margaret Dyer (88), possessed 'a pair of beads', that is, a set of rosary beads.

John Assheby (175b) bequeathed his signet ring to his son George, who in turn bequeathed it to his son Thomas.[155]

Occupations: farming: Although almost everyone was involved in farming to some extent, farm animals, equipment and crops only feature in a few of the testaments.

Occupations: crafts and trades: Workshops, whether within the house or in outbuildings, would have been included in the will proper, but the equipment in them would usually be included in the testament, as was the baker's equipment of Thomas Spenser (248).

Appointment of executors: Usually towards the end of their testaments, testators named their executors, frequently appointing their spouse and/or other family members, or else business or social acquaintances in the locality. One or more **supervisors** of the executors, usually of higher social standing, might be named as well. Executors and supervisors might also be members of the clergy. Bequests were usually made to executors in recompense for their labour or 'pains' in executing the will, the amount varied, not only according to the wealth of the testator but perhaps also according to amount of work expected of the executors. Occasionally one or more of the executors renounced their appointment, leaving the execution to the other(s), (e.g. 46, 56) but their reasons are not recorded. Perhaps the one left to administer the will was considered perfectly competent, or impossible to work with.

The residue: After all the specific bequests, the testator usually bequeathed the residue of all their goods and chattels to the executor(s) to dispose of, sometimes for the health of the testator's soul.

Sealing: After the testament had been written and read out to the testator and witnesses, a seal might be applied to the document. Witnesses' names were sometimes added. In later original wills that have also been registered it is clear that, while witnesses were named in the original wills, they might not be listed in the registered will.

---

[155] To Thomas 'my signet with my Armes in it, which was my Grauntfathers and bequethid unto me by my Fader in his last will'. (TNA, PROB 11/18/196, will of George Asshby, 13 March 1515)

The form of the will proper

The will, more correctly, the last will (*ultima voluntas*), was a legal document, the main purpose of which was to convey instructions or requests to the testator's feoffees with respect to real estate.

Feoffees: Because testators were not allowed by law to bequeath real estate, a practice called 'enfeoffment to use' been developed, whereby the holder of property enfeoffed (that is, conveyed the property to) feoffees or trustees, to his or her 'use'. In other words, the feoffees held the property on behalf of the original holder and since they held it to his or her 'use', the feoffees could, subsequently, be told what to do with it. Thus in their last will the testator would request the feoffees to hand over the 'estate' or title in the property, or certain parts of it, to other named beneficiaries. A handful of the documents here include what is, effectively the testator's last will. Only three mention feoffees: John Mertok (120) regarding his manor of Warehache in Ware; George Wynkborn (225) regarding his property in the parishes of Rickmansworth and Watford called 'Croxleys, Julyans lond & dellys'; Thomas Sywarde (174) had enfeoffed his house to five named individuals and he had also surrendered his copyhold lands into the hands of two named people to the use his wife during her life time and then to his heirs.

Lands: Testators' descriptions of their lands varied enormously, from the simple 'all my lands and tenements' of John atte Hyde (51), to named lands or properties. John Holtyng (240) bequeathed 'all my londes frehold & copyhold callid Harry Smythes & Waterdell'.

The probate sentence

It was the responsibility of the executors named in the will to obtain probate. The probate sentence was a certificate of approval added to the original will (whether that consisted of testament only, or testament and will proper) by the court. Some were very short, others quite detailed. The first part of the probate sentence usually stated that the will had been proved 'before' (Latin *coram*) the archdeacon or his official (sometimes named), and gave place and date. Occasionally a member of the clergy was commissioned to act on behalf of the official, when he was termed a 'commissary' (no. 55). Within the probate sentence was the grant of administration, in which the executors present were named and 'power [to act] reserved' to those not present.

In general, an inventory should have been taken of the personal possessions of the deceased, valued by competent persons, and exhibited in the probate court before probate could be granted. Some historians have assumed that the practice of drawing up an inventory only began following an act of 1529.[156] However, the survival of earlier inventories clearly suggests otherwise and even where early inventories have not survived, as in Hertfordshire, references to them, for example in probate sentences, indicate that they had existed. In this collection an inventory in mentioned three times, firstly in the unusual circumstances of the vicar, Henry Bornwash (49), who had died intestate. An inventory of his goods had been made but it was not submitted to the archdeacon's court 'because his goods were set aside by the collector of the Lord Pope because the said vicar was chaplain to the Lord Pope by bull'. Lettice Danyell (167) had also died intestate, and, rather than grant letters of administration, the archdeacon, Richard Runham, instructed her son Thomas to pay her creditors and make a 'true inventory' of her goods. In the probate sentence of John Assheby's will proved in the Prerogative Court of Canterbury on 1 July 1499, his executors were required to exhibit a 'full & faithful inventory' before the feast of St Bartholomew (24 August).

In theory the whole probate sentence should have been copied into the register by the probate clerk, but this did not always happen. For each will published here the whole of the probate sentence given in the register has been given in translation to show the variations that might occur. Another reason is to provide the name of the archdeacon, or his representative, as these names are not recorded in many other documents.

---

[156] Cox and Cox have drawn attention to earlier regulations concerning inventories in N. and J. Cox, 'Probate inventories: the legal background, part 1', *The Local Historian*, 16 (1984), pp.133–145, p.133.

Editorial conventions

General

Paragraphing has been added to aid the reader.

The probate clause has been translated in full (whether short or long). It is given in italics to make it distinct from the will itself.

Where there is no commendation of the soul and/or committal of the body for burial this has been noted. These sections were not necessarily missing in the original will: it is clear that some wills were condensed by the probate clerk to save space.

Abbreviations such as 'In &c' have been reproduced as written.

Roman numerals have been converted to figures.

Numbers have been written in full in bequests (e.g. four sheep) but sums of money have been written in figures (e.g. 3s 4d).

Alternative meanings, or missing words have been given in plain text in square brackets [thus].

Insertions in the document have been indicated with angled brackets \thus/.

Deletions have been struck through ~~thus.~~

Editorial comments such as illeg (for illegible), or damaged, have been given in italics in square brackets: [*illeg*] [*damaged*].

In the will of Petronilla Dier (32), words that she spoke regarding the identity of her executors are given in double inverted commas: " ".

English wills

These have been reproduced in full.

Regular palaeographic abbreviations have been expanded silently.

The spelling is somewhat erratic, but is mostly phonetic, so if the meaning is unclear read the words aloud.

The use of [*sic*], meaning 'that is what has been written', has been minimised.

Latin words in English wills given in italics e.g. *de Insula*.

Latin wills

There has been some editing in these wills. Repetitive phrases have been omitted: for example, I bequeath (*Lego*), Next (*Item*).

English words given in Latin wills have been shown in single inverted commas: ' '.

Datum has been translated as 'Given (at)' rather than 'Dated (at)': it refers back to the place and date stated at the beginning of the will.

parens and its variations (usually *parentorum*) has been translated as 'parents' but it might mean 'ancestors'.

Some Latin words have been given in italics following their translation where the meaning is in doubt or unusual.

dominus = sir; *magister* = master; *Magister* = Master (See Glossary.)

Pre-Reformation Wills from

Rickmansworth Parish

(1409-1539)

Pre-Reformation Wills from Rickmansworth Parish

1. Simon Canoun[1]   **reference BL Add MS 6057, fol. 26r**
will: undated   **probate: 23 May 1409**[2]

The testament of Simon Canoun was proved in the presence of Brother Simon Wyndsore, commissary in this matter, in the year 1409, the meaning of which follows in these words.

In the name of God, Amen, &c.

Firstly I bequeath my soul to God &c.

To the fabric of the church of Rykm[er]sworth 2s; to each of the clerks of the same 3d.

To Agnes my daughter a cow; to Magot[3] my daughter a cow.

Indeed the residue of all my goods I give to Agnes my wife; her and my son John I ordain my executors by these present [writings].

2. John Canoun[4]   **reference BL Add MS 6057, fol. 26r**
will: undated   **probate: 23 May 1409**

The testament of John Canoun was proved in the year 1409, in the presence of Brother Simon Wyndsore, commissary in this matter, the meaning of which follows in these words.

In the name of God, &c.

Firstly I bequeath my soul to God &c.

To the light of the Blessed Mary of Rykm[er]sworth a sheep; to the bells of the same church a sheep.

Indeed the residue of all my goods I give and bequeath to John atte Forde and John atte Hille, whom I ordain my executors by these present [writings].

---

[1] At the manor court held on the Tuesday next after the feast of St Mark the Evangelist 8 Henry IV (26 April 1407) Simon Canoun had been granted a section of the lord's (i.e. the abbot's) river called Pyghtellesburne to make a sluice for catching fish. (fol. 25r)

[2] Proved at the court of the manor of Croxley held on the Thursday after Ascension Day 10 Henry IV (23 May 1409); the manor belonged to the cellarer of St Albans Abbey. In 1409, Brother Simon Wyndsore was cellarer.

[3] The text is a sixteenth century copy of the original: her name is written as *Magote* [Latin; dative case].

[4] Perhaps the John Canoun who was Simon's son.

3. John atte Forthe[5] reference BL Add MS 6057, fol. 28v

will: 6 March 1415/16 **probate: 24 September 1416**[6]

The testament of John atte Forthe was proved in the presence of Brother Michael Cheyne, cellarer and commissary in this matter, the meaning of which follows in these words.

In the name of God, Amen. On 6 March in the year of our Lord 1415/16, I John atte Forthe being of sound mind make my testament in this manner.

Firstly I bequeath my soul &c, my body to burial in the churchyard of the Blessed Mary of Rickmersworth.

To the vicar of the aforesaid church 2s; to John Streteman 8d; to John Bramenhangre 8d.

Indeed the residue of all my goods not bequeathed I give and bequeath to my son Richard that he may &c. And him I ordain my executor &.

And he was granted administration in form of law and he gave his oath.[7]

4. John atte Well reference: 1AR5r

will: 8 March 1416/17 **probate: 9 November 1417**

In the name of God, Amen. On 8 March 1416/17, I John atte Well, of whole mind, make my testament in this manner.

First I bequeath my soul to God, the Blessed Mary & all the saints; my body to be buried in the churchyard of the Blessed Mary of Rykm[er]sworth.

I bequeath 100s 6s 8d [*£5 6s 8d*] for a priest to celebrate for my soul and the souls of my parents; to the fabric of Rykm[er]sworth church 13s 4d; to the light of the Trinity 12d; to the light of the Crucifix 12d; to the light of St Mary 12d; to the light of St Edmund 12d; to the light of St Katherine 2s.

To the fabric of the church of Chalffunte St Peter 3s 4d.

---

[5] John atte Forthe was one of the manorial jurors at the courts held on Thursday after the feast of St Augustine the bishop 1 Henry V (31 August 1413) and Thursday after the feast of St Michael the Archangel 2 Henry V (4 October 1414). (fol. 27v) He may well have been the John atte Forde who was John Canoun's executor.

[6] The will was proved at the court held on the Thursday after the feast of St Matthew 4 Henry V (24 Sept 1416)

[7] The court book records that Richard took over his father's manorial holding. The heriot was an ox, priced 8d. He was over age. He paid 10s for his entry fine and for the right to marry. The lord abbot had released him from the harvest services due from the holding, i.e. mowing, haymaking, ploughing and harrowing owing to the lord for an annual payment of 10s and 2 capons. His will is no. 6 below.

To John Stretman 6d; to John Bramynagger 6d.

To the bridge of Woxbrygge 6s 8d.

To Isabel, daughter of my son John, one cow; to the daughter of my brother 13s 4d; to each of my servants one quarter of barley.

The residue of all my goods I give and bequeath to Joan my wife, which Joan atte Well of Glehamste & John Tylyr I ordain executors by this present [testament].

Proved on 9 November in the year above said [1417].

5. William Creke reference: 1AR10v
will: 14 September 1425 probate: 14 January 1425/6

In the name of God, Amen. On the feast of the exaltation of the Holy Cross [14 September] in September 1425, I William Creke of Rycm[er]yswurthe, being in sound mind, make my testament in this manner.

First I bequeath my soul to God, the Blessed Mary [and] all the saints; and my body to be buried in the churchyard of the church of the Blessed Mary of Ricmerswurth.

I bequeath to the same church 12d; to the vicar of that church 12d; to sir Henry 6d; to the two clerks 12d. I leave 12d to be distributed among the poor on the day of my burial.

The residue of all my goods not bequeathed above I give & bequeath to Katherine my wife for burying my body, and that she may settle my debts and distribute for the health of my soul as may seem best to her to do.

I ordain and constitute the said Katherine my wife and William my son executors. [Given on] the day and year abovesaid.

Proved before the archdeacon on 14 January in the year above said [1425/6].

6. Richard at the Furde reference: 1AR10v
will: 11 January 1425/6 probate: 11 February 1425/6

In the name of God, Amen. On 11 January 1425/6, I Richard at the Furde[8] of Ricm[er]s', being sound in mind, make my testament in this manner.

First I bequeath my soul to God & the Blessed Mary & all the saints; my body to be buried in the churchyard of the Blessed Mary of Ricm[er]swurthe.

I bequeath to ten poor people of the aforesaid parish five measures of wheat to be divided among them in equal portions.

To my son John six sheep; to my son William as many [as to John].

---

[8] In the margin his name is given as Ric' at forde

The residue of all my goods not bequeathed, I give and bequeath to Joan my wife for my burying and for paying my debts and also for distributing among the poor for my soul as may seem best to her to do.

I ordain and make the aforesaid Joan my wife my executrix & Thomas Stretman & John Wymond supervisors, and furthermore my debts to be paid by the hands of the said Thomas & John.

This testament was proved before W[illiam] Alnewyke, archdeacon, on 11 February 1425/6.

7. Richard Yan, farmer of Croxley[9]   reference: 1AR10v
will: 12 February 1426[10]   probate: no clause

In the name of God, Amen. On 12 February 1426 I Richard Yan, farmer of Crokeslee in the parish of Rykem[er]sworth, being in sound mind make my testament in this manner.

First I bequeath my soul to Almighty God, the Blessed Mary and all His saints; & my body to be buried in the churchyard of the Blessed Mary of Ricm[er]swurthe.

I bequeath to the light of the Holy Cross of the same church 20d; to the light of the Blessed Mary 20d; to the light of St Edmund 3s 4d.

To Lettice my servant one 'bulloc'; to my father my lined cloak.

The residue of all my goods not bequeathed above I give and bequeath to my wife Katherine for burying my body, and paying my debts and also for disposing for my soul as may seem best to her to do, and the aforesaid Katherine my wife, William Yan and Richard Syngar [I make] my executors.

Given the day and year abovesaid.

[*No probate clause; the preceding will was proved on 11 February 1425/6.*]

---

[9] His status is given as *firmarius*, meaning that he was the lessee of the manor of Croxley, paying rent for it to the abbey of St Albans; he was, therefore, the tenant of what is now Croxley Hall Farm.

[10] The preceding will in the register was proved on 11 February 1425/6 and the following will later in 1426, so it is probable that Yan's will was written on 12 February 1426 according to modern dating (as happened occasionally). There is no probate clause.

8. Richard Suward   reference: 1AR11r
will: 23 July 1426   probate: c.6 October 1426

In the name of God, Amen. On 23 July 1426, I Richard Suward, sound in mind, make my testament in this manner.

First I bequeath my soul to God & the Blessed Mary & all the saints; and my body to be buried in the churchyard of the Blessed Mary of Rycm[er]swurth.

I bequeath to the fabric of the same church 2s 6d.

All my moveable goods to my daughters, that is, Helen and Agnes, to be divided between them in equal portions by my executors; to Henry my son 40s from my tenement in which I now dwell to be paid to him by the hand of his brother John.

The residue of all my goods not bequeathed above I give and bequeath to Henry my son and Thomas Wodeward for burying my body and paying my debts and distributing from them for my soul as may seem best to them to do, and the aforesaid Henry and Thomas Wodeward I make, ordain and constitute my executors, the day and year above said &c.

Proved before the archdeacon [no date, next will proved on 6 October 1426]

9. Maud[11] Horsman   reference: 1AR13v
will: 23 January 1427/8   probate: 5 May 1428

In the name of God, Amen. On 23 January 1427/8, I Maud Horsman of Rykm', being in sound mind, make my testament in this manner.

First I bequeath my soul to Almighty God, the Blessed Mary [and] all His saints; & my body to be buried in the churchyard of the Blessed Mary of Rykm'.

To the church of Saret one sheep [*illeg*]; to the two clerks of Rykm' 4d.

To John [*Joh'i*] Horsman one ?enamelled pot.[12]

The residue of all my goods I give and bequeath to John Meryweder for my burial and for paying my debts & disposing for my soul as may seem best to him to do, and the aforesaid John & Roger Lucas I make, ordain and constitute my executors.

This testament was proved at Rickmansworth before William Alnewyke, archdeacon of the monastery of St Alban on 5 May 1428 &c.

---

[11] The Latin for Maud is *Matilda*.

[12] *una[m] olla[m] enea[m]*

10. Maud Dyer   reference: 1AR13v
will: 1428   probate: 5 May 1428

In the name of God, Amen. In the year of our Lord 1428 [no other date], I Maud Dyer of Rykm', of sound mind, make my testament in this manner.

First I bequeath my soul to Almighty God, the Blessed Mary & all His saints; and my body to be buried in the churchyard of the Blessed Mary of Ryk'.

I bequeath to each light in the said church 6d; to the two clerks 4d; to the high altar one 'towele'.

The residue of all my goods not bequeathed I give & bequeath to Roger my son and Thomas Wodwarde for burying my body and for paying my debts and for disposing for the health of my soul as may seem best to them, and I make and constitute the said Roger and Thomas my executors.

This testament was proved at Rickmansworth before William Alnewyke, archdeacon of the monastery of St Alban, on 5 May in the year above said [1428].

11. Idiota Colyer   reference: 1AR13v
will: not dated (?early 1428)   probate: 5 May 1428

In the name of God, Amen. I Idiota Colyer of Rykm', being of whole mind, make my testament in this manner.

First I bequeath my soul to Almighty God, the Blessed Mary and all His saints; and my body to be buried in the churchyard of Rykm'.

I bequeath to the altar of St Edmund one 'towele'. I will that John Carter will celebrate for my soul, and my husband's [soul] and for all the faithful departed two trentals of St Gregory.

The residue of all my goods not bequeathed I give and bequeath to John Carter to dispose for the health of my soul as may seem best to him, whom I make and constitute my executor, & John Bramanger supervisor that he may implement the abovesaid.

This will was proved before William Alnewyke, archdeacon of the monastery of St Alban on 5 May in the year abovesaid [1428].

12. John Rowe   reference: 1AR13v
will: 28 February 1427/8   **probate: 8 May 1428**

In the name of God, Amen. On 28 February 1427/8,[13] I John Rowe of Rykm' of sound mind make my testament in this manner.

First I bequeath my soul to God, the Blessed Mary and all His saints; my body to be buried in the churchyard of the Blessed Mary of Rykm'.

I bequeath to the fabric of the said church 2d; to the two clerks 2d.

The residue of all my goods I give and bequeath to John Rowe, my son, to bury my body and to dispose for the health of my soul as seems best to him to do, whom I constitute and ordain my executor.

This testament was proved before William Alnewyke, archdeacon of the monastery of St Alban on 8 May in the year abovesaid [1428]; & [administration] was committed &c.

13. William Spicer   reference: 1AR14r
will: 20 July 1428   **probate: 9 August 1428**

In the name of God, Amen. On 20 July 1428, I William Spicer of Rykm[er]sworth, of sound mind, make my testament in this manner.

First I bequeath my soul to God, the Blessed Mary and all His saints; and my body to be buried in the churchyard of the church of the Blessed Mary of Rykm' next to my parents.

I bequeath to the work of the great 'le hers' 6s 8d; to the vicar to celebrate divine service for my soul, my parents' souls & all the faithful departed 2s; to each of the clerks 12d.

The residue of all my goods I give and bequeath to Agnes my wife and John Baldwyn for burying my body and disposing for my soul, whom I make and constitute my executors by these presents.

This testament was proved on 9 August in the year abovesaid [1428].

---

[13] The date is incomplete. It should be 28 February 1427 [i.e. 1427/8]; the clerk has written *MCCCC oct'*. The probate year is as in the preceding will, which is clearly *MCCCC vicesimo oct'*, i.e. 1428.

14. Walter Selwode reference: 1AR16v
will: 2 February 1428/9 probate: no clause[14]

In the name of God Amen. On the 4 Nones of February [2 February] 1428/9, I Walter Selwode of Rekem[er]sworth, sound in mind but thinking of my mortality, make my testament in this manner.

First I bequeath my soul to Almighty God, the Blessed Mary and all his saints; my body to be buried in the churchyard of the church of the Blessed Mary of Rekem[er]sworth aforesaid.

I bequeath to to the light of the Holy Cross one sheep; to the light of the Blessed Mary one sheep; to the light of St Edmund one sheep; to the two parish clerks to each of them 4d.

The residue of all my good not bequeathed I give and bequeath to Christine my wife[15] for burying [my body] [*damaged*] and distributing for the health of my soul as may seem best to her to do, and the aforesaid Christine [*the page is torn; no more*]

15. William Whithbrede reference: 1AR74v[16]
will: 13 February 1429/30 probate: 11 March 1429/30

In the name of God, Amen. On 13 February 1429/30, I William Whithbrede of Rykm[er]sworth make my testament in this manner.

First I bequeath my soul to the Almighty & to the Blessed Virgin Mary the mother of Christ; & my body to be buried in the churchyard of the parish church of Ryk'.

To the vicar 2s; to each clerk of the said church 12d; to the fabric of the said church 6s 8d.

To John my son remaining in Lond'[17] 12 sheep.

The residue of my goods I give & bequeath to Cecily my wife, whom I ordain & constitute executrix of this testament.

This testament was proved before the archdeacon on 11 March in the year above said [1429/30].

---

[14] Neither this nor the two preceding wills have dates of probate, they have been written in a different hand from the rest of the page. The preceding will is that of John Elfred (17), which was written on 2 September 1431.

[15] Her will is no. 18.

[16] This will has been recorded out of sequence, much later in the register. Probate was definitely granted on 11 March 1429/30. Somewhat irregularly, the next entry in the register records the induction of sir Richard Astwode as vicar of Bushey on the last day of May 1430.

[17] *lond' com[m]oranti*

16. John Elverede   reference: 1AR15r
will: 12 April 1430   probate: no clause

In the name of God, Amen. On 12 April 1430, I John Elverede of Rykm[er]sworth, by the favour of the Lord, sound in mind, make my testament in this manner.

First I bequeath my soul to Almighty God, the Blessed Virgin Mary & all the saints of God; and my body to be buried in the churchyard of the parish church of the Blessed Mary of Rykm[er]sworth.

I bequeath to the high altar of the said church 18d; to the light of the Holy Trinity 12d; to the Sepulchre light of the said church 8d; to the light of the Holy Cross 6d; to the light of the Blessed [Mary] there 6d; to the light of the Blessed Edmund there ~~6d~~ 3d; to the adult male clerks of the parish 12d.

To Isabel my wife 20 sheep; to John Elverede my son, the elder, six sheep, four measures of wheat, four measures of malt, four measures of oats; to Ralph Elverede six sheep, four measures of wheat, four measures of barley, four measures of oats; to John Elverede the younger my son six sheep; to Nicholas my son one sheep.

To John Arnolde one sheep, four measures of wheat, four measures of oats; to Richard Hamounde one sheep; to John Slynger one sheep; to John Colman one sheep; to John Warde one sheep; to John Marion one sheep; to John Baldwyn one sheep.

The residue of all my moveable goods I give and bequeath to Isabel my wife and to John my son, the younger, that they may divide the said goods equally between them and dispose for my soul as may seem best to them to implement this my testament and faithfully carry it out.

I make and ordain the said Isabel my wife and John my son, the younger, my executors.

Proved &c [no details] [preceding will proved on 1 April 1430]

17. John Elfred   reference: 1AR16v
will: 2 September 1431   probate: no clause[18]

In the name of God, Amen. On the 4 Nones of September [2 September] 1431, I John Elfred, of sound mind, praise be given to God, make my testament in this manner.

First I bequeath my soul to God Almighty, the Blessed Virgin Mary and to all his saints; & my body to be buried in the churchyard of the church of the Blessed Mary of Rykem[er]sworth.

---

[18] See note to William Selwode (14).

I bequeath to the high altar of the same 12d; to the fabric of the same church 12d; to each of the lights of the altars there 12d; to each poor person of the town 6d.

To Roger Bourynger for his labour in implementing my testament 5s; to Richard ?Sibles for his labour about the same 5s.

The residue of all my goods not bequeathed I give to the said Roger and Richard for repairing the defective roads around the town of Rikem[er]sworth aforesaid; the same Roger and Richard to fulfil this testament as they would answer for it before the High Judge, and I make and constitute them executors.

[*no probate clause*]

18. Christine Selwode, widow   reference: 1AR17r
will: 26 December 1431   probate: no clause[19]

In the name of God, Amen. On 26 December 1431, I Christine Selwode, widow, of Rykem[er]sworthe, being in widowed state, thanks be to God of sound mind, make my testament in this manner.

First I bequeath my soul to the Blessed Trinity, Father, Son and Holy Paraclete; and my body to be buried in the churchyard of the parish church of the Blessed Mary of Rykem[er]sworth aforesaid.

I bequeath to the high altar of the said church for my tithes [forgotten] and other failings 20d.

To the fabric of the church of St Peter of Chalfunte [*illeg*] & a pan.

The residue of all my goods, my debts faithfully paid, I give to John Wymond, smith, Thomas Gilbe and John Suward of the aforesaid parish church, whom I ordain, constitute and make my executors of my said testament.

[*no probate clause*]

19. Joan Stretman, widow   reference: 1AR17v
will: 12 April 1432   probate: no clause[20]

In the name of God, Amen. On 12 April 1432, I Joan Stretman, widow, ?praised be God, being in sound mind, make my testament in this manner.

First I bequeath my soul to Almighty God, the Blessed Virgin Mary & all the saints of God; & my body to be buried in the churchyard of the parish church of the Blessed Mary of Rikem[er]sworth.

---

[19] None of the wills on folio 17r has a probate clause.

[20] None of the wills on folio 17v has a probate clause.

I bequeath to the high altar of the said church 12d; to each of the parish clerks of the same 4d; to the [light] of the Blessed Trinity of the same 6d; to the light of the Holy Cross of the same 6d.

And all my other goods I bequeath to Thomas Stretman of Rim[er]sword that he may dispose those goods for the health of my soul [and] to the honour of God as may seem best to him; the same Thomas I ordain, constitute and make executor of this my testament.

[no probate clause]

20. Richard Clerke   reference: 1AR19r
will: 4 November 1432   **probate: 15 November 1432**

In the name of God, Amen. On 4 November 1432, I Richard Clerke of Rykm', of sound mind, make my testament in this manner.

First I bequeath my soul to God, the Blessed Mary and all the saints; & my body to be buried in the churchyard of the Blessed Mary of Rykm' aforesaid.

I bequeath to the high altar of the same one ram; to the light of the Blessed Edmund one ewe.

To Thomas my brother one ewe with its lamb.

The residue of all my goods I give and bequeath to Alice my wife, she to faithfully implement my testament. I ordain and make her my executrix.

This testament was proved on the 15th day of the month aforesaid [November 1432]

21. Joan at the Welle, widow   reference: 1AR17v
will: 7 December 1432   **probate: no clause**

In the name of God, Amen. On 7 December 1432, I Joan at the Welle, widow, being in my sound mind, make my testament in this manner.

First I bequeath my soul to Almighty God, the Blessed Mary and all His saints; & my body to be buried in the churchyard of the Blessed Mary of Rickmers'.

I bequeath to the high altar of the same 4d; to each of the parish clerks of the same 4d.

To Simon Croyle 4d.

I bequeath all of my other goods to Thomas Boterfeld and William Randulf to dispose as seems best to them for the health of my soul, and the same Thomas and William I make executors of my said testament.

[no probate clause]

22. John Bayly reference 1 AR 20v
will: no date **probate: no clause [1433]**[21]
John Bayly of Rykm[er]sworth died in the year of our Lord above said [1433] and
bequeathed 6d towards wax; he gave the residue of his goods to his wife Ellen,
whom he constituted his executrix.

23. John at the Hyde reference: 1 AR 21v
will: 8 January 1433/4 **probate: 13 February 1433/4**
In the name of God, Amen. On 8 January 1433/4, I John atethyde [at the Hyde] of
Rykm[er]sworth, of sound mind, make my testament in this manner.
First I bequeath my soul to Almighty God, the Blessed Virgin Mary and all the
saints of God; & my body to be buried in the churchyard of the Blessed Mary of
Rykm[er]sworth.
I bequeath to the high altar in the name of tithes forgotten 5s; to each of the parish
clerks 2s; to the light of the Holy Trinity 12d; to the light of the Blessed Mary 12d; to
the light of the Blessed Katherine 3s 4d & one measure of wheat.
To John my son 6s 8d; to William my son 6s 8d; to Richard my son 6s 8d; to
Thomas my son 6s 8d; to Alice my daughter 6s 8d; to Agnes Baker 3s 4d & one
measure of wheat; to Joan Colyer 5s; to Isabel my daughter 6s 8d; to each of my
children aforesaid four sheep; to every single one of my godchildren [space] 12d.
To 12 poor people of my parish [or, co-parishioners] to each of them 4d.
To John Tyler the elder 6s 8d & to Thomas Buttyrvylde 6s 8d.
The residue of all my moveable goods I bequeath to Thomas Buttyrvylde & John
Tyler aforesaid that they may dispose, distribute and spend to the honour of
Almighty God for the health of my soul & the soul of Joan my wife & all the faithful
departed as may seem best to them to carry out the instructions, and the same
Thomas and John I constitute my executors to faithfully execute this testament.
This testament was proved on 13 February in the year above said [1433/4]

---

[21] This will is recorded in a brief sentence in the register with no date for the will or probate
but the page is dated 1433. The testator's name and parish are only recorded in the margin.

24. William at the Hyde[22]   reference: 1AR22r
will: 27 January 1433/44   probate: 13 February 1433/4

In the name of God, Amen. On 27 January 1433/4, I William at the Hyde, of sound mind, make my testament in this manner.

First I bequeath my soul to God &c; & my body to be buried in the churchyard of the Blessed Mary of Rykm'.

I bequeath to the high altar 6d; to each of the lights there 4d; to either of the parish clerks 8d; to 12 poor people of the same parish 12d; for the reparation of the same church 12d.

To Thomas Buttyrvild 20d.

The residue of all my goods I give to the same Thomas to dispose for my soul & I ordain him executor of this testament.

This will was proved on 13 February [year not stated][23]

25. John Tyler, 'maltman'   reference: 1AR24r
will: 28 March 1434   probate: no clause [1434][24]

In the name of God, Amen. On 28 March 1434, I John Tyler 'maltman' of Rykm[er]sworth, by the grace of the most Blessed Trinity languishing [but] in my sound mind, make my testament in this manner.

First I bequeath my soul to Almighty God, the Blessed Virgin Mary & all the saints of God; & my body to be buried in the churchyard of the parish church of the Blessed Mary of Rykmersworth aforesaid.

I bequeath to the high altar of the same church 3s 4d; to John Bramangre parish clerk 12d; to Thomas Streteman parish clerk 12d; to each each[*sic*] there in the same church 12d; to each of four poor men on the day of my burial 4d; to Simon Croile, poor man, 12d; to the fabric of the parish church of the Blessed Mary of Rykmersworth aforesaid 3s 4d; to the fabric of the parish church of St Peter of Chalfunte [*deletion*] 6s 8d.

To [*illeg*][25] of the parishioners for the bridge of the vicarage 12d; to the high road from my house leading to the [?][26] high way 6s 8d; to each of my godchildren 4d.

---

[22] Perhaps the son of John (23).

[23] *Wills at Hertford* gives 1433/4, so that same day as John at the Hyde.

[24] *Wills at Hertford* gives 1434.

[25] Meaning a representative; might be ?'wante' or 'warde'.

[26] Should be 'king's', but that is not what has been written.

To Richard my son 6s 8d; to Thomas my son 6s 8d; to Margaret my daughter 6s 8d; to Roger son of John Daye 6s 8d.

To the light of the Holy Cross in Rykmersworth church aforesaid 3s 4d; to poor people on the 30th day after my obit 2s; to Henry Bergwasch[27] my vicar and curate 6s 8d; to Thomas Botervylde, 'Maltman', 6s 8d.

The residue of all my goods I give and bequeath to Sarah my wife to pay my debts and to do other works of mercy for the health of my soul & for its best sustentation. I ordain, constitute and make The said Sarah my wife and Roger Daye I ordain, constitute and make my executors to well and faithfully carry out my testament, and the aforesaid vicar & Thomas to be supervisors of this my testament.

[*No probate clause*]

26. Joan Belche, widow   reference: 1AR23r
will: 12 May 1434   probate: 10 September 1434

In the name of God, Amen. I Joan Belche, widow of Rykm', of sound mind, on 12 May 1434, make my testament in this manner.

First I bequeath my soul to God Almighty, the Blessed Mary and all the saints; & my body to be buried in the churchyard of the church of the Blessed Mary of Rykm' aforesaid.

I bequeath to the high altar there 6d; to either clerk 6d; to each altar outside the chancel 6d; to the fabric of the same church [6d *deleted*] four measures of wheat; to the great light of the Blessed Virgin one sheep; to the vicar of Saret 6s 8d; to the parish church of Saret two sheep.

To Thomas Godthanke one brass vessel, one pan, six ?gallon vessels, one 'tripod', two silver spoons; to John Rowe one brass vessel, two gallon vessels, & one pan, six gallon vessels & one 'tripod' of iron, two [*deletion*] silver spoons, one pair of sheets; to Roger Belch one cow, one pair of sheets; to Thomas 'of the felde' one brass pan, one gallon vessel and one measure of wheat & one measure of malt; to John Sansum one pair of sheets & two 'virgat' de blanket'; to Margery Bryan one pig and one measure of wheat; to Thomas Davy 12d; to Henry Holm 6d; to Katherine Frowe one sheet & 6d; to Henry Kynge one measure of wheat & two measures of malt

The residue of all my goods I bequeath to the aforesaid Thomas Godthanke & John Rowe, and the same I ordain, constitute and make my executors to well & faithfully execute this testament. *This testament was proved before the Archdeacon on 10 September in the year abovesaid [1434].*

---

[27] The vicar at this time was Henry Bornwash.

27a. Thomas Daye   reference: 1AR76r[28]
will: 8 January ?1435/6   probate: 28 January 1435/6

In the name of God, Amen. In the month of January on the 8th day last past, I Thomas Daye of Rykm[er]sworth, being in my sound mind, praise to the most Blessed Trinity, make my testament in this manner.

First I bequeath my soul to Almighty God, his most blessed Mother & all the saints of God; and my body to be buried in the churchyard of the principal church of the Blessed Mary of Rykm[er]sworth aforesaid.

To the vicar of the same, my curate, 3s 4d; to John Bramanger parish clerk 6d 12d; to Thomas Stretman parish clerk 6d; to the fabric of the said parish church 13s 4d.

To the king's highway between the tenement of William Flete[29] & barn of Helen Bayly 6s 8d.

To Agnes, wife of John Cartere 2s 4d & three sheep; to Alice wife of Simon my mother[30] 12d, one pair of sheets, eight measures of barley, two measures of wheat, one 'blanket' & one 'coverlet'; to Alice the wife of Simon at the Verne 3s 4d; to Margaret daughter of the same one sheep; to Katherine her sister one sheep; to Agnes her sister one sheep; to Margaret the wife of William Wymond one yoked [or, *large*] heifer; to John son of John Cartere one sheep; to Richard his brother one sheep; to Elizabeth his sister one sheep; to William son of Richard Slynger & Margery his sister one heifer to be shared between them; to Maud Kyng widow 4d and one measure of barley & to her sister Katherine 4d; to Avice Roter widow 4d & one measure of malt; to John Kape four sheep; to Simon Croyle 4d & to Isabel Colle 4d; to Thomas Davy 4d; to John Rowe one measure of wheat; to Katherine Frowe 4d; to Walter a poor man 4d & one russet gown; to John Batte one measure of wheat; to Richard Godfrey one measure of wheat; to Simon Webbe one measure of wheat; to William the poor man dwelling with me one measure of wheat & one

---

[28] The will of Thomas Daye, reference 1AR76r, is not listed in the *Index of Wills at Hertford*. It appears to be have been recorded out of sequence, as probate was granted in January 1435 [1435/6]; the other will on folio 76r was granted probate on 3 March 1435/6. The will of Thomas Daye, reference 1AR26r (27b) is very similar but the two probate dates are different.

[29] Probably referring to the More. Flete had first acquired property in Rickmansworth shortly before 1401. He acquired Britwell in 1410, and The More, Ashleys and Batchworth in 1416. (See H. Falvey, 'William Flete: More than just a castle builder', *The Ricardian*, vol. X, no. 124 (March 1994), pp.2–15.)

[30] 'wife of Simon' has been crossed out here; the following bequest is to 'Alice the wife of Simon at the Verne'

measure of barley;[31] to Walter Daye two measures of malt; to each of those whom I raised from the holy font [*i.e.* godchildren] one sheep.

The residue of all my goods not bequeathed I bequeath to John Cartere & Richard Slyngere that they may dispose of those goods for the health of my soul as they would wish to answer for when examined in the presence of God [on Judgement Day], and them I constitute my executors to carry out faithfully my testament. *This testament was proved on xxviij [28] day of January MCCCCxxxv [1435]* [1435/6]

27b. Thomas Daye
reference: 1AR26r

will: 8 January ?1435/66   **probate: 12 February 1435/6**

In the name of God, Amen. On 8 January last past I Thomas Daye of Rykem[er]sworth, being in my sound mind, praise to the most Blessed Trinity, make my testament in this manner.

First I bequeath my soul to Almighty God, the Blessed Virgin Mary & all the saints of God; & my body to be buried in the churchyard of the parish church of the Blessed Mary of Rykem[er]sworth aforesaid.

I bequeath to the vicar of the same, my curate, three shillings four pennies; to John Bramangre parish clerk 12d; to Thomas Streteman parish clerk 6d; to the fabric of the said church 13s 4d.

To the king's highway between the tenement of William Flete and the barn of Ellen Bayly 6s 8d.

To Agnes the wife of John Cartere 3s 4d & three sheep; to Alice wife of Simon,[32] my mother, 12d & one pair of sheets, eight measures of barley, two measures of wheat, one 'Blankete' & one 'coverlet'; to Alice wife of Simon 'at the verne' 3s 4d; to Margaret daughter of the same one sheep; to Katherine her sister one sheep; to Agnes her sister one sheep; to Margaret the wife of William Wymond one yoked [*or*, large] heifer; to John son of John Cartere one sheep; to Richard his brother one sheep; to Elizabeth his sister one sheep; to William son of Richard Slyngere & Margery his sister one heifer between them; to Maud Kyng widow 4d & one measure of barley & Katherine her sister 4d; to Avice Roter widow 4d & one measure of malt; to John Kape one sheep; to Simon Croile 4d; to Isabel Colle 4d; to Thomas Davy 4d; to John Rowe one measure of wheat; to Katherine Frowe 4d; to Walter the poor man 4d & one russet gown; to John Batte one measure of wheat; to

---

[31] The version on 1AR26r has 4d (iiij d) to William the poor man as well as grain.

[32] 'wife of Simon' has been crossed out in the version on 1AR76r.

Richard Godfrey one measure of wheat; to Simon Webbe one measure of wheat; to William the poor man dwelling with me 4d, one measure of wheat & one measure of barley; to Walter Daye two measures of malt; to each of those whom I raised from the font one sheep.

The residue of all my goods not bequeathed I bequeath to John Cartere & Richard Slyngere that they dispose of those goods for the health of my soul as they would wish to answer for when examined in the presence of God [on Judgement Day] and them I constitute my executors to carry out faithfully my testament.

The above testament was proved before us, John Peyton, archdeacon of the monastery of St Alban, on 12 February in the year above [1435/6][33]

28. John Deye   reference: 1AR28r

will: 27 November 1436   **probate: 5 February 1436/7**

In the name of God, Amen. On 27 November 1436, I John Deye of Rykem[er]sworth, in my sound mind, the Blessed Trinity be praised, make my testament in this manner.

First I bequeath my soul to Almighty God; & my body to be buried in the churchyard of my parish church of the Blessed Mary of Rykem[er]sworth.

I bequeath to the high altar of the same [church] 12d; to both parish clerks 8d; to the light of the Blessed Trinity 8d; to the light of the Holy Cross 12d; to the light of St Katherine 12d; to the light of St Edmund 6d; to Simon Croylle 8d; to the fabric of the aforesaid church 3s 4d.

The residue of all my goods I bequeath to Isabel my wife, Roger my son & Richard Roberd, and the same I ordain and make executors of this my testament that they may faithfully implement and fulfil it.

This testament was proved on 5 February in the year above said [1436/7]; & administration was granted to Roger and Richard, and to Isabel when she shall come.

29. Thomas Godthank   reference: 1AR30r

will: 28 April 1437   **probate: no clause [1437]**[34]

In [the name] of God &c. I Thomas Godthank of Rykm[er]sworth, in my sound mind, make my testament &c.

---

[33] There is no explanation in the register as to why probate was granted twice.

[34] *Wills at Hertford* gives 1437.

First I bequeath my soul to God &c.[35]

I bequeath to the fabric of the church of Ryk' 3s 4d; to sir Thomas, chaplain in the same, 6d; to John Brannengre 6d; to Thomas Stretman 6d.

To William my son my best gown and my 'baselard'; to Richard my brother one other gown after the first of the best; to John Rowe one other gown; to Marg' my niece one new gown with one tunic.

To the light of the Blessed Ed[mund] 12d.

To Thomas son of Thomas Wynkefeld one lamb; to John son of John Randulf one lamb.

The residue of all my goods I give and bequeath to Margery my wife for her sustentation and that of my children.

The executors of this my testament I constitute and ordain Margery my wife and John Rowe aforesaid, & Richard my brother supervisor.

Written at Rik' on 28 April 1437.

[*no probate clause*]

30. John Wynkeburn   reference: 1AR28v
will: 8 May 1437   probate: 4 July 1437

In the name of God, Amen. On 8 May 1437, I John Wynkeburn, being in my sound mind, make my testament in this manner.

First I bequeath my soul to Almighty God; and my body to be buried in the churchyard of my parish church of the Blessed Mary of Rykem[er]sworth.

I bequeath to the light of Rood in the same church 5s; to the light of the Blessed Edmund in the same 5s; to John Brammanger 3s 4d; to Thomas Stretman 2s.

To Simon Croile 20d; to ?Thomas my servant 20s.

The residue of all my goods I give and bequeath to Joan my wife that she may do for my soul as may seem best to her for the faithful execution of the same. The said Joan I ordain and make executrix, and John my elder son to be her supervisor.

This present testament was proved on 4 July [1437]; and because the executrix at that time was unable to come to receive the administration, it is given to the vicar of Rickmansworth in order that he should commit the administration to the same executrix, first administering the oath [to her] in the form sworn.

---

[35] No mention of burial place.

31. John atte Welle   reference: 1AR29v
administration only: died on 20 March 1437/8
John atte Welle of Rikm[er]sworth died intestate on 20 March 1437/8 &[36]
administration of his goods was granted to Robert Gybbe of the same place.

32. Petronilla Dier (widow)   reference: 1AR30r
will: [18 &] 20 March 1437/8   probate: no clause
In the name of God, Amen. On 20 March 1437/8, I Petronilla Dier, by the
intercession of the Blessed Trinity, being in my whole mind, make my testament in
this manner.

First I bequeath my soul to Almighty God, the most Blessed Virgin Mary & all the
saints of God; and my body to be buried in the churchyard of the parish church of
the most Blessed Virgin Mary in the town of Rikmersworth.

I bequeath to the high altar of the same [church] one ewe; to the present vicar of the
same 12d.

I bequeath to John Dyere my son a belt of black leather with silver decoration; to the
same a silver spoon of my better spoons; to the same a cow if it can be done, that is
to say, saving the customs of the lord of the Monastery of St Albans and of the
aforesaid church. I bequeath to Agnes my daughter one spoon of my better spoons;
to Margaret Diere my best kerchief; to John Diere the coverlet of my bed, the best; to
Nicholas Clerk one large chest and one pair of sheets; to the same one cow if it can
be done saving the customs of the lordship and church aforesaid; to the same
Nicholas & Agnes his wife one feather bed; to Nicholas Clerk one silver spoon of my
better spoons; to Alice wife of Roger Lucas one gown and a black undergarment; to
John and Richard, sons of John Diere, to each of them one silver spoon not of the
best.

To the woman placing my body in the shroud one chemise; to two poor women, to
each of them, one chemise; to the light of the Blessed Mary one ewe; to my six
godchildren, to each of them one ewe.

To Petronilla, the daughter of Agnes Clerk, one candlestick, one salt-cellar (or
saucer) and six pieces of tin;[37] to Cecily, the daughter of John Diere, the residue of
the vessels, candlesticks and saucers.

---

[36] The & seems to imply that this is the date on which he died rather than the day on which
administration was granted. Other entries on the folio do not give any clues.
[37] perhaps meaning dishes made from tin

To the fabric of the church 6d; to sir Thomas our chaplain 6d; to John Brannanger 6d; to Thomas Streteman 6d.

Indeed, Petronilla, widow, above written, on the 18 day of the month abovesaid began to make this testament & constituted and made John Dyere executor of the same, and on the 20 day she completed that same [testament] and on the advice of Roger Lucas, [she] admitted to it Nicholas Clerk that he might be executor with him [*i.e.* John Dyere] of this testament so saying "to execute faithfully my testament I ordain, make and constitute John Diere and with him Nicholas Clerk my executors". These being witnesses our vicar, John Brannanger,[38] Thomas Stretman, Roger Lucas & others.

Written the year, month and day above said.

[*no probate clause*]

33. Peter atte Stirte

[note of probate]

reference: 1AR32r

probate: 20 May 1439

Memorandum that the testament of Peter atte Stirte was proved before us on 20 May 1439 & it was his will that his wife should have half of all his goods after his debts had been paid & Robert atte Stirte his son should have the other half, to whom administration was granted &c.

34. Sarah Tyler, widow

will: 16 June 1439

reference: 1AR33r

probate: 20 May 1440

In of God &c. On 16 June 1439, I Sara Tyler of Rykmersworth, widow, make my testament in this manner, &c.

[*No committal of soul or burial clause.*]

I bequeath to the high altar of the church of Rykmersworth one cloth, my best; to the same 12d.

To Simon Croyle poor man 6d; to Thomas Tylere a green bed; to Margaret Quadych one 'coverlyt'.

The residue of my goods I give to Richard Tylere of Ryk' to pay my debts, whom I ordain my executor.

This present testament was proved on 20 May 1440; and administration was committed to the aforesaid executor, who was sworn in form of law.

---

[38] This man was not the vicar. He and Thomas Stretman were parish clerks; the vicar was Henry Bornwash.

35. Thomas Roos (weaver)   reference: 1AR36r
will: 16 August 1441   **probate: 27 September 1441**

In the name of God, Amen. On 16 August 1441, I Thomas Roos of Rykm[er]sworth make my testament, &c.

[*No committal of soul or burial clause.*]

To the vicar for tithes forgotten a lambkin.

To Henry my son all my equipment pertaining to the art of weaving; to each of those carrying my body to the church 1d; to John my son one 'doublet'.

To John Tanner 5s that he may give them to an honest priest for celebrating for my soul; to Thomas Stretman 2d.

I will that all my debts and all the customs and expenses of obsequies and burial being paid and all my last will being observed, done and carried out, that then all my gear and equipment remaining in my house at Bacheworth be delivered to Margery my wife.

The residue of all my goods I give to Richard[39] Brannanger & Henry Roos my son, whom I ordain my executors.

Probate of this testament granted 27 September in the year above [1441]; and administration was granted to Richard the aforesaid executor; the other executor did not appear.

36. John Lovett   reference: 1AR37r
will: 6 December 1441   **probate: 6 February 1441/2**

In the name of God, Amen. On 6 December of the year above said [1441],[40] I John Lovett of Rym[er]sworth, of sound mind, make my testament, &c.

[*No committal of soul or burial clause.*]

I bequeath to the fabric of the same church three sheep.

To Alice my daughter one heifer & six sheep; to Denise the wife of William my son six sheep; to Thomas the son of my son three sheep; to Thomas my servant three sheep.

Indeed one half of the residue of all my goods I bequeath to Agnes my wife and and the other half of them I bequeath to my son William.

I ordain and make the said Agnes my wife executrix of this testament.

---

[39] Definitely Richard, not John.

[40] The date 'the feast of the nativity of Our Lord 1441' is written (in full in Latin) at the top of the folio.

The above testament was proved on 6 February in the year above written [1441/2]; and administration of the goods of said testament was granted to the executrix above written, sworn in form of law.

37. John Dyer

reference: 1AR37r

will: 18 January 1441/2   probate: 2 February 1441/2

In the name of God, Amen. On 18 January 1441/2, I John Dyer of the town of Rym[er]sworth, of sound mind, make my testament, &c.

[No committal of soul or burial clause.]

I bequeath to the high altar there one sheep; to each clerk 6d; to the light of the Blessed Cross 12d; to the new bell being made there 12d; to the fabric of the said church 12d.

To John my son four sheep; to Richard my son four sheep; to each of my godchildren whom I raised from the font one sheep.

The residue of all my goods I give and bequeath to Margaret my wife and I ordain and make her executrix.

In witness whereof, I have placed my seal.

The above testament was proved on 2 February in the year above written [1441/2]; and administration of the goods of the said testament was granted to the executrix above written, sworn in form of law.

38. Richard Robard

reference: 1AR41r

will: 17 November 1442   probate: 21 January 1443/4

In the name of God, Amen. On 17 November 1442, I Richard Robard of Rym[er]sworth, of sound mind &c, make my testament &c.

First I bequeath my soul to God &c; & my body to be buried in the churchyard of my parish church of Rym[er]sworth.

I bequeath to the high altar there 6d; to the light of the Blessed Mary in the nave of the church 4d; to the great light there 4d; to the work of the chapel of the Blessed Virgin Mary 4d; to the light of the Blessed Katherine 4d; to each parish clerk of the aforesaid church 6d.

To John Roberd my brother eight measures of barley & to William Slyngar eight measures of barley.

The residue of all my moveable and immoveable goods I give and bequeath to Agnes my wife, & I ordain and make her executrix of this my testament, & the aforesaid John and William her assistants.

Written at Rym[er]sworth &c.

The above testament was proved on 21 January 1443/4; and administration of the goods of the said testament was granted to the executrix above said, sworn in form of law.

39. Henry Panter   reference: 1AR42r
will: 20 May 1444   **probate: 30 August 1444**
In the name of God, Amen. On 20 May 1444, I Henry Panter of Rym[er]sworth, of sound mind &c, make my testament &c.

First I bequeath my soul to God &c; & my body to be buried in the churchyard of the parish church of Rym[er]sworth aforesaid.

I bequeath to the chapel of the Blessed Mary situated in the churchyard of the said church 3s 4d; to the bell of the same church newly set up 12d; to my curate there now living 3s 4d; to John Brannanger parish clerk 6d; to Thomas Stretman parish clerk 6d.

All my other goods I give and bequeath to Cecily my wife for the sustentation of her life; and the same Cecily I ordain and make executrix of this my testament &c.

The above testament was proved on the penultimate day of August in the year above written [1444]; and administration of all the goods was granted to the executrix of the above written testament, sworn in form of law.

40. Baldewin Rous, esquire   reference: 1AR50v
will: 15 August 1446   **probate: 4 March 1446/7**
On the day of the Assumption of the Blessed Virgin Mary [15 August] 1446, I Baldewin Rous, esquire, of Rykem[er]sworth in the exempt jurisdiction of the Monastery of St Albans, of sound mind and whole memory, but fearful, being on the point of death, make my testament in this manner.

First I bequeath my soul to Almighty God & all his saints; & my body to be buried in the churchyard of my parish church of Rikm[er]sworth aforesaid.

I bequeath to the fabric of the same church 6s 8d.

To Paul my servant two gowns.

Moreover the residue of all my goods not bequeathed I give and bequeath to Katherine my wife, whom I constitute my executrix that she may dispose of them for my soul as may seem best to her to do.

Given at Rikm[er]sworth aforesaid on the day & year above said.

This present testament was proved, approved and favoured in the presence of us, William Albon, doctor of canon law, archdeacon of the exempt jurisdiction of the monastery of St Alban in the diocese of Lincoln on 4 March 1446/7; &

administration of all the goods yet existing in the jurisdiction with regard to this testament was granted to the executrix named in the same, sworn in form of law. Given under my aforesaid official seal on the day & year abovesaid.

41. William Poonde   reference: 1AR49v
will: 24 October 1446   probate: 6 November 1446

In the name of God, Amen. I William Poonde of Rykem[er]sworth make my testament in this manner, that is to say, on 24 October 1446.

First I bequeath my soul to God &c.

To the work of the church there two sheep; to the works of the same two of my trees growing on my land; to the little one of the serving boys called William one sheep with a lamb. \& 40[?d] to the reparation of the common way/.[41]

The rest of my moveable goods I give and bequeath to Emmot my wife and John my son, that they may dispose of it according to the said will for the health of my soul.

That this my testament may be well and faithfully executed I appoint and constitute them as my executors.

The present testament was proved on 6 November in the year above [1446]; and administration &c was granted to the executrix above named, sworn in form of law.

42. John Hereward   reference: 1AR50r
will: 4 January 1446/7   probate: 31 January 1446/7

In the name of God, Amen. On 4 January 1446/7, I John Hereward of Rykem[er]sworth, being of sound mind &c, make my testament in this manner &c.

First I bequeath my soul to God &c; & [my] body to be buried in the churchyard of the Blessed Mary of Rykem[er]sworth aforesaid.

I bequeath to the high altar of the said church 3s 4d; to each of the four lights in the body of the church 10d.

To the way adjacent to the place called 'Fowle slowgh' 20d.

The rest of my goods, wherever they are, I dispose through John Seward of Rykem[er]sworth for the health of my soul; and I ordain and appoint him executor of this my testament.

Proved on the last day of the month aforesaid [31 January 1446/7], & administration was granted to John Seward above named, sworn in form of law.

---

[41] [added in the margin]: *& xl ad rep[ar]acio[n]em vie comune*

43. John Holtyng   reference: 1AR50v
will: 8 January 1446/7   **probate: 17 March 1446/7**

In the name of God, Amen. I John Holtyng of Rykem[er]sworthe, being in my
sound mind, on 8 January 1446/7 make my testament in this manner.

First I bequeath my soul to Almighty God; & my body to be buried in the
churchyard of the parish church of the Blessed Mary of Rykem[er]sworth.

I bequeath to the lights of the Holy Cross, the Blessed Edmund, the Blessed
Katherine & the chapel of the Blessed Mary, to each of them one sheep.

To each of my children one sheep.

Of this my testament I ordain & make executrix my wife called Bennet.[42]

*The above testament was proved on 17 March in the year as above [1446/7]; and
administration of all the goods concerned in the said testament was granted to
Bennet, executrix named above, sworn in form of law; & she was released from
[providing] a final account, saving all rights whatsoever.*

44. William Smyth   reference: 1AR53r
will: 4 December 1447   **probate: 20 January 1447/8**

Because [man] born of woman, living for a short time, is filled with many miseries,
on that account, I William Smyth of Rykmansworth,[43] knowing [that] nothing is
more certain than death [and] nothing more uncertain than the hour of death,
wishing in my prosperity to provide for the health of my soul, in the name of the
holy and undivided Trinity, Father, Son & Holy Spirit, on 4 December 1447, I
ordain and make my testament in this manner.

First, I commend my soul to Almighty God & to the Blessed Mary his Mother & to
all his saints; & my body to holy burial.

I bequeath to the light of the Blessed Trinity 2d; to John Brangangre 2d; to Thomas
Stretman 2d.

To each of my sons and daughters one sheep.

I bequeath the value of one damask gown, in English a 'Motlay', to the repair of a
certain way called 'Pyssyng daill'.

My blue gown to Peter, husband of my daughter; one coat to John Wynkefeld.

The residue of all my goods not bequeathed above, my debts firstly being paid and
my funeral expenses deducted, I give and bequeath to Alice my wife & Roger
Brownyng whom I ordain & constitute to be my true & legitimate executors.

---

[42] The Latin for Bennet is *Benedicta.*
[43] Unusually, the 'modern' spelling.

These being witnesses: Thomas Mees priest & John Wyckeborn the younger &
many others.

*The above testament was proved and favoured before us &c on 20 January in the
year as above [1447/8]; and administration of all the goods concerned in the said
testament was granted to the executors above named, sworn in form of law; & they
were released from rendering to us a final account, saving all rights whatsoever; &
they were acquitted.*

45. John Gybbes   reference: 1AR54v
will: 6 March 1447/8 [English]   probate: no clause but *c.*25 March 1448[44]

In dei nomine, Amen. I John Gybbes in my good mende, beyng the 6 day of March
in the yer of owr lord 1447/8, make & ordeyne my testament in this maner.
Fyrst I bequethe my sowle unto almyghty god & my body for be beryed in the
chirch yerd of our Lady in Rykm[er]sworth.
Item I be quethe unto oure Lady lygt in the seid chirch 12d. Item I be queth un to
the reparacion of the said chirch 12d. Item unto the lygt in oure lady chapell 12d.
Item unto eche of the clerkys of the seid chirch 6d.
Item unto John Tyler, the sone of Thomas Tyler, six ewen & in mony 6s 8d. Item
unto Richard Tyler his brother 3s 4d. Item to the older ~~John~~ Jone the doughter of
Thomas Tyler two ewen & in mony 3s 4d. Item unto yonger Jone here soster one
ewe.
Item I be queth unto the reparacion of the hy way at Poleyns 12d.
Item unto Margerye Swanlond a pogge[*sic*]. Item unto John Tyler my blew gowne.
Item unto Jone Gybbes & to Margrete her soster, the dowghtryn of William Gybbes,
eche of hem a lamb. Item unto the older Jone the doughter of Thomas Tyler a basyn
& lavour. Item unto the said Jone a bras pot containing by estimation a galon. Item
unto John Tyler a posnet of bras containing a potell. Item seven pec' of pewter vessel
I be queth the oon half unto John Tyler & the todyr half unto the older Jone his
soster. Item I be queth unto Alison Lucas 20d. Item unto yongge Jone the doughter
of Thomas Tyler 12d. Item unto Kateriine Gybbes the Wyf of Thomas Gybbes one
ewe. Item unto John Gybbes the sone of Thomas Gybbes a shep. Item unto John
Spryngold a ewe. Item I be queth unto Thomas Gybbes 20d. Item unto William
Gybbes 20d. Item unto William Arnewy 3s 4d.

---

[44] The page is headed (in Latin) 'the feast of the Annunciation of the Blessed Virgin Mary
AD 1448, William Albon'.

And this will forto be fulfylled I make & ordeyne myn executours William Arnewy, Thomas Gybbes & William Gybbes.

In Wytenesse her of I have set my seal the day & the yer above wretyn.

[*No probate clause*]

46. Thomas Edred

46. Thomas Edred	reference: 1AR58r
will: 26 September 1448	probate: 2 October 1449

In the name of God, Amen. On 26 September 1448, I Thomas Edred of Rykm[er]sworth, being in my sound mind, make & ordain my testament in this manner.

First I bequeath my soul to Almighty God, the Blessed Virgin Mary & indeed to all the saints of God; & my body to be buried in the churchyard of the church of Rykm[er]sworth, that is to say, between the chapel of the Blessed Mary & the wall there of the said church.

To the high altar of the said church 4d; to the light of the Holy Cross 12d; to the reparation of the same church 20d; to each of the parish clerks 6d; to the chapel of the Blessed Mary there 4d.

That this my testament be well & faithfully carried out I ordain and make my wife Joan & Thomas Boterfeld, 'Maltman', my executors.

In witness whereof to this my present testament, my last will, I have placed my seal.

Proved &c 2 October 1449; & [administration] was committed &c to Joan, executrix named, sworn in form of law; Thomas Boterfeld renounced administration.

47. Thomas Gybbes

47. Thomas Gybbes	reference: 1AR56v
will: 14 March 1448/9	probate: 3 May 1449

Since nothing in this world is more certain than death & since nothing is more uncertain than the hour of death, thus it is that I Thomas Gybbes of Rykem[er]sworth, being in my whole mind, on 14 March 1448/9, ordain & make my testament in this manner.

First I commend my soul to the most blessed Trinity & the Blessed Virgin Mary & all the saints of God; & my body to holy burial in the churchyard of the parish church of Rykm[er]sworth.

To the high altar of the same 12d; to John Brannger 4d; to Stretman[*sic*] 4d; to the beam [*trabi*] of the Blessed Mary 6d; to the altar of the Blessed Edmund 6d; to the altar of the Blessed Katherine 6d.

To Alice recently my servant six sheep.

The residue of my goods not bequeathed above, my debts firstly paid & my funeral expenses deducted, I give and bequeath to Joan my wife & to Thomas my son the elder, whom I make, ordain & constitute my true & legal executors.

These being witnesses: John Bramanger, Richard Gybbes & others.

Proved &c 3 May 1449; administration was committed to Thomas, one of the executors named, sworn in form of law; right of administration being reserved to Joan the other named executor if she wishes to take it up.

48. Roger Bryan   reference: 1AR59v

will: 16 November 1449   **probate: 31 January 1449/50**

In the name of God, Amen. On 16 November 1449, I Roger Bryan of Rykem[er]sworth[45] being sick in body but sound in mind, make my testament in this manner.

First I bequeath my soul to God & the Blessed Virgin Mary & to all the saints; & my body to be buried in the churchyard of the parish church of the Blessed Mary of Rykem[er]swort aforesaid.

To the vicar of the same church for a mortuary [payment] my best gown.

To Adam Hardegrype of Rysselepe my woollen tunic; to my sister, wife of the same Adam, two sheep.

To the light of St Edmund of the said church of Rykem[er]swort one sheep; to the fabric of the pavement of the aforesaid church one sheep.

For well and faithfully implementing this my will I constitute and ordain as my executors Henry Suward of Rykem[er]swort & William son of the same & the residual part of all my goods not bequeathed I commit to the disposition and execution of my aforesaid executors that they may dispose [it] annually on my anniversary as shall seem best to them, my executors, for my soul.

These are the debts that are owed to me the aforesaid Roger: firstly Richard Goddyntonge of Rykem[er]swort 6s 8d; Roger Belch of the same 5s 8d; Roger Adam of the same 40d; Robert Merchaunt of the same 2s 9d.

These witnesses being present: sir John parish chaplain & the aforesaid Richard.

Probate &c the last day of January the year abovesaid 1449/50;[46] and administration was committed &c to Henry Suward executor named in the testament, sworn in form of law; administration being reserved to William named in the testament, if he wishes to take it up.

---

[45] In every other instance in this will the spelling 'Rykm[er]swort' is used.

[46] The year is written out in full at the top of the page.

49. Henry Bornwash, vicar   reference: 1AR62v

died: 10 March 1450/1

[*margin*] Master Henry Bornwash lately vicar of Ryk'

Henry Bornwash, vicar of Rykm[er]sworth, died intestate on 10 March the year above said [1450/1]; therefore the inventory of his goods by John Wymond & John Bremangre [is not] attached as is made plain in it. It is missing because his goods were set aside by the collector of the Lord Pope because the said vicar was chaplain to the Lord Pope by bull.[47]

50. Richard Gybbe   reference: 1AR67r

will: 4 October 1452   **probate: 13 April 1453**

In &c. On 4 October 1452, I Richard Gybbe of Rykm[er]sworth, of sound mind & good memory, make my testament in this manner.

First I commend my soul to Almighty God, the Blessed Mary & all the saints; & my body to be buried in the churchyard of the parish church of St Mary of Rykm[er]sworth aforesaid.

To the said church for oblations 20d; to the fabric of my mother church of St Alban 8d; to John Bramanger 8d; to the light of St Mary in the chancel of the said church of Ryk' 8d.

The residue of all my goods I give and bequeath to the sustentation and support of Alice my wife and of Richard Hamond my son,[48] whom I ordain and make my executors.

Given the year and day above said.

Proved on 13 April 1453 &c.

51. John atte Hyde   reference: 1AR66r

will: 8 October 1452   **probate: 2 March 1452/3**

In &c. On 8 October 1452, I John atte Hyde of Rykm[er]sworth within the peculiar jurisdiction of St Albans, in the diocese of Lincoln, being in my sound mind and whole memory, make my testament in this manner.

First I commend my soul to Almighty God, the Blessed Mary & all the saints; & my body to be buried in the churchyard of the parish church of St Mary of Ryk' aforesaid.

---

[47] See the Introduction, pp. xxx–xxxi, for some details of Bornwash's career.

[48] Definitely says *filij mei* – perhaps Richard Hamond was his wife's son by an earlier marriage.

To the high altar of the said church 12d; to the light of St Mary in the chancel of the said church of Ryk' 12d; to the reparation of the mother church of St Alban 12d.

I will that Isabel my wife shall have my tenement & my lands, with all their appurtenances and all their profits, until my son and heir William comes to his legal age. The same William my son, by permission of the lord [of the manor], I will that the said Isabel my wife shall have under her rule and discipline while he is under his aforesaid legal age. And afterwards, the said William my son, when he shall come to his right age, and be possessed of my said tenement & my lands, I will that the said Isabel my wife shall have her home and sojourn within my said tenement at the same time & suitable food from the profits and appurtenances of my said tenement & my lands for the term of her life. And if it should happen that the aforesaid William my son should leave this light [*i.e.* die] while the said Isabel my wife & his mother is living, then I will that the same Isabel my wife shall have & possess my said tenement & my aforesaid lands for the term of her life.

The residue of all my goods, principally after the payment of my debts, I give & bequeath to the said William my son & his heirs according to the custom of the manor & to the said Isabel my wife, whom I make and ordain my executrix; & Thomas Botervyle, 'maltman', in all things to be her assistant and supervisor. Given at Ryk' aforesaid the year & day abovesaid.

Proved &c 2 March in the year above said [1452/3]; & administration was committed to the executors[sic] named within, sworn in form of law.

52. Thomas Wodeward   reference: 1AR67v
will: 22 November 1452   probate: 13 April 1453

In &c. On 22 November 1452, I Thomas Wodeward of Rykm[er]sworth in the peculiar jurisdiction of the monastery of St Alban, in the diocese of Lincoln, being of sound mind & whole memory make my testament in this manner.

First I commend my soul to Almighty God, the Blessed Mary & all the saints; & my body to be buried in the churchyard of the parish church of Ryk' aforesaid.

To the high altar of the aforesaid parish church 12d; to John Bramanger & Thomas Stretman, clerks of the said parish church, 12d, to each 6d; to the sustentation of the lights of St Edmund & St Katherine the martyrs 8d, to each 4d; to the sustentation of lights burning before the Crucifix & the Glorious Virgin in the chancel of the before-written church 8d, to each 4d.

The residue of all my goods I give & bequeath to Joan my wife.

She and John Wymond I make my executors that they may do, ordain and dispose thereof as seems best to them to please God and speed my soul.

Given the year, day & place above written.
Proved 13 April 1453 &c.

53. William Crek, esquire   reference: 1AR66v
will: 29 November 1452   probate: 24 January 1452/3

In &c. On the penultimate day of November 1452, I William Crek of
Rykmersworth, esquire, in the diocese of Lincoln, under and subject to the peculiar
jurisdiction of St Albans, of sound mind and good memory, fearing to be in
imminent peril of death, make my testament & last will in this manner.

First I commend my soul to Almighty God, his mother the glorious Virgin Mary &
all the saints; & my body to be buried in the churchyard of the parish church of Ryk'
aforesaid next to the body of Julian, formerly my wife.

To the high altar of the said church for tithes forgotten & other failings 6s 8d; to the
reparation & sustentation of the said parish church 13s 4d; to the reparation of the
chapel of St Mary situated in the churchyard of the said parish church 6s 8d.

I will and command that first and principally all my debts be paid; after which
payment and satisfaction and the services of my lands done, I will that Katherine my
wife have a third part of all my moveable goods, both grain and utensils, so that the
aforesaid Katherine my wife neither during my lifetime, nor after my death, shall
alienate or remove any goods secretly without my knowledge and [the knowledge
of] my executors. If she were to do this, I will that she will neither have nor enjoy
that third part of my moveable goods bequeathed to her, unless she immediately
returns those moveable goods thus abstracted into the hands of my executors,
without fraud, deceit or decrease.

I bequeath to Joan and Agnes my daughters, when they shall come to years of
maturity for their marriages 40 marks, that is, to each of them 20 marks received
from the profits and rents of my manor of Mykelfeld & its appurtenances. And if
my said daughters shall pass from this life unmarried, then the aforesaid 40 marks
shall be disposed for the health of my soul, of my parents and of my friends.

I give and bequeath to Thomas my son all my lands and tenements both free and
unfree, wherever they be, which lands and tenements I am able to give, bequeath,
assign and sell, holding them to himself and the heirs of his body lawfully begotten.
And if he should pass from this life without heirs of his body lawfully begotten, then
I will that the next heirs of my said manor of Mykelfeld shall then have all my
abovesaid lands and tenements, holding them to them and the heirs of their body
lawfully begotten and being begotten forever.

To Margaret Whytman, widow, 6s 8d & annually for her life 6s 8d arising from the profits of my said manor of Mykelfeld.[49]

To Joan [*Joha[n]ne*] my servant 6s 8d.

To John Bramanger & Thomas Stretman, to each of them, 20d; to each poor person dwelling in the parish of Rykm[er]sworth who are then living, 4d in alms.

To Alice Fylle my servant for her pay being in arrears & out of recognition 10s; to Christine Wymond my gown of scarlet or with fur for its lining;[50] to John Bennyng for his good service to me recently 13s 4d; to John Bryght my servant 6s 8d and my protective tunic called in English 'un jakke' & a protective burette called 'un salet' & my best bow; to Richard Cleve my servant 6s 8d.

The residue of all my goods not bequeathed, I will that they are in the disposition, judgement and will of Bartholomew Halley, John Creke, esquire, sir John Wynton perpetual vicar of the church of Rykm[er]sworth, & Thomas Waleys, whom I make, ordain & constitute to be my executors, that they may do, ordain & dispose as seems best to them to please God and benefit my soul.

In witness of these present I have placed my seal.

Given at Ryk' aforesaid, on the year, day and month above written.

Proved &c 24 January [1452/3]; & [administration] was committed &c to John Creke & Thomas Waleys, executors named in the testament &c, sworn; administration reserved to the other executors &c.

54. Andrew Ragon   reference: 1AR69r
will: 1 June 1454   probate: 20 July 1454

In &c. On 1 June 1454, I Andrew Ragon of Rykm[er]sworth, of sound mind & whole memory, make my testament in this manner.

First I commend my soul to Almighty God, the Blessed Mary & all the saints; & my body to be buried in the churchyard of the parish church of Rykm[er]sworth aforesaid.

To John Branangre & Thomas Stretman 4d, to each 2d.

To Roger my son my better gown and my best hood.

Of this my testament and last will I make and ordain my wife Alice, my son Robert & William Dryver my executors by these present [*writings*]; and discrete men [*i.e.*

---

[49] See the Introduction p. xlvi for a brief summary of the complicated dispute between William Creke and Richard Whitman from (at least) 1433 to 1435. Twenty years later Creke made provision for a substantial annual payment to Richard's widow, Margaret.

[50] The Latin is unclear, perhaps either his scarlet gown or one that has a fur lining.

supervisors] John Wynton, vicar of the parish church of Rykm[er]sworth aforesaid & John Wymond of the same.

Given the year, day & place abovesaid.

Proved &c 20 July in the year abovesaid [1454]; & they were released, saving all rights whatsoever &c.

55. Joan Wodeward   reference: 1AR78r
will: 14 November 1454   probate: 22 February 1454/5

In &c. On 14 November 1454, I Joan Wodeward of Rykm[er]sworth, of sound mind & whole memory, make my testament in this manner.

First I commend my soul to Almighty God, the Blessed Mary & all the saints; & my body to be buried in the churchyard of the parish church of Rykm[er]sworth aforesaid.

To the high altar of the said church for tithes forgotten and other failings 12d; to sir John, vicar of the said church, 12d; to the reparation of the chapel of St Mary situated in the churchyard of the aforesaid church 12d; to the reparation of the said parish church two sheep; to the lights of the Holy Trinity, St Mary, St Edmund and St Katherine four sheep, to each light one sheep; to John Bramanger parish clerk 6d; to Thomas Stretman clerk 4d.

The residue &c I will to be at the disposition and will of Thomas Botervyle, John Wymund & Roger Adam, whom I ordain, make & constitute my executors.

Given the day & year abovesaid.

Proved &c 22 February [1454/5] &c.

56. John Syward   reference: 1AR78r
will: 4 January 1454/5   probate: 15 March 1454/5

In &c. On 4 January 1454/5, I John Syward of Rykm[er]sworth, of sound mind & good memory, make my testament in this manner.

First I commend my soul to Almighty God, the Blessed Mary & all the saints; & my body to be buried in the churchyard of the parish church of St Mary of Ryk' aforesaid.

To the high altar of the said church for tithes forgotten & other failings 3s 4d; to the reparation of the chapel of St Mary situated in the churchyard of the said church one sheep; to the reparation of my parish church one sheep.

To John Bramanger 4d; to Thomas Streteman 2d; to Henry Wymond 2d; to William Chambre 12d.

Of this testament & my last will I make, constitute & ordain Clemence my wife & John Wynkeburn the younger my executors.

Given the year, day & place above said.

Proved &c 15 March the year abovesaid [1454/5]; & administration was committed to Clemence, executrix herein named; John Wynkeburn her co-executor renouncing; &c she was sworn in form of law.

57. Richard Slynger   reference: 1AR78r
will: 20 January 1454/5   probate: 1 March 1454/5

In &c. On 20 January 1454/5, I Richard Slynger of Rykm[er]sworth, of sound mind & whole memory, make my testament in this manner.

First I commend my soul to Almighty God, the Blessed Mary & all the saints; & my body to be buried in the churchyard of the parish church of Ryk' aforesaid.

To the high altar of the aforesaid church for tithes forgotten & other failings 12d; to the lights of St Edmund and St Katherine two sheep.

To Katherine the daughter of Richard Playter one sheep; to John Slynger my brother my better gown.

To William my son & Margaret my wife all my moveable goods to each of them part, & of this my testament & last will I make, constitute and ordain William my son and Henry Syward my executors.

Given the year, day and place above written.

Proved &c 1 March [1454/5] &c; [William] sworn; administration of the same reserved to Henry Syward if he shall come &c.

58. John Wynkeburn the elder   reference: 1AR81r
will: 8 March 1454/5   probate: 1 October 1455

In &c. On 8 March 1454/5 I John Wynkeburn the elder of Rykm[er]sworth, of sound mind & whole memory, make my testament in this manner.

First I commend my soul to Almighty God, the Blessed Mary & all the saints; & my body to be buried next to the grave of my father in the churchyard of the parish church of St Mary of Ryk' aforesaid.

To the reparation & sustentation of the parish church of Ryk' aforesaid 6s 8d; to the lights of the Holy Trinity, St Edmund & St Katherine in the aforesaid church 2s, to each of them 8d; to Thomas Stretman 12d; to John Bramanger 8d.

To each of my spiritual sons and daughters one ewe; to Joan Gape two ewes; to William Wynkeburn one bushel of wheat & two bushels of malt; to Katherine the daughter of the said William one ewe.

I will that I shall have one trental for my soul &c.

To Isabel my wife in money paid out and in household goods to the value of £10; to my two daughters Alice & Rose 8 marks, to each of them 4 marks, when they shall come to their age of marriage, and if it should happen that they should die before their marriageable age, then I will that the said 8 marks be spent in pious uses for the health of my soul & of my friends' [souls].

The residue &c I will to be at the disposition, ordering and will of Joan [Edelyn] my mother, Isabel my wife & John my brother, whom I ordain, make and constitute my executors that they may dispose and ordain as seems best to them to please God and speed my soul &c.

Proved 1 October 1455; & [administration] was committed to the executors named &c.

59. Helias Stokker reference: 1AR79r
will: 29 April 1455 probate: 2 June 1455

In &c. On the penultimate day [29] of April 1455, I Helias Stokker of Rykm[er]sworth, of sound mind & whole memory, make my testament in this manner.

First I commend my soul to Almighty God, the Blessed Mary & all the saints; & my body to be buried in the churchyard of the parish church of St Mary of Ryk' aforesaid.

To the high altar of the same church 4d.

The residue &c I give & bequeath to Katherine my wife, whom I make my executrix that she may dispose [of it] as seems best to her to please God &c.

Proved &c 2 June in the year above said [1455] &c.

60. Joan Edelyn[51] reference: 1AR83r
will: 8 October 1455 probate: 26 June 1456

In &c. On 8 October 1455, I Joan Edelyn of Ryk', of sound mind &c.

First to God &c; & my body to be buried in the churchyard of the parish church of Ryk' aforesaid.

To the said parish church 1 silver chalice [*or,* cup] to the value of 4 marks & the 4 marks which are in the hands of Thomas Hende of Trynge for rent of land let to him at farm.

---

[51] Mother of John Wynkeburn the elder (58) and of his brother, also John.

To the fabric of the monastery of St Alban 20 marks, which the said Thomas Hende owes me for money lent to him.

To John Wynkeburn my son 29 marks, which Thomas Hende owes me for rent of land let to him at farm.

To the fraternities of the Holy Trinity & St Katherine the virgin & martyr one large spit and one 'Aundyerne'.

To Alice my granddaughter two small spits & one small brass jar called 'le posnet'; to William Whytele one brass jar.

The residue of all my goods not bequeathed I will shall be at the ordering and will of John Wynkeburn my son, whom I ordain, make & constitute my executor.

Given at Ryk' aforesaid, the year & day above said.

Proved &c 26 June 1456 &c; and [the executor] was released, saving all rights whatsoever.

61. Nicholas Turnour   reference: 1AR83r
will: 22 October 1455   probate: 26 June 1456

In &c. On 22 October 1455, I Nicholas Turnour of Ryk', of sound mind &c, make my testament in this manner.

First I commend my soul to Almighty God &c; & my body to be buried in the churchyard of the parish church of Ryk' aforesaid.

To the high altar of the aforesaid church &c 12d; to the lights of the Crucifix, the Holy Trinity, St Mary & St Katherine 16d, to each of them 4d; to the chapel of the Blessed Mary *de Insula*[52] 6d.

I will that after my decease, & that of Margaret my wife, my lands and tenements in Ryk' aforesaid be sold & with those monies coming from them a priest may be found to celebrate for me and my forebears immediately for one year in the said parish church of Ryk'.

The residue &c I will shall be at the disposal, ordering & will of Margaret my wife, whom I make, ordain & constitute my executrix

In presence of the honest men William Revell & Andrew Turnour, son of the said Nicholas, & others. Given &c.

Proved &c 26 June 1456 &c; and [the executor] was released &c.

---

[52] The chapel of St Mary of the Island, located in the churchyard.

62. Thomas Holtyng   reference: 1AR83r
will: 10 May 1456   probate: 26 June 1456

In &c. On 10 May 1456, I Thomas Holtyng of Rykm[er]sworth, of sound mind & whole memory, make my testament in this manner.

First I commend my soul to Almighty God &c; & my body to be buried in the churchyard of the parish church of Rykm[er]sworth.

To the high altar of the said church &c 20d; to Thomas Stretman 12d.

The residue &c I give & bequeath to Joan my wife that, my debts paid, she may dispose for the health of my soul &c, whom I make & ordain my executrix, given &c.

Proved &c 26 June 1456 &c; and [the executrix] was released.

63. Margaret Slynger,[53] late wife of Richard   reference: 1AR85r
will: 20 October 1456   probate: 4 December 1456

In &c. On 20 October 1456, I Margaret Slynger, late the wife of Richard Slynger, of Rykm[er]sworth, of sound mind & whole memory, make my testament in this manner.

First I commend my soul to Almighty God; & my body to be buried in the churchyard of the parish church of Rykm[er]sworth aforesaid.

To the high altar of the said church for tithes forgotten and other failings 12d; to the reparation of the aforementioned church 6d; to the chapel of the Blessed Mary *de Insula* 6d; to the reparation of the common way leading from the said town of Ryk' as far as Schepcote 6s 8d.

To Agnes Davy one mantle; to Julian the wife of Thomas Godfray one tunic called 'le Frende'; to Margery, daughter of the said Thomas, one candlestick and one salt-cellar; to the three godsons & goddaughters whom I raised from the holy font 18d, to each of them 6d; to Isabel Cake [*or*, Cave] one cover; to Joan Davy, daughter of John Davy, one candlestick & one sheet.

The residue &c at the will of William Slynger, whom I ordain and make my executor &c.

To the parish clerks 8d, to each of them 4d.

Proved 4 December in the year above said [1456].

---

[53] *Wills at Hertford* has 'Olyng'. It is Margaret Slyng[er]: her husband Richard's will is no. 57.

64. Richard Vern   reference: 1AR87v
will: 4 April 1457   **probate: 18 May 1457**

In &c. On 4 April 1457, I Richard Vern of Rykm[er]sworth, of sound mind & whole memory, make my testament in this manner.

First I bequeath my soul to Almighty God; & my body to be buried in the churchyard of the parish church of Rykm[er]sworth aforesaid.

To the high altar of the said church for tithes forgotten & other failings 12d; to the reparation and sustentation of the said church of Ryk' 20d; to Thomas Stodley & Thomas Stretman, parish clerks 8d, to each of them 4d.

To Margaret my wife and Richard my son all my moveable goods, my debts being paid.

Of this present testament and my last will I make, ordain and constitute executors the aforesaid Margaret my wife and Richard my son, that they may dispose and order as seems best to them to please God and speed my soul.

Given at Ryk' aforesaid the year and day above said.

Proved &c 18 May in the year above said [1457].

65. Roger Bowryng   reference: 1AR88r
will: 16 April 1457   **probate: 9 July 1457**

In the name of god, Amen. On 16 April 1457, I Roger Bowryng of Rykm[er]sworth, of sound mind and whole memory, make my testament in this manner.

First I commend my soul to Almighty God, the Blessed Mary & all the saints; & my body to be buried in the churchyard of the parish church of the Blessed Mary of Rykm[er]sworth aforesaid.

To the high altar of the aforesaid parish church for tithes forgotten & other failings 3s 4d.

To Katherine my granddaughter a brass pot, a brass pan, a pair of sheets, a cover and a 'blanket'; to Joan my wife all and singular my household utensils, except those bequeathed to the aforesaid Katherine my granddaughter; to my aforesaid wife Joan two quarters of wheat and two quarters of barley.

I will that my lands and tenements be sold and that the money coming shall pay my debts. I will that, my debts having been paid, I have a priest celebrating in the said church of Rykm[er]sworth for a quarter of a year for my soul and the souls of my friends.

Of which above testament and my last will I make, ordain and constitute John Wynkburn of Rykm[er]sworth aforesaid and John Webbe of the same my executors. In the presence of the discrete men William Weller & William Revell.

Given at Rykm[er]sworth aforesaid the year and day above said.
Proved &c 9 July [1457]; and [the executors] were released.

66. Thomas Trot　　　reference: 1AR92r
will: 3 July 1458　　　probate: 31 July 1458
In &c. On 3 July 1458, I Thomas Trot of Rykm[er]sworth, of sound mind and whole memory, make my testament in this manner.
First I commend my soul to Almighty God, the Blessed Mary & all the saints; & my body to be buried in the parish church of the said town of Rykm[er]sworth.
To the high altar of the aforesaid church for tithes forgotten & other failings 3s 4d.
I will that all my other goods not bequeathed to be at the disposition, ordering and will of Alice my wife, whom I constitute, ordain and make my executrix.
In the presence of these discrete men: John Wynton, vicar of the aforesaid church of Rykm[er]sworth & John Wakyngton, learned man [*l[ite]rato*], witnesses summoned for this.
Given the year and place above written.
Proved &c the last day of July in the year above said [1458] &c.

67. John Gybbes　　　reference: 1AR99r
will: 4 June 1459　　　probate: 15 May 1460
In &c. On 4 June 1459, I John Gybbes of Rykm[er]sworth, of sound mind &c.
First I bequeath my soul to Almighty God, the Blessed Mary &c; & my body to be buried in the churchyard of the parish church of Ryk' aforesaid.
To the high altar of the said church for tithes forgotten & other failings 12d; to the reparation of the chapel of St Mary *de Insula* 4d; to James Kelly, parish clerk, 4d; Thomas Stretman, the other parish clerk, 4d; to Peter Prentyse 4d.
The residue of my goods not bequeathed I will that that they be at the disposition, ordering and will of Thomas Gybbes, my brother, & Richard Hamond of Rykm[er]sworth aforesaid, whom I ordain, make & constitute my executors.
Given at Ryk' aforesaid the year and day &c.
Proved 15 May 1460 &c.

68. John Wynkfeld   reference: 1AR97r
will: 20 June 1459   **probate: 4 October 1459**

In &c. On 20 June 1459, I John Wynkfeld, of sound mind & memory, make my testament in this manner.

First I give my soul to the Almighty, the Blessed Mary & all the saints; & my body to be buried in the churchyard of Rykm[er]sworth.

To the high altar of the said church for my tithes forgotten & other failings 8d; to the two parish clerks, to each of them 4d.

The residue &c I will that it be at the will and disposition of Alice my wife, whom I make, ordain and constitute my executrix.

Proved &c 4 October in the year above said [1459].

69. Katherine Turnour, late wife of Richard   reference: 1AR97r
will: 20 July 1459   **probate: 3 October 1459**

In &c. On 20 July 1459, I Katherine Turnour of Rykm[er]sworth, lately the wife of Richard Turnour of the same, of sound mind & good memory, make my testament in this manner.

First I commend my soul to Almighty God, the Blessed Mary & all the saints; & my body to be buried in the churchyard of the parish church of Rykm[er]sworth aforesaid.

To the high altar of the aforesaid church for tithes forgotten and other failings one sheep; to James Kelly, parish clerk, 8d; to Thomas Stretman his fellow 8d; to John Bramanger 8d; to Peter Prentyse 4d; to the reparation of the great bell recently broken 20d; to the light of the Holy Trinity one sheep; to the light of St Mary 4d; to the light of St Katherine 4d; to the light of St Nicholas the bishop & confessor 2d; to the light of St Christopher 2d.

The residue &c I will that it be in the disposition, ordering & will of Roger Adam & of Richard Bayle, smith, whom I ordain, make & constitute my executors.

Given &c.

Proved &c 3 October in the year above said [1459].

70. Agnes Wodeward   reference: 1AR120r
died: 24 July 1459   administration: 14 November 1467[54]

On 14 November 1467 administration of the goods of Agnes Wodeward, lately of Rykm[er]sworth, who died intestate on 24 July 1459, was granted to John Wodeward of the same [place] &c.

71. William Randolff   reference: 1AR102v
will: 10 March 1462   probate: 28 April 1462

In &c. On 10 March 1461 [1461/2], on I William Randolff of Ryk', of sound &c. [*No committal of soul or burial clause.*]

To the high altar of the aforesaid church for tithes forgotten & other failings 12d; to the reparation of the aforesaid parish church 12d; to each light in the said church 4d; to each parish clerk 4d.

The residue of all & [singular] my goods I will that they be at the ordering, disposition & will of Andrew my son, Thomas Buttervyle, 'maltman', of Ryk' aforesaid & Thomas Lambard of Chalfunt St Peter, that they may ordain & dispose &c, whom I ordain, make and constitute my executors by these presents. *Proved &c 28 April 1462.*

72. Thomas Gybbes, of Herynghers   reference: 1AR102v
will: 10 May 1462   probate: 19 May 1462

In &c. On 10 May 1462, I Thomas Gybbes of Herynghers in Rykm[er]sworth, of sound mind &c.

First I bequeath my soul to Almighty God, the Blessed Mary &c; my body to be buried in the churchyard of the parish church of Rykm[er]sworth aforesaid.

To the high altar of the said church for tithes forgotten and other failings 3s[*sic*]; to the reparation and maintenance of the aforesaid church half a quarter of wheat and four quarters of malt; to James Kelly, Thomas Streteman, John Bramanger and John Streteley, to each of them 6d; to each of the lights in the aforesaid church 4d.

I will that Brother Thomas Hamyngford celebrate for half a year for my soul and the souls of my father and my friends.

The residue of my goods not bequeathed, I will that they be at the disposition and will of Richard Hamond and Roger Belche, whom I ordain, make and constitute my

---

[54] No indication why administration was only granted 8 years later; year of death definitely 1459.

executors; and I make John Wynton, perpetual vicar of the aforesaid church of
Rykm[er]sworth, in all and singular my supervisor.
Proved &c 19 May in the year above said [1462].

73. Rose Gybbes, widow of Thomas   reference: 1AR103r
will: 20 May 1462   probate: 21 May 1462[55]

In &c. On 20 May 1462, I Rose Gybbes, lately the widow of Thomas Gybbez of
Herynghers in Rykm[er]sworth, of sound mind &c.
[*No committal of soul*]; & my body to be buried in the churchyard of the parish
church of Rykm[er]sworth aforesaid, next to the grave of Thomas lately my
husband.[56]
To the high altar of the aforesaid church 3s 4d; to the reparation of the chapel of St
Mary 'de Iland' 20d; to the lights of the said church 2s; to each parish clerk 4d.
The residue of all my goods not bequeathed I will that they be in the disposition &
ordering of John Wynton, vicar of the aforesaid church, Thomas Hamyngford
chaplain, Richard Hamond & Roger Belche, whom I make & constitute my
executors that they may dispose and order as seems best to them to please God &
profit my soul.
Proved &c 21 May in the year above said [1462].

74. William at Welle, woolman   reference: 1AR111v–112r
will: 8 November 1462   probate: 19 October 1464

In &c. On 8 November 1462, I William at Welle of the parish of Rykm[er]sworth, in
the county of Hertford, 'Wolman', sound in mind yet sick in body, make my
testament in this manner.
First I bequeath my soul to Almighty God &c; & my body for ecclesiastical burial in
the churchyard of the parish church aforesaid, between Margery and Rose my wives.
To the works of the said church being done & to the sustentation of the lights in the
same 40s; to the vicar of the said church 13s 4d; to each chaplain being at my masses
and exequies on the days of my burial & celebration on the thirtieth day, to each of
them 12d; to the parish clerks of the said church, to each of them on the same days
8d; to each of the other clerks singing on those days in masses & my exequies on the
aforesaid days each of them 4d.

---

[55] Probate date is definitely 21 May, i.e. the day after the will was made.
[56] Not mentioned in her husband's will (72); it seems likely that they were both ill.

To John my son in English money £20; to William my son in English money £20.
[*At this point the following note is in the margin in the same hand as the main text; indicated here in* { }] {Note that £40 is lacking from John's legacy and £20 from William's legacy.[57] And if one of them should die then £10 of the share of the deceased should pass to the monastery of St Albans.}

To Agnes my daughter, wife of John Seybroke of Harpeden, 66s 8d; to Joan my daughter 20s; to Joan Jaket my kinswoman 20s; to William the elder, son of Margaret[58] my wife, 40s; to Agnes, daughter of the same, 66s 8d.

To the works of the parish church of Trenge in the county of Hertford 20s; to the sustentation of the light of St Mary the mother of our Lord Jesus Christ in the parish church of Aylesbury 20s.

To John Walloxton of Isnamstede Cheyne 40s.

& the same John and Margaret my wife I make my executors for the execution of this my testament.

[*fol. 112r*] The residue of all my goods I give & bequeath to the aforesaid executors, that they, having God before their eyes, will pay my debts & dispose of those goods for my soul, the souls of my parents & benefactors & all the faithful departed as may seem best to them to perform for the health of my soul.

In which &c; this my present testament sealed with my seal, given the month and year above said.

Proved &c 19 October 1464.

75. Richard Vale (miller)   reference: 1AR106v
will: 30 March 1463   **probate: 30 April 1463**

In &c. On the penultimate day of March 1463, I Richard Vale of Rykm[er]sworth, of sound mind &c, make my testament in this manner.

First I commend my soul to Almighty God, the Blessed Mary & all the saints; & my body to be buried in the churchyard of the parish church of Ryk' aforesaid.

To the high altar of the aforesaid church 12d; to the reparation of the said church 3s 4d.

---

[57] The meaning is unclear, but there are at least two possibilities: 1) John and William had been left money by a grandparent and this had not yet been given to them; 2) their father William changed his mind and there was an addition written on the original will stating that he wanted them to have more than the £20 recorded.

[58] Definitely Margaret here and Margery earlier: she is his current (presumably third) wife.

I bequeath to Brother Thomas Hemyngford for celebrating for my soul & the souls of my father and mother for half a quarter of one year 16s 8d; to each priest being at my exequies 4d; to each parish clerk 2d; I bequeath to the chapel of the Blessed Mary *de Insula* one pound of wax.

To Julian my servant one green-coloured gown lately my wife's, one red-coloured tunic, one silver spoon & 5s in money; to Margaret Wymond one blue coloured tunic called 'a frend' lately Alice my wife's, one green-coloured mantle, one silver spoon & 5s in money; to John Quyntyn my servant[59] all & singular my instruments [*i.e.* tools] pertaining to the craft of milling & my murrey-coloured gown; to the said John & John Ware my bed in which I lay; to Joan Myller, Margaret Wymond & the above written Julian all & singular the veils called 'kercheves' which were lately Alice my wife's; to the aforesaid Julian a good pair of sheets & two pairs of medium; to the aforesaid Margaret two pairs of sheets of the better [*sort*]: to Joan Turnour, wife of William Turnour, my best brasen vessel called 'le Cawdron'.

The residue of all my goods not bequeathed I give & bequeath to Valentine my son, that he may have and possess it for his own use, without impediment and retention of my executors.

Of this my testament & last will I make, ordain & constitute the aforesaid Valentine my son, William Turnour & John Quyntyn my executors.

In the presence of these discrete men, William Hamond & William Webbe, called for the purpose, the year, day & place above written.

This was proved on the last day of April in the year above said [1463].

76. Thomas Buttervyle   reference: 1AR111v
note of administration: 8 April 1465

On 8 April 1465 the testament of Thomas Buttervile of Ryk' was proved & administration of the same was granted to Isabel, wife of the said Thomas.

77. John Tyler   reference: 1AR114v
will: no date [?1466]   probate: 31 July 1466

In &c. I John Tyler of the parish of Rykm[er]sworth make &c.

To the high altar of the aforesaid church 6d.

The residue &c I give & bequeath to Margaret my wife, whom I̶ ̶m̶a̶k̶e̶ and John Botervyle I make my executors &c \Given/

Proved on the last day of July 1466.

---

[59] The word used is 'fa[mu]lo', from *famulus*; slightly different in meaning from *serviens*.

78. John Tymberlake   reference: 1AR114v
will: no date   probate: [?31 July 1466][60]

John Tymberlake of the parish of Rykm[er]sworth made his nuncupative will in the presence of sir John Wynton, vicar.

He bequeathed his soul to God &c.

He bequeathed to the church of Rykm[er]sworth 8d.

The rest of his goods he gave & bequeathed to Robert Tymberlake his son, whom he constituted his executor &c.

Proved &c; & administration was granted to the executor above written.

79. William Gybbys   reference: 1AR116v-117r
will: 24 August 1466   probate: 21 October 1466

In &c. On 24 August 1466, I William Gybbys, of sound mind, make my testament in this manner.

First I bequeath my soul to Almighty God &c; my body to be buried in the churchyard of the Blessed Virgin Mary in the parish of Rykm[er]sworth.

First to the principal altar 12d; to the cathedral church of St Alban one bushel of wheat; to the two holy water clerks of the said church, to each of them one bushel of wheat.

To Edward my oldest son six sheep & one best pan, and I give and bequeath to him my cottage with all its appurtenances called 'lokers' & one spoon; to Denise my daughter to William my second son six sheep and one spoon; to Hugh my third son six sheep & one spoon; to Joan my daughter six sheep & one spoon; to Denise my daughter six sheep & one spoon; to Agnes my daughter six sheep & one spoon & one cooking-pot; to Denise the younger my daughter six sheep & one best pan; to Rose my daughter six sheep & the second best pan; to Margaret my daughter six sheep and one second best jar.

To John my servant eight sheep; to Edward my servant four sheep; to Lettice my servant twenty sheep and one cow of 'brendyld' colour with one blue coloured gown.

To Alice my spiritual daughter [*i.e.* goddaughter] three sheep; to all my goddaughters six sheep to be distributed among all of them.

To Isabel Deye[61] half a bushel of wheat; to Alice Abelle half a bushel of wheat.

---

[60] No probate date, but the preceding will (John Tyler, 77) was proved on 31 July 1466.

[61] Or perhaps Dreye

45

To the light of the Holy Cross one bushel of wheat; to each of the lights of the aforesaid church, one after the other, one bushel of wheat.

To Denise Axtell one cow & to Joan my daughter one cow.

The residue of all my goods not bequeathed, my debts being fully paid, I give and bequeath to Simon Rolffe & William Davy to dispose in the best way for me and in the better way for my soul, or else they will respond for me in the presence of God on the day of Judgement. And I will that they have for their labour, each of them, 6s 8d.

And I ordain, make and dispose them to be my executors, so that having my authority in all, that my moveable and unmoveable goods, wherever they be, will be divided and distributed between them.

Proved on 21 October the year abovesaid [1466]; & [the executors] had their acquittance.

80. John Creke   reference: 1AR118r
will: 10 March 1466/7   probate: 2 May 1467

In &c. On 10 March 1466/7, I John Creke of the parish of Rykm[er]sworth, of sound mind but sick of body, make my testament in this manner.

First I bequeath my soul to Almighty God &c; & my body to be buried in the church of the Holy Cross of Saret.

To the aforesaid church 20s; to the high altar of the same church 3s 4d; to the high altar of the church of Rykm[er]sworth for oblations and tithes forgotten 3s 4d; to the poor to be distributed amongst them 3s 4d.

To William Myles a gown; to Robert Clyffe 20d. I bequeath to my two male servants to be divided between them 3s 4d; to my two female servants to be divided between them 3s 4d; to Robert Gayte 6s 8d; to John Dyer my godson a lamb; to Peter Halley my armour.

The residue of my goods not bequeathed above I give & bequeath to Agnes my wife for maintaining her and my son John & for his governing and keeping.

And the same Agnes I make, ordain and constitute executrix of this my present testament & last will by these presents.

Given the day and year above said.

Proved on 2 May 1467; and the executrix swore in form of law that she, Agnes, would pay such debts and bequests of both John Creke and of William Creke.[62]

---

[62] Perhaps referring to debts and legacies still due from the will of William Creke (53), of which John was one of the executors.

81a. Roger Adam (mercer)   reference: 1AR117v-118r
will: 7 April 1467   probate: 16 April 1467

[*The whole will has been crossed out in the register; another version (81b) was granted probate on 20 August 1467.*]

[*margin*] Roger Adam, void because it follows with other additions.

In &c. On 7 April 1467 I Roger Adam of Rykm[er]sworth, of sound mind & whole memory, make my testament in this manner.

First I bequeath my soul to Almighty God, the Blessed Mary & all the saints; & my body to be buried in the churchyard of the parish church of Ryk' aforesaid.

I bequeath to the high altar of the church of Ryk' aforesaid for tithes forgotten & other offences 6s 8d.

To Julian my wife all & singular my goods which are, & indeed are, in my house where I dwell in the said town of Ryk', except one coverlet, one pair of 'blanketts', one pair of sheets with a mattress & a 'bolster' & white seeler, part of the same, which I give & bequeath to sir Thomas Barre, chaplain, &c. Also except the 'Merceryware' in my shop, which I give & bequeath to Walter Barre, reserving to myself all the wax there & two chests with the goods locked in them &c. Also except a brass pan of four gallons capacity & a brass pot in which I am accustomed to seal my ?*episanas*,[63] which I give and bequeath to Alice my daughter &c. To the aforesaid Julian my wife all & singular the money which is owed to me by the Reverend Father & Lord, his lordship George, Archbishop of York & chancellor of the kingdom of England,[64] with this condition, that she pay all & singular my debts & that she give to sir Thomas Barre, chaplain, £6 13s 4d to celebrate for my soul & those of my parents for one whole year in the university of Oxford or in the parish church of Ryk' aforesaid. And if the aforesaid Julian my wife refuses to do these things, then I will that the aforesaid money be taken into the hands of my executors that they shall do as above [*fol. 118r*] I have commanded & bequeathed &c.

To James Kelly & Thomas Stretman, parish clerks, 4s, to each of them 2s.

The residue of all my goods not bequeathed I will shall be at the disposal, ordering & will of William Revell & Giles Stokker of Ryk' aforesaid, whom I make, ordain & constitute my executors.

In the presence of these discrete men: William Syward & Henry Wymond, summoned & required in witness of these premisses.

---

[63] The other version has *thesauas* ('treasure').

[64] Archbishop George Neville held the manor of the More at this time; presumably he had purchased some items on credit from Roger Adam.

Given the year, day & place above said.
Proved on 16 April in the year above said [1467].

81b. Roger Adam (mercer)   reference: 1AR119v
will: 7 April 1467   **probate: 20 August 1467**

In &c. On 7 April 1467 I Roger Adam of Rykm[er]sworth, of sound mind & whole memory, make my testament in this manner.

First I bequeath my soul to Almighty God, the Blessed Mary & all the saints; & my body to be buried in the churchyard of the parish church of Rykm[er]sworth aforesaid.

I bequeath to the high altar of the church of Rykm[er]sworth aforesaid for tithes forgotten & other offences 6s 8d.

To Julian my wife all & singular my goods which are, & indeed are, in my house where I dwell in the said town of Rykm[er]sworth, except one coverlet, one pair of blankets, one pair of sheets with a mattress & a 'bolster' & seeler of white linen, part of the same, which I give & bequeath to sir Thomas Barre, chaplain, &c. Also except the 'Merceryware' in my shop, which I give & bequeath to Walter Barre, reserving to myself all the wax there & two chests with the goods sealed in them &c. Also except a brass pan of four gallons capacity & a brass pot in which I am accustomed to seal treasure, which I give and bequeath to Alice my daughter &c. Also I will that the aforesaid Julian my wife shall have all & singular the money & debts which are owed to me by the very Reverend Father in Christ & Lord, his lordship George, Archbishop of York & chancellor of the kingdom of England, and by others, with this condition, that she pay all & singular my debts & that she give to sir Thomas Barre, chaplain, her son, £6 13s 4d to celebrate for my soul & those of my parents for one whole year in the university of Oxford or in the parish church of Rykm[er]sworth aforesaid. And if the aforesaid Julian my wife refuses to do these things, & my executors do not wish to discharge them, then I will that the aforesaid money & debts be taken into the hands of my executors that they may pay my debts as above I have commanded & perceived.

To James Kelly & Thomas Stretman, parish clerks, 4s, to each 2s; to the parish church of Rykm[er]sworth aforesaid a decent silver chalice, to the value of 10 marks. I will that the lights & candles of the Holy Trinity & St Christopher be sustained & maintained in the manner & form previously observed in the aforesaid parish church for five years immediately after the day of my end. I will that my anniversary be done & celebrated annually for ten years immediately after my death. To the reparation of the way called Waleyslane 6s 8d.

I release, bequeath & assign all & singular my goods, things, animals, chattels, clothing, lands & services being in my lands & tenements in Baccheworth within the aforesaid parish of Rykm[er]sworth or in each other place wherever they are to William Revell & Giles Stokker, whom I ordain, make & constitute my executors that they may dispose & ordain for the health of my soul, my parents, benefactors, friends & all the faithful departed, whom I make my executors, in the presence of these discrete men: William Syward & Henry Wymond, required & summoned in witness of these premisses.

Given the year, day & place above said.

This present last & whole testament of the within named Roger, deceased, was proved in our presence &c on 20 August of the within written year [1467]. And administration was committed &c [to the executors, who were] sworn in form of law & admitted. Note elsewhere on 16 April in the year abovesaid another last testament, not complete, of the said Roger was exhibited to us; we have obliged them [the executors], bound by their corporal oath to God on the Holy Gospel, that they are exhibiting the true & whole testament. Therefore they have thus exhibited it to us; it is agreed by us that it is allowed; it is approved by these presents. Given under our official seal 20 August the year abovesaid.

82. Joan Brownyng, widow   reference: 1AR125v
will: 18 June 1469   probate: 8 March 1469/70

In &c. I Joan Brownyng, widow, of the parish of Rykm[er]sworth, of sound mind & in my healthy memory, make my testament in this manner.

First I bequeath my soul to Almighty God & the Blessed Mary & all the saints; and my body to be buried in the churchyard of the parish church of Rykm[er]sworth aforesaid.

I will that there be said for my soul a trental of masses within one year; to the lights of the said church 12d; to the bell of the said church 12d.

To my grandson called Yele a gown of 'blewe' colour; to the said Yele a belt of 'Russet' colour; to the said Yele a cover of 'mbre'[65] colour; to the said Yele a brass pot.

The residue of all my goods not bequeathed I give & bequeath to William Revell & Maud his wife, & of this my testament I ordain, make & constitute the said William Revell my executor & the said Maud my executrix that they dispose for my soul as seems best to them to do.

---

[65] Probably meaning 'umber' (light brown).

In witness &c, in this my present testament I have placed my seal.
Given at Rykm[er]sworth aforesaid 18 June 1469
Proved &c 8 March 1469/70; administration of the goods &c was granted to William
Revell, executor named in the testament; he was sworn; power reserved to the other
executor.

83. Roger Fosakyrley   reference: 1AR127r
will: 18 August 1469   **probate: 22 October 1470**
In &c. On 18 August 1469, I Roger Fosakyrley of Rykm[er]sworth, of sound mind
&c;
[*No committal of soul*]; & my body to be buried in the churchyard of the parish
church of Ryk' aforesaid.
To the high altar of the said church for tithes forgotten & other failings 20d; to
James Kelly & Thomas Stretman, clerks of the aforesaid parish church, 8d, to each
of them 4d.
The residue &c I give & bequeath to Joan my wife, whom I make, ordain &
constitute my executrix that she dispose for her own use & pray for the health of my
soul. Given &c
Proved on 22 October 1470.

84. Isabel Boterfeld, widow   reference: 2AR9r
will: 2 December 1470   **probate: 25 May 1472**
In &c. On the Sunday next before the feast of St Nicholas 1470 [2 December 1470],[66]
I Isabel Boterfeld, widow, of sound mind &c;
[*No committal of soul*]; & my body to be buried in the churchyard of St Peter of
Chalfhunte.
To the high altar of Ryk' for my tithes forgotten 12d; to the light of the most Blessed
Virgin Mary there in the chapel 6d.
To the high altar of Chalfhunt aforesaid one sheep; to St Peter there, next to the
high altar, 4d; to the light of the Holy Cross of Chalfhunt aforesaid 4d; to the light of
the Blessed Mary there 4d.
The residue of all my goods &c I give & bequeath to William Boterfeld & Thomas
my sons, whom I make & ordain my executors that they distribute & dispose it for
the health of my soul.
Proved on 25 May 1472.

---

[66] Feast of St Nicholas is 6 December.

85. Richard Botervyle   reference: 2AR2r
will: 7 September 1471   probate: 13 September 1471

In &c. On 7 September 1471, I Richard Botervyle of the parish of Rykm[er]sworth, of sound mind, make &c.

First I bequeath my soul to Almighty God &c; and my body to be buried in the churchyard of the parish church of Rykm[er]sworth aforesaid.

To the high altar of the same church for my tithes forgotten 12d; to James Kelly, the head clerk of the same parish, 4d & to John Stretman 2d.

The residue of my goods not bequeathed above I give & bequeath to Joan Botervyle, my wife, for her sustentation & our children's & that she may dispose the same for the health of my soul, & the same Joan, John Botervyle & Thomas Botervyle I make, ordain & constitute my executors by these present [writings].

Given &c

Proved on 13 September the year above said [1471].

86. John Wyllyes   reference: 2AR9r
will: 16 November 1471   probate: 27 May 1472

In &c. On 16 November 1471, I John Wyllyes of the parish of Rykm[er]sworth &c. [*No committal of soul or burial clause.*][67]

To the high altar of the said church 12d.

To one Austin [*or,* Augustinian] friar one sheep.

The residue &c I give & bequeath to Henry Wyllyes my father & the same Henry I make my executor by these presents.

Proved on 27 May 1472.

87. Thomas Wyllyes   reference: 2AR9r
will: 12 December 1471   probate: 27 May 1472

In &c. On 12 December 1471, I Thomas Wyllyes of the parish of Rykm[er]sworth, of sound mind &c.

[*No committal of soul or burial clause.*]

To the high altar of the said church 12d.

To my two brothers & my four sisters, to each of them, four sheep; to my two brothers aforesaid, to each of them, two bullocks; to Richard Kyng three sheep & one bullock.

---

[67] All of the wills on folio 9r have been condensed; this has been done by the clerk and is not (necessarily) the exact text of the original will.

I will that a chaplain shall have 33s 4d to celebrate for my soul in the aforesaid church for one quarter of a year.

To the church of Rykm[er]sworth 6s 8d and to the church of Saret 6s 8d and to the church of Isnamsted[68] 6s 8d.

The residue &c I give & bequeath to Henry Wyllyes my father & the same Henry I make my executor by these presents.

Proved on 27 May 1472.

88. Margaret Dyer, widow   reference: 2AR6v
will: [no date] 1471   probate: 17 January 1471/2

In &c. In the year 1471, I Margaret Dyer, of Rykm[er]sworth, widow, of sound &c. [*No committal of soul or burial clause.*]

To the high altar of the said church 12d; to the image of the Holy Cross of the parish church of Saret one sheep.

To Maud Revell a silver ring; to John Dyer my son a mazer & four silver spoons; to Margaret, wife of the said John, a gown not of the better [sort], a belt trimmed with cherry-red & a pair of beads; to John Rugmer two silver spoons.

The residue of all my goods &c I will be disposed through the hands of William Revell and the said John my son in pious and charitable uses for the health of me, my parents and my friends as they would be willing to answer for before the High Judge.

I make ordain, make and constitute them executors of this my testament & last will. Given the year & day above said.

Proved on 17 January [1471/2]; acquitted.

89. Peter Arstok   reference: 2AR7r
administration: 30 January 1471/2

On 30 January in the year above said [1471/2],[69] administration of the goods of Peter Arstok, of the household of the lord archbishop of York, dying at Rykm[er]sworth [i.e. at the More], was committed to William Singylton, clerk, &c.[70]

---

[68] One of the old names for Chenies.

[69] 1471 is written clearly (in Roman numerals) at the top of the folio

[70] For a brief discussion of the careers of Peter Arstok (89) and Thomas Shorthouse (90), see H. Falvey, 'Some members of the household of George Neville, Archbishop of York', *The Ricardian*, vol. XXII (2012), pp.55-58.

90. Thomas Shorthouse　　　　　　reference: 2AR7r
administration: 8 February 1471/2
On 8 February in the year above said [1471/2], administration of the goods of
Thomas Shorthouse, of the household of the lord archbishop of York, dying at Ryk',
[i.e. at the More], was committed to Thomas Tewson, clerk, &c.

91. Richard Tyler　　　　　　reference: 2AR9r
will: 18 March 1471/2　　　　　　**probate: 25 May 1472**
In &c. On 18 March 1471/2, I Richard Tyler of Ryk', of sound mind &c.
[*No committal of soul or burial clause.*]
To the high altar of the said church 4d; to all the lights in the said church 8d.
The residue &c I give & bequeath to Goda[71] my wife that she may have & possess it
for her livelihood & support & that she pray for my soul.
I make & constitute her my executrix &c.
Proved on 25 May 1472.

92. John Buterfeld　　　　　reference: 2AR9r
will: 8 May 1472　　　　　**probate: 25 May 1472**
In &c. On 8 May 1472, I John Buterfeld of Ryk', of sound mind &c.
[*No committal of soul or burial clause.*]
To the high altar of the said church 4d; to the light of the Holy Crucifix one lamb.
The residue &c I give & bequeath to Joan my wife for her own support & livelihood
& to pray for me.
And I make, ordain & constitute her my executrix, &c
Proved on 25 May the year above said [1472].

93. Robert Marchand, butcher　　　　　　reference: 2AR9r
administration: 27 May 1472
On 27 May 1472 administration of the goods of Robert Marchaund, 'bocher', late of
Rykm[er]sworth, dying intestate, was granted to Joan, relict of the said Robert, & to
John Marchaund of the same [place].

---

[71] This is definitely her name; according to Trice-Martin (*The Record Interpreter*, p.457)
there is no English equivalent.

94. Margaret Benfeld, widow   reference: 2AR10r
will: 8 June [year omitted]   probate: 19 June 1472

In &c. On 8 June [year omitted] I Margaret Benfeld of Rykm[er]sworth, widow, of sound &c.

[*No committal of soul or burial clause.*]

To the high altar of the said church 12d; to each of the lights being in the said church 4d.

The residue &c I will that it be at the disposition, ordering & will of John Buttervyle of Ryk' aforesaid, whom I ordain, make & constitute my executor of this my testament & last will, &c.

Proved on 19 June 1472.

95. Joan Buttervyle, widow   reference: 2AR10r
will: 25 June 1472   probate: 27 July 1472

In &c. On 25 June 1472, I Joan Buttervyle of Rykm[er]sworth, widow, of sound &c; [*No committal of soul*]; & my body to be buried &c next to the grave of Richard Buttervyle lately my husband.

To the high altar of the said church 8d; to the repair of the aforesaid church 8d; to James Kelly, parish clerk, 4d; to the repair of ropes of the bells of the said church eight pounds of hemp.[72]

The residue &c I will that it be converted & disposed for the support of my children if they shall survive [me], if not then I will that it be disposed in pious & charitable uses for the health of my soul, of my husband, my children & all the faithful departed by the hands of John Goodwynne of Woburn, my brother, & of John Bottervyle of Ryk' aforesaid, whom I make, ordain & constitute my executors.

In the presence of these honest men: James Kelly & Roger Daye, having been called & required as witnesses in the premises.

Given &c

Proved on 27 July in the year above said [1472].

---

[72] The Latin is not clear but this seems to fit: *viij ll' canab'.*

96a. John Ayleward the elder   reference: 2AR13v
will: 20 September [1472]   probate: 8 June 1473

In &c. On 20 September in the year abovesaid[*sic*], I John Ayleward the elder of Ryk' &c.
[*No committal of soul or burial clause.*]
First to the church of Ryk' aforesaid 8d & to all of the lights in the same church 12d.
The residue &c I give and bequeath to Ellen my wife for her support, and I make her my executrix.
Proved on 8 June in the year above said [1473]

96b. John Ayleward the elder[73]   reference: 2AR14r
will: 20 September 1472   probate: 8 June 1473

In &c. On 20 September 1472, I John Ayleward the elder of Rykm' make my testament &c.
First I bequeath my soul to God &c; [*no burial clause*].
To the high altar 8d and to all of the lights in the same church 12d & to the fabric of the said church 6s 8d, which John Thrustell owes me.
The residue &c I give and bequeath to Ellen my wife for her support, and I make her my executrix by these presents.
Proved &c on 8 June 1473.

97. John Bremangre   reference: 2AR12r
administration: 17 January 1472/3

On 17 January 1472/3 administration of the goods of John Bremangre of Rykm[er]sworth, deceased, was granted to John Bremangre of London, his son.

98. Henry Seward   reference: 2AR13v
administration: 8 June 1473

On 8 June in the year above said [1473][74] administration of the goods of Henry Seward of Ryk', deceased, was granted to William Seward of the same &c.

---

[73] Entered a second time, with a few more details.

[74] This is the next entry after the will of John Ayleward the elder; probate year 1473.

99. Guy Stokker   reference: 2AR14r
will: 30 June 1473   probate: 26 July 1473

In &c. On the last day of June 1473, I Guy Stokker of Rykm[er]sworth, of sound mind & whole memory, make my testament in this manner.

First I bequeath my soul to Almighty God, the Blessed Mary & all the saints; & my body to be buried in the churchyard of the parish church of Rykm[er]sworth aforesaid.

To the high altar of the aforesaid church 6s; to all of the lights in the aforesaid church 6s.

To Denise, Christian, Margaret and Joan my daughters, to each of them ten sheep; to Isabel, daughter of William Cornell, a young cow, that is 'An hekfer'; to Margaret, daughter of John Phelyp, another young cow; to Ralph my son two cows; to Thomas Becham two sheep.

To each of my [god]sons whom I raised from the font one sheep.

To Thomas & Henry, parish clerks, 16d, to each of them 8d; to Thomas Hemyngforth, vicar of Saret, ten marks to celebrate for my soul and my parents' [souls] for one year in the church of Rykm[er]sworth aforesaid.

Of this my testament & last will I make, constitute & ordain my executors Elizabeth my wife, John Fybuyn & John Mertok

in the presence of these honest men: John Wynkeburn & Richard Nevyle called and required as witnesses of the premises.

Given the year, day & place above written.

Proved & approved &c 26 July the year above said [1473]; & administration was committed to Elizabeth & John Fybuyn, executors, they being sworn; administration reserved to John Mertok; & the aforesaid executors have been acquitted.

100. Thomas Audytor [or Andytor]   reference: 2AR15r
will: 10 July 1473   probate: 30 September 1473

In the name of God, Amen. On 10 July 1473, I Thomas Audytor of Rykm[er]sworth, of sound mind &c.

[*No committal of soul or burial clause.*]

To the high altar of the said church 3s 4d & to the fabric of the church of St Alban 4d; to the chapel of St Mary *de Insula* one ewe; to the light of St Katherine in the same church one sheep & to the house called 'the Chyrchehowse' two sheep & for the repair of the king's high way proceeding between Bottis pyghtyll & Mapilcrosse 3s 4d.

I will that a wax candle be found on Sundays & feast days burning at the time of the Mass before St Peter at the high altar in the church of Chalfont St Peter.

To each of my spiritual sons 2d.

The residue of my goods &c I give & bequeath to Denise my wife, & the same Denise & John Carter I make my executors of this present testament & Andrew Randolff supervisor of the same by these presents.

Given &c.

Proved on the last day of September in the year above said [1473].

101. Thomas Gybbes   reference: 2AR15v
will: 31 August 1473   probate: 7 October 1473

In &c. On the last day of August 1473, I Thomas Gybbes of Rykm[er]sworth, of sound &c, make my testament in this manner. First &c.

[*No committal of soul or burial clause.*]

To the high altar of the said church 12d; to the reparation of the aforesaid parish church 12d; to the church of the monastery of St Alban 4d; to the repair of the king's highway called Ryggeweylane one bushel of wheat.

To John my son my great table in my house of Kendale & my best doublet; to Margery my daughter one brass pot, one candlestick, one shallow bowl, one platter, one dish & one salt of tin [*or*, pewter]; next[75] one mattress, one cover, one pair of sheets & one salt cellar for salt.

The residue &c I give & bequeath to Ellen my wife, that she may pay my debts, which Ellen & Roger Thorn of Abbots Langley I make my executors.

In the presence of the discrete men John Gybbes & Thomas Warde, called and summoned as witnesses in the testamentary premises.

Given the day & year above written.

Proved on 7 October &c [1473] &c; [Ellen] sworn; administration reserved to Roger Thorn if &c.

102. Agnes Meryweder   reference: 2AR15r
administration: 30 September 1473

Agnes Meryweder died & named her executors sir John Wyton, vicar of Ryk', & John Horseman of the same; to whom was committed administration of all the goods of the said deceased was committed &c, on the last day of September in the year above said [1473].

---

[75] Legatee not stated, perhaps Margery again.

103. William Revell   reference: 2AR18r
will: 29 November 1474   probate: 24 December 1474

In &c. On the penultimate day of November 1474, I William Revell of
Rykm[er]sworth, of sound mind & whole memory, make my testament & last will
in this manner.

First I commend my soul to Almighty God, the Blessed Mary & all the saints; & my
body to be buried in the churchyard of the parish church of Rykm[er]sworth, next
to the grave of my parents.

To the high altar of the said church for tithes forgotten & other failings 12d; to the
church of the monastery of St Alban 20d; to the two parish clerks 8d, to each 4d.

To the aforesaid church twenty quarters of malt in the following manner: that is, the
first year after my decease five quarters at the time of year that shall seem most
opportune to Maud, my wife & executrix, and thus year by year in the same way
until the twenty quarters of malt be finished and fully paid by the hands of my said
wife & executrix, her heirs, deputies & assigns ?to the use of the guardians & ruling
wardens of the said church for six years after my death. I bequeath, perceive, dispose
& will that immediately after my decease there be paid & handed over by the hands
of the said Maud my wife & executrix, three cows in my keeping & disposed by the
hands & ordering of said wardens of the said parish church of Rykm[er]sworth for
the time being under my following charge, mandate, bequest & order, that is, that
they shall have, keep or dispose by his or their deputies for five years then
immediately following the said three cows accounting for the profit and increase,
arising not only from them but also from the aforesaid malt, to the most honest &
powerful men of the aforesaid parish church to that they pay & oblige [them] to
render account for the things received & spent [for] the aforesaid church. After
those five years, that is in the sixth year of my passing, I will that then & in
perpetuity there be had, held & kept my anniversary & obit, and my wife's, my
parents' & my benefactors in the manner & form that here follows: I will &
prescribe that a great mass of our anniversary be offered for five pennies to the
honour of the five wounds of Christ & of his passion, & in three other masses in
such a way for each of them one penny & for three priests then being at our
exequies 12d, each of them 4d; And to the poor of the parish then & not otherwise
in alms 25d[sic] & whatever is left over from the said profit & increase to remain to
the work of the said church for ever.

This ordinance I perceive to be observed for ever in the accustomed and customary
form of exequies, with lights & ringing of bells used in each parish church. And if
the above said wardens of the said parish church shall be found to be negligent in

the observance above required, then I will that two honourable men from the parishioners be found & required to faithfully observe and do all the above written, elected & taken up by the discretion of the vicar of the said church & of four venerable men of the said parish.

I will, ordain and order that Maud my wife & executrix, her heirs & assigns shall serve & keep for five years immediately after my decease our anniversary honestly & by honourable custom as this custom & laudable usage should be.

And of this my testament & last will I make, ordain & constitute Maud my wife executrix & disposer of my goods.

These honest men, Richard Nevile & Thomas ?Warde having been summoned & required by me to ?be present when my seal was affixed in faith & witness. Given the day, year & place above said.

Proved &c on 24 December in the year above said [1474].

104. John Tollowe reference: 2AR20r
will: 15 July 1475 [English] **probate: 9 October 1475**

In dei nomine, Amen. The 15 day of the moneth of Jule in the yer of our lorde 1475, I John Tollowe of the paryssh of Rykm[er]sworth, hole of mynde and of gode remembrance in this wyse &c.

Fyrst I bequeth my sowle to all myghty god &c; [*no burial clause*].

Also I bequeth to the hye awter for my tythes forgoten 3s 4d.

All the residue of all my godes meveable & unmeveable I geve to my wyffe Elizabeth Tollowe to dispose for my sowle as she thynketh best.

And her I make myn executrice and John Bryce my son in lawe anoder of myn executoures.

And in witnesse &c.

Proved &c on 9 October [1475].

105: Stephen Stalon reference: 2AR20r–20v
will: 8 October 1475 **probate: 30 October 1475**

In &c. On 8 October 1475, I Stephen Stalon of Ryk', of sound mind & whole memory, make my testament in this manner.

First I commend my soul to Almighty God, the Blessed Mary & all the saints; & my body to be buried in the churchyard of the parish church of Ryk' aforesaid.

To the high altar of the said church 3s 4d; to the church of the monastery of St Alban 20d; to Thomas Hemyngforth, vicar of the parish church of Saret, one sheep or 12d; to the light of St Mary in the church of Ryk' one sheep or 12d; to Thomas Warde & Henry Wymond, parish clerks, to each of them one sheep or 12d.

To Katherine Martyn my daughter one bullock & three sheep; to my other four daughters, to each of them three sheep; to Isabel, daughter of Katherine Martyn my daughter, three sheep; to William Martyn three sheep.

To the repair of the king's highway which leads from redeheth to the bridge called Caysebrigge 13s 4d.

Of this my testament & last will above written I make Alice my wife, Roger & William my sons & Richard Hamond my executors, leaving to the said Roger, William & Richard my executors, for their labour, to each of them, 6s 8d.

The residue of all my goods not bequeathed I will to be at the disposing, ordering & will of Alice my wife, executrix as abovesaid, with the supervision & advice of John Wynton, vicar of Ryk' aforesaid, whom I make, ordain & constitute in all above written my supervisor.

In the presence of the honest men John Horsman & William Holtyng, witnesses to the premises, called, specially required & summoned; & I placed my seal in this testament with my hand. Given the year, day & place above said.

Proved &c on 30 October in the year above said [1475]

106. Giles Roose *alias* Gardyner   reference: 2AR22r
will: 26 February 1475/6   **probate: 4 May 1476**

In &c. On 26 February 1475/6, I Giles Roose, otherwise called Gardyner, of sound mind & memory but sick in body, make my testament in this manner.

First I bequeath my soul to God, the Blessed Mary & all his saints; & my body to be buried in the churchyard of the Blessed Mary of Rykm[er]sworth.

To the high altar of the same church 8d.

The residue of all my goods I give & bequeath to Joan my wife, whom I constitute my executrix to dispose for the health of my soul as seems best to her to do.

Proved &c on 4 May 1476; & acquitted.

107. John Boterfeld   reference: 2AR25v
will: 20 May 1476   **probate: 31 May 1477**

In &c. On 20 May 1476, I John Boterfeld of Rykm[er]sworth, of sound mind & good memory I make &c.

First I bequeath my soul to God &c; & my body to be buried in the churchyard of the parish church of Ryk' aforesaid.

To the high altar of the said church for tithes &c 12d; to the light of the Holy Cross 8d; to the image of the Holy Trinity 2d; to the image of St Mary the Pieta 2d; to the image of St Katherine there 4d; to the chapel of the Blessed Mary there 8d; to the two parish clerks 8d.

The residue &c I give & bequeath to Agnes my wife, [*damaged*] Tredewey & Robert Boterfeld, whom I ordain, make & constitute my executors, that they may ordain &c. Given the day & year abovesaid.

Proved on the last day of May the year above said [1477]; & the said executors were released from their office [i.e. their role was complete]

108. Philip Kyng   reference: 2AR23r
will: 18 September 1476   **probate: 15 October 1476**

In &c. On 18 September 1476, I Philip Kyng of Rykm[er]sworth, of sound mind & good memory, make my testament in this manner.

First I bequeath my soul to Almighty God, the Blessed Mary & all the saints; & my body to be buried in the churchyard of the parish church of Rykm[er]sworth aforesaid.

To the high altar of the said church for tithes neglected & forgotten & also for other failings 6s 8d; to the vicar of the said church to pray for my soul 3s 4d; to the church of the exempt monastery of St Alban 12d; to the two parish clerks, to each of them 4d; to each of the lights of the said parish church 12d.

I will that my debts having been paid & other expenses & charges owed to anyone done, whatever remains of my goods shall be for George my son & Marion my daughter, according to the discretion, view & will of Walter atte Dene & Margaret his wife, my daughter, whom I make, constitute & ordain executors of this my present testament & last will.

In the presence of the honest men, William Seward & Thomas Warde, called & summoned & required witnesses to the premises.

Given the year, day & place above said.

Proved &c on 15 October in the year above said [1476]; & they [the executors] had their acquittance.

109. Joan Bowryng, widow reference: 2AR24r
will: 12 November 1476 probate: 18 December 1476

In &c. On 12 November 1476, I Joan Bowryng of Rykm[er]sworth, widow, of sound mind & memory, make my testament in this manner.

First I bequeath my soul to Almighty God, the Blessed Mary & all the saints; & my body to be buried in the churchyard of the parish church of Rykm[er]sworth aforesaid.

To the church of the monastery of St Alban 4d; to the house called 'le chirchehous' of the said parish of Rykm[er]sworth one towel; another towel to the aforesaid parish church for wiping the hands of godfathers & godmothers in the holy place after the baptism of infants.

The residue of my goods not bequeathed I will that, my debts being paid, Henry Smyth dispose it, whom I ordain, make & constitute my executor.

In the presence of these honest men: John Mertok & Thomas Warde, they being called & summoned as witnesses to these premises.

Given the day and year above said.

This testament was proved & favoured in the presence of us &c on 18 December the year above said [1476]; & administration of the goods concerned in the above testament was granted to Henry Smyth, named in the testament, sworn in form of law & he was acquitted.

110. Roger Belche reference: 2AR24r
will: 1 December 1476 probate: 17 December 1476

In &c. On 1 December 1476, I Roger Belche, of sound mind & memory make my testament in this manner.

First I bequeath my soul to Almighty God, the Blessed Mary & all his saints; & my body to be buried within the churchyard of the church of the Blessed Mary of Rykm[er]sworth.

To the high altar of the same church 12d; to the lights of the same church, that is, to St Katherine 8d, to the Holy Cross 8d, to St Edmund 8d, to the Holy Trinity 8d, to St Clement 8d; to the reparation of the bells of the same church 12d.

To Roger my son 16s 8d; to my sons Richard three sheep, Edward six sheep, Thomas six sheep and to my daughters Joan one sheep, Katherine two sheep & Marion two sheep; to each of my godchildren one sheep.

The residue of all my goods not bequeathed, my debts & necessary expenses being paid, I give & bequeath to Joan my wife, William Belche & John Belche my sons, that they, having God before their eyes, order & dispose it for the health of my soul as seems best to them to do.

And them, Joan my wife, William and John my sons, I make, ordain & constitute executors of this my testament.

Richard Wynkefeld, John Buturfeld & others being called specially & summoned as witnesses to this.

The above testament was proved & favoured in the presence of us &c on 17 December the year within-written [1476]; & administration of the goods relating to this testament was granted to Joan and William, executors named in the testament & sworn in form of law. The right of administration of the same testament was reserved to John Belche, the other executor named therein if he should wish to take upon himself the administration; & it happened that the said John did take it up; & the aforesaid executors have been acquitted.

111. Henry Willeys   reference: 2AR24r
will: 16 December 1476   probate: 14 January 1476/7

In &c. On 16 December 1476, I Henry Willeys of Rykmansworth, of sound mind & in my whole memory, make my testament in this manner.

First I bequeath my soul to Almighty God, the Blessed Mary & all the saints; & my body to be buried in the churchyard of the parish church of Rykm[er]sworth aforesaid.

To the high altar 12d; to the vicar of Saret 12d; to the parish church 3s 4d; to the church of Saret 3s 4d; to each of my spiritual sons & daughters a lamb.

I will that my wife have half of all my moveable goods if she does not remain unmarried; if she remains unmarried she to have all my goods.

To Roger More 4d; to Thomas Stretman 4d.

Of this my testament I ordain, make & constitute Joan my wife my principal executrix, Roger Willeys her son[76] my executor, & Thomas Wrekyll of Watford supervisor of this my testament, that they dispose for my soul as seems best to them to do.

This present testament was proved & favoured in our presence &c on 14 January in the within-written year [1476/7]; & administration of all the goods &c was committed to the executors named herein, who were sworn in form of law & they were released from [producing] a final account &c, saving all rights whatsoever.

---

[76] Definitely her son: *filium eius*

112. William Gardyner reference: 2AR25r
will: 3 March 1476/7 probate: 22 March 1476/7

In &c. On 3 March 1476/7, I William Gardyner of Rykm[er]sworth, of sound mind &c.

First I bequeath my soul to God &c; [*no burial clause*].

To the high altar of the said church for tithes forgotten & other failings 12d; to the chapel of the Blessed Mary *de Insula* 4d; to the church of the monastery of St Alban 4d; to the vicar of the church of Saret 4d; to Thomas Warde, parish clerk, 4d; to Thomas Stretmen, poor man, 2d.

To Margery my daughter one sheep, one sheet & three pieces of pewter called 'pewter vessell'.

The residue &c I will be at the disposition & will of Joan my wife, Roger & John my sons, whom I make & constitute my executors &c.

Proved &c on 22 March in the year abovesaid [1476/7]; & they had their acquittance.

113. William Bullok, gentleman[77] reference: 2AR26r
will: 24 April 1477 probate: 17 June 1477

In &c. On 24 April 1477, I William Bullok of Rykm[er]sworth in the county of Hertford, gentleman, of sound mind and whole memory, make my testament and my last will in this manner.

First, I bequeath and commend my soul to Almighty God my Creator and Saviour, the Blessed Mary & all the saints; & my body to be buried in the parish church of Rykm[er]sworth aforesaid.

To my mother church the exempted monastery of St Alban 20d; to the high altar of the parish church of Rykm[er]sworth aforesaid 12d; to my same parish church of Rykm[er]sworth one cow; to St Mary *de Insula* one wax candle weighing one pound.

To Agnes Bullok my granddaughter my good [singular] being with John Blunt; to Robert Bullok my grandson my chain [*cathenam*] of gold & my 'jaket' of green damask; to Agnes Revell my best cow; to Thomas Blunt, Elizabeth Blunt, Eleanor Blunt, Alice Blunt and Joan Blunt, to each of them, one bullock.

To the two parish clerks, to each of them, 4d.

---

[77] His wife's will is no. 193.

I will that my marriage gown be sold and out of the money received from it a priest shall be hired to celebrate for my soul in the parish church of Rykm[er]sworth aforesaid.

I will, ordain and command that there shall be kept, maintained and commemorated two anniversaries for the soul of Margery Letterford my godmother [*commatris*], according to the counsel, meaning and discretion of Alice my mother, John Bullok the younger my brother and Maud my wife, out of the cost [*i.e.* value] of the goods and belongings of the aforesaid Margery, deceased, who had made me her co-executor with Alice my mother and John junior my brother abovesaid for as long as the goods aforesaid shall last and endure.

The residue of all my goods whatsoever, moveable and unmoveable not bequeathed, I give and bequeath to the disposition and will of Maud my wife, whom I ordain, make and constitute my executrix that she may dispose and ordain as seems best to her to please God and profit my soul completely.

The discrete men John Bullok the younger my brother, Thomas Warde, John Gardiner and John Brewode being witnesses to the premises, summoned, called and required, together with the appending of my seal in witness of the premises. Given the year, day and place above said.

This present testament was proved & approved & favoured &c on 17 June in the year abovesaid [1477]; & the aforesaid executrix was released from office & had her acquittance.

114. Thomas Baldewyn　　　　reference: 2AR26v
will: 12 September 1477　　　probate: 1 October 1477
In &c. On 12 September 1477, I Thomas Baldewyn of Rykm[er]sworth, of sound mind &c.
[*No committal of soul or burial clause.*]
To the high altar of the said church 12d; to the church of the monastery of St Alban 4d; to the fabric of the church of Ryk' aforesaid one sheep; to the chapel of St Mary *de Insula* one sheep; to the parish church of Saret one sheep; to the parish church of Isnamstede one sheep; to Thomas [Warde], parish clerk, 4d; to John Gardyner 2d.
The residue &c I give & bequeath to Joan my wife, whom I make my executrix.
In the presence of the honest men John Baldewyn & Richard Wyngfeld, witnesses in the premises.
Proved &c on 1 October in the year abovesaid [1477]; & she had her acquittance.

115. John Wellys   reference: 2AR27r–27v
will: 7 October 1477   probate: 27 March 1478

In the name of God, Amen. On 7 October 1477, I John Wellys of the parish of Rykmersworth, of sound mind yet sick in body, make my testament in this manner. First I bequeath my soul to Almighty God my creator, the most Blessed Mary his mother & all the saints of the heavenly court; & my body to be buried in the churchyard of St Peter in the town of St Albans next to the Cornewell 'chapell'[78] beside Richard Newbury, brother of Alice my wife, if it should happen that I die within the town of St Albans.

My house called Bowrynges with its appurtenances & my meadow called Hermytage there, with all its appurtenances situated & lying in Rykmersworth aforesaid in which I am seised at the time of the making of this my last will, I give & bequeath to Alice my wife, holding to her & hers according to the custom of the manor there for ever.

The reversion of all the lands & tenements called Shepartes & Groves with [*fol. 27v*] their appurtenances, all of which ought to descend to me after the death of Margaret Honerce, late the wife of William Wellys my father now deceased, I give & bequeath to the said Alice my wife, holding to her & hers according to the custom of the manor there for the term of the life of the said Alice, holding to her under the following conditions, that is, each year for the space of three years immediately following after the said lands & tenements come into the use or hands of the said Alice, that the said Alice shall distribute to four worthy priests, or to one suitable priest, whichever shall seem best to her to do, to celebrate for my soul, & for the souls of my father & my mother & for the souls of all our friends & benefactors in Rykmersworth aforesaid.

I will that after the decease of Alice my wife that that tenement called Shepartes with its appurtenances shall remain to Agnes my sister, wife of Thomas Saybrok of Harpeden, holding to her & hers according to the custom of the manor there forever.

I will that after the decease of Alice my wife that that tenement called Groves with its appurtenances shall remain to Alice Saybroke, daughter of Agnes Saybroke, my sister, holding to her & hers according to the custom of the manor there for ever.

I bequeath to the said Alice my wife 100 shillings to be paid to me, my heirs & executors by John Martok of Rykmersworth & Margaret his wife on the feast of the

---

[78] The Cornwall chapel, first mentioned in 1440, stood in St Peter's churchyard on an unknown site. (*VCH Herts*, vol. II, p.420)

nativity of St John the Baptist 1478. I will that the other 100 shillings owed to me, my heirs and assigns paid on the said feast of the nativity of St John the Baptist by the aforesaid John Martok & Margaret his wife to be disposed by the said Alice my wife in the following manner. That is: in the first year out of the said £10 that four nobles[79] be delivered to four priests, or to one suitable priest, which ever seems best to her to do, to celebrate for my soul, the souls of my father & mother & in the second year four nobles, in the third year four nobles, and in the fourth year 20s in from as above paid for the health of our souls.

To Thomas Saybroke & the said Agnes Saybroke my sister the half part of my vessels called 'Harnesshid vessell'; to Agnes my servant my long blue linen robe. The residue of all my goods not bequeathed, I give & bequeath to the said Alice my wife, whom I make my executrix & John Newbury my executor by these presents, the month and day above written.

Made at St Albans in the presence of Master John Wellis, chaplain 'de le Charnell', then its confessor & mine.

This present testament was proved & approved & favoured &c on 27 March 1478; & administration of the goods &c was committed the within-named executors, who were sworn in form of law.

116. William Lovet   reference: 2AR28v
will: 24 March 1477/8   probate: 2 October 1478

In &c. On 24 March 1477/8, I William Lovet of Rykm[er]sworth, of sound mind & whole memory, make my testament &c

[*No committal of soul or burial clause.*]

To the high altar there for tithes forgotten & other offences two sheep; to the church of the monastery of St Alban 4d.

The residue of all & singular my goods &c I give & bequeath to Denise my wife, whom I constitute, ordain & make my executrix.

In the presence of the discrete men Thomas Warde & John Gardyner, called & summoned in witness of the premisses.

Given &c.

Proved 2 October [1478] &c; & she had her acquittance.

---

[79] One noble = 6s 8d; so four nobles = 26s 8d.

117. Richard Carter   reference: 2AR33r
will: 6 April 1479   **probate: 11 September 1479**
In &c. On 6 April 1479, I Richard Carter of Rykm[er]sworth, of sound mind &c, make my testament &c
[*No committal of soul*]; & my body to be buried in the churchyard of the parish church of Ryk' aforesaid.
To the high altar of my said parish church 12d; to the church of the monastery of St Alban 8d & to the light of the Holy Cross 12d;[80] to the light of St Katherine 6d & to each altar within the said church 4d; to the light of the Blessed Mary of Pity 4d; to my parish church one ewe; to the chapel of St Mary *de Insula* 4d.
To the repair of the king's highway leading from the tenement of me, the said Richard, to the tenement of Guy Gape 3s 4d.
I bequeath to Joan my daughter 20 sheep & moveable goods to the value of 6s 8d.
Of this &c I make & ordain Andrew Randolffe of Ryk' aforesaid & Thomas Buttervyle of Chalfont St Peter my executors.
In the presence of these honest men: Thomas Warde & John Gardyner, witnesses to the premisses &c.
Proved &c 11 September the year abovesaid [1479]; & they were released &c.

118. John Rolff the elder   reference: 2AR38v
will: 8 April 1479   **probate: 12 October 1480**
In &c. On 8 April 1479, I John Rolff the elder of Rykm[er]sworth, of sound mind &c.
[*No committal of soul or burial clause.*]
To the high altar of the said church 8d; to the reparation of the said church 12d; to the church of the exempt monastery of St Alban 6d; to Thomas Warde, parish clerk, 4d; to John Gardyner the other parish clerk, 2d.
& to John Bacon 2d, Anastasia Taillour 2d & John de Valo[ur] 2d.
The residue of my goods not bequeathed I will be at the disposition, will & ordering of John Rolff my son the elder, whom I ordain, constitute & make my executor.
In the presence of the honest men Henry Coton & Thomas Warde, called & summoned in witness of the premises.
Given the year, day & place above said.
Proved on 12 October 1480; & he had his acquittance.

---

[80] Probably in the church of St Mary rather than of St Alban.

119. Robert Pursell   reference: 2AR33v
will: 15 August 1479   probate: 7 October 1479
In &c. On 15 August 1479, I Robert Pursell of Rykm[er]sworth, of sound mind &c
[*No committal of soul*]; & my body to be buried in the churchyard of the parish
church of Ryk'.
To the high altar of the said church 12d; to the church of the exempt monastery of
St Alban 4d.
The residue &c I will to be at the disposal & ordering of Joan my wife & John
Wynkburn, her father, whom I ordain, make & constitute my executors.
In the presence of these honest men: Thomas Warde & John Grey, witnesses &c.
Proved on 7 October the year above written [1479]; & they had their acquittance.

120. John Mertok   reference: 2AR33r
will: 23 August 1479   probate: 11 September 1479
In &c. On 23 August 1479, I John Mertok of Rykm[er]sworth, being vigorous in
body, of sound mind & healthy memory, make my testament & my last will in this
manner.
First I commend my soul to Almighty God, the Blessed Mary, St Alban the
protomartyr and all the saints; & my body to be buried in the parish church of
Rykm[er]sworth aforesaid near the grave of my son John.
To the church of the monastery of St Alban 6s 8d; to the high altar of the church of
Rykm[er]sworth aforesaid for my tithes forgotten & other failings 6s 8d; to the high
altar of the parish church of Ware, in the diocese of London, 6s 8d.
I will & command that I shall have a priest to celebrate for my soul and the souls of
my parents and friends in the parish church of Rykm[er]sworth aforesaid for one
year immediately [after my death].
To Agnes my daughter for her marriage 20 marks of good money of England.
I will, order, command and require that William Staneley of Burley in the County of
Rotoland[81] esquire, John Wynkburn of Rykm[er]sworth aforesaid, yeoman of the
king's chamber, & Robert Forthe of Aylesbury in the county of Bucks, 'yoman', my
feoffees of and in my manor with all its appurtenances called Warehache, situated
within the parish of Ware in the county of Hertford,[82] shall make release and entry

---

[81] Burleigh, in the county of Rutland
[82] According to the *VCH* there was a manor in Ware called 'Waters alias Martocks, now
Mardocks'. John Mertok is not mentioned in that account but the name is highly suggestive.
(*VCH Herts*, vol. 3, p.390)

[&c], or their attorneys, to my wife Margaret or her feoffees;[83] and my wife Margaret, her heirs and assigns to have and hold it freely and quietly for ever. However, I will and command that she shall immediately [allow] George, Hugh and Alice, my and her sons and daughter, to share my goods, true and material, according to the discretion, view and advice of John Wynton, perpetual vicar of the parish church of Rykm[er]sworth aforesaid, and the aforesaid John Wynkburn, yeoman of the king's chamber, whom I make, ordain and constitute with my aforesaid wife Margaret, my executors, that they and she shall do, regulate and dispose of all and singular my goods as they would wish to answer for in the presence of Christ the Lord and for the good of my soul.

These honest men being present: Thomas Russell and William Slynger, they being called and required as witnesses to these present [writings].

In which present testament I have placed my seal; given the year, day and place above written.

Proved on 11 September the year above written [1479]; & they were released &c, saving all rights &c.

121. Roger Gardyner   reference: 2AR33v
will: 17 September 1479   **probate: 7 October 1479**

In &c. On 17 September 1479, I Roger Gardyner of Rykm[er]sworth, of sound mind &c.

My soul[*sic*]; & my body to be buried in the churchyard of the parish church of Ryk' aforesaid.

To the high altar of the said church 8d; to the exempt monastery of St Alban 4d.

To Katherine my daughter when she shall come to her years of maturity for her marriage 20s.

The residue of my goods &c I will that it be in the will & disposition of Alice my wife, Joan my mother & John my brother, whom I ordain executors.

In the presence of the honest men, Thomas Warde & Richard Warde. Given &c.

Proved &c on 7 October the year above written [1479]; & they had their acquittance.

---

[83] Margaret Martock is mentioned in the *VCH* account.

122. Alice Gardyner, late wife of Roger   reference: 2AR34v
will: 5 October 1479   probate: 23 October 1479

In &c. On 5 October 1479, I Alice Gardyner, late the wife of Roger Gardyner[84] of the parish of Rykm[er]sworth, in the county of Hertford, also called St Mary 'in le Yland', of sound mind & whole memory, make my my testament in this manner.

First I bequeath my soul to Almighty God, the Blessed Mary the begetter of God & all the saints of God; & my body to be buried in the churchyard of the aforesaid church.

I bequeath my best animal that I have for my mortuary and principal legacy; to the high altar of the aforesaid church 20d; to the vicar of the same church 20d to be disposed for the health of my soul; to the reparation of the house of the oft-mentioned church[85] four measures of barley.

To John Gardyner, brother of my husband, four measures of barley & one pair of sheets; to Joan Gardyner, mother of my husband, two pairs of sheets; to Joan Gardyner, wife of my husband's brother, one gown & one pair of sheets.

The residue of my goods &c I give & bequeath to Thomas Russell, my father, of Chalfont St Giles, whom I make my executor, that he dispose of as seems best &c for the health of my soul & of my children.

Given &c

These being witnesses: John Brusch, John Rolfe, Thomas Russell & Joan Turnour & Isabel Russell with other trustworthy persons.

Proved &c on 23 October the year above written [1479]; & he had his acquittance.

123. Joan Gardyner[86]   reference: 2AR35r
will: 13 October 1479   probate: 11 November 1479

In &c. On 13 October 1479, I Joan Gardyner of Rykm[er]sworth, of sound mind &c. First I bequeath my soul to God &c; [*no burial clause*].

To the high altar of the said church 8d; to the church of the exempt monastery of St Alban 4d.

To John Blaksalt 4d; to John, son of Roger my son, deceased, 20d; to Joan Turnour my green gown & to Agnes Davy my green mantle.

The residue &c I give & bequeath to John my son, whom I make &c my executor that he may dispose it &c.

---

[84] So her husband Roger (no. 121) had died before 5 October.
[85] Meaning the church-house
[86] Mother of Roger (no. 121)

These being present as witnesses to the premises: Richard Warde & John Blaksalt &c Given &c.

Proved &c on 11 November [1479] &c; & he had his acquittance.

124. John Gardyner[87]   reference: 2AR35r
will: 16 November 1479   probate: 27 November 1479

In &c. On 16 November 1479, I John Gardyner of Rykm[er]sworth make my testament in this manner.

First I bequeath my soul to God &c; & my body to be buried in the churchyard of the parish church of Ryk' aforesaid.

To the high altar 12d; to the church of St Alban 4d; to the vicar of Saret 8d & to sir John[88] 8d; & to Agnes Shepey one sheet; to the reparation of the church 12d & to each light in the same church 4d.

To Thomas Warde one sheet & to Katherine Warde 4d; to Richard Warde a green coloured gown that was my brother's; to Joan Coton[89] one good sheet & to Thomas Coton 4d.

To the chapel of the Blessed Mary 4d; & to each of my godsons & daughters 4d.

To the daughter of William Belche one sheep & to the daughter of John Belche one sheep; to John Edward 2d & to John Tyler 2d.

The residue &c I give & bequeath to Joan my wife, & the same Joan my wife & John Wynton, vicar of Rykm[er]sworth I make my executors of this my present testament &c.

Proved &c on 27 November in the year abovesaid [1479]; & they were released &c.

125. John Belche   reference: 2AR36r
will: 20 December 1479   probate: 31 December 1479

In &c. On 20 December 1479, I John Belche of Rykm[er]sworth &c.

First I bequeath my soul to Almighty God, the Blessed Mary &c; [*no burial clause*].

To the high altar of the said church 8d; to the church of the exempt monastery of St Alban 2d; to the fabric of the said church of R' aforesaid 12d; to Thomas Warde, parish clerk, 4d.

---

[87] Brother of Roger (no. 121) and son of Joan (no. 123); so four adult members of one family died within two months of each other.

[88] John Wynton, vicar of Rickmansworth

[89] Or perhaps Soton.

The residue of all my goods I give & bequeath to Agnes my wife that she may be sustained & live, & pray for my soul, which Agnes & William Belche, my brother, I make & constitute my executors.

These honest men being present as witnesses: John Buttervyle[90] & William Baron &c.

Proved &c on the last day of December in the year abovesaid [1479]; & they had their acquittance.

126. John Buttervyle   reference: 2AR36r
will: 26 December 1479   probate: 31 December 1479

In &c. On 26 December 1479, I John Buttervyle of Rykm[er]sworth, of sound mind & in my healthy memory, make my testament in this manner.

First I commend my soul to Almighty God, the Blessed Mary &c; & my body to be buried in the churchyard of the parish church of R' aforesaid.

To the high altar of the said church 6d; to the church of the monastery of St Alban 4d; to the light of the Crucifix my best sheep; to the reparation of the wax candles called 'torches' 8d.

The residue of all of my goods, after the payment of my debts, I will that they be disposed for the support of Christine my wife & of our children, which Christine & William Buttervyle my father I make & ordain my executors.

In the presence of the honest men Richard Wynkfeld & John Baldwyn, summoned & required as witnesses of the premises.

Given &c.

Proved &c on the last day of December in the year abovesaid [1479]; & they had their acquittance.

127. Robert Buttervyle   reference: 2AR37r
will: 13 January 1479/80   probate: 5 February 1479/80

In &c. On 13 January 1479/80, I Robert Buttervyle of Rykm[er]sworth, of sound mind & hole memory, make my testament &c.

[*No committal of soul or burial clause.*]

To the high altar of the said church 12d; to the church of the monastery of St Alban 4d; to the light of the Holy Cross & of St Katherine 2d; to St Mary *de Insula* 4d; to Thomas Warde, parish clerk, 4d.

---

[90] His will (no. 126) was made 6 days later, on 26 December, and was granted probate on 31 December, the same day as Belche's was.

The residue &c I will be in the disposition of John Blakewell, whom I make, ordain & constitute my executor &c.

Proved &c on 5 February the year &c [1479/80]; & he had his acquittance, saving all rights whatsoever.

128. Robert Bytterley   reference: 2AR36v
administration: 29 January 1479/80

Administration of the goods of Robert Bytterley, late of the parish of Rykm[er]sworth, because he died intestate, was granted to Isabel, relict of the said Robert, Master Richard Lessy, William Robyns esquire, James Cawode gentleman & sir Thomas Hemmyngforth, vicar of Saret, on 29 January 1479/80.[91]

129. John Gryse   reference: 2 AR 40r
administration: 20 December 1481

On 20 December in the year above said [1481] administration of the goods of John Gryse, late of Ryk' deceased, was committed to Nicholas Dunsworth, saving all rights whatsoever; [*added later*] & on 28 June 1484 the aforesaid Nicholas & Isabel, relict of the said John, had their acquittance.

130. John Rydale   reference: 2AR41v
will: 24 November 1482   probate: 3 December 1482

[*This will has been crossed out in the register; the reason is given in the margin; here the reason has been reproduced after the main text.*]

In the name of God, Amen. On 24 November 1482, I John Rydale of Rykm[er]sworth, of sound mind, make my testament in this manner.

First I bequeath my soul to Almighty God, the Blessed Mary & all the saints; & my body to be buried in the porch of the parish church of the Glorious Virgin Mary of Rykm' aforesaid.

To the high altar of the aforesaid church for tithes forgotten 3s; to the mother church of St Alban martyr 6d & to the two parish clerks 8d; to sir Thomas Coton 10s for celebrating a trental for my soul & the souls of my parents & friends.

I will that the residue of all my goods remain to Katherine my wife[92] for term of her life if she remain unmarried & after her death all the said goods I give & bequeath to Margaret my daughter; & if it should happen that Katherine should marry, then I

---

[91] For Bytterley and the high status of his administrators, see the Introduction, pp. xliv–xlv.
[92] Her will is no. 163.

will that the said goods be divided by my executors between the said Katherine my wife & Margaret my daughter.

Furthermore, I will that Margaret my daughter have my tenement in Rykm[er]sworth after the decease of Katherine my wife & if the said Margaret should die without heirs, then the said tenement to be sold after her death & the money arising be distributed for our souls in pious & charitable uses.

I ordain & constitute the aforesaid Katherine, sir Thomas Hemyngforth, vicar of Rykm[er]sworth, & John Wynkborn my executors of this my present testament, that they may dispose for my soul as seems best to them to please God & profit the health of my soul.

Given the day & year above said.

Probate &c on 3 December the year above written [1482]; & administration was committed &c to the executors named; & they had their acquittance, saving all rights whatsoever; on the oath of the said Katherine [administration] will be committed to her on these premisses by the vicar or to others in her name.

[margin] Thus was this testament cancelled. It was refuted in presence of master Thomas Newlond, archdeacon; because great exceptions were placed by trustworthy witnesses, call all those with an interest in this matter to come to Rykmersworth.[93]

131. Elizabeth Stokker   reference: 2AR41v
administration: 2 January 1483

On 2 January 1482 [1482/3] administration of the goods of Elizabeth Stokker, late of Rykm[er]sworth, who died intestate, was committed to John Felypp & John Stokker of the same [place].

132. John Wynkburn   reference: 2AR42r
will: 5 August 1483   probate: 22 August 1483

In the name of God, Amen. On 5 August 1483, I John Wynkburn, of sound mind, make my testament in this manner following.

First I bequeath my soul to Almighty God, the Blessed Mary & all the saints; & my body to be buried in the parish church of the Blessed Mary of Rykm[er]sworth.

To the vicar there in the name of my mortuary one grey-coloured colt; to the high altar of the said church for my tithes & oblations forgotten & negligently done 20s;

---

[93] Indicating that the archdeacon would hold an enquiry into the circumstances surrounding the making of this will and its contents.

to the fabric of the same church, wherever there shall be most need & opportunity 40s.

To Joan Pursell my daughter 10 marks; to Joan Bugberd 5 marks; to Thomas Seward 40s; to Robert Pygot 6s 8d; to Agnes Wymond 10 marks; to John Webbe 6s 8d; to William Holtyng 20s; to William Colyer 6s 8d.

To the repair of the king's highway leading from the town of Rykm[er]sworth aforesaid to London 40s.

To Joan my wife & Nicholas my son £50 equally divided between them; to George my son £50; to John Melsham the elder 40s; to Ralph Bukberd 5 marks; to William Bukberd 40s; to each of the three sons of Agnes Wymond 6s 8d.

I will that immediately after my decease a certain suitable priest be hired to celebrate in the aforesaid church for three whole years for the health of my soul & of my parents' [*souls*] and indeed of Katherine & Margaret my wives, & of all my deceased benefactors.

Of this testament I make, ordain & constitute executors George Danyell, esquire, Joan my wife, George my son & Joan Pursell my daughter that they dispose the residue of my goods not bequeathed in this [testament], after my obsequies & funerals completed, for the health of my soul and of those aforesaid, as may seem best to them to do.

In witness whereof, I have placed my seal.

These being witnesses: sir Thomas Hemyngforth, vicar of Rykm[er]sworth, Henry Wheler, Thomas Russell & others.

Given the day & year above said.

This present testament was proved & approved and favoured before us, John Rothebury, archdeacon, &c, on 22 August in the year abovesaid [1483]; and [administration] was committed &c to the executors named within, sworn in form of law; & they had their acquittance; saving all rights whatsoever.

133. Richard Hamond   reference: ?AR45r
will: 27 July 1484   probate: 7 August 1484

In &c. On 27 July 1484, I Richard Hamond of Rykm[er]sworth, of sound mind but being infirm in my body, make my testament &c.

First I bequeath my soul to God &c; & my body to be buried &c.

To the high altar for tithes forgotten 6d; to sir John de Herscolo 20d for celebrating five masses for the wounds of Christ; to each of the lights of the church 4d; to the mother church 6d; to the reparation of the new chapel 12d; to each parish clerk 4d.

To Lettice Preest 3s 4d; to John Dowghty two sheep & two measures of wheat; to my four spiritual sons, to each of them 4d; to Ann Hamond & Joan Hamond 8d.

I will that Katherine my wife shall have my cottage in Rykm[er]sworth for term of her life, having surrendered it into the hands of Thomas Creke esquire, bailiff, absent & outside the town, in the presence of suitable witnesses; & after the decease of the said Katherine I will that the said cottage be sold by my executors & the supervisor of my testament & the money arising be disposed part to Thomas Hamond my son & part to Henry my son according to the discretion of my executors & my supervisor, but I will that the most part of the total value of the cottage be used & disposed to a suitable priest for celebrating for my soul & the souls of all my benefactors while its lasts.

The residue &c I give & bequeath to Katherine my wife & Henry my son, whom I ordain & constitute my executors of this my testament & last will, [&] I ordain & make master Thomas Hemyngforth, vicar, supervisor, & that the executors will act according to the advice of my same supervisor.

Given at Rykm[er]sworth the year & day above said.

Proved &c on 7 August in the year abovesaid [1484]; & they were released.

134. Nicholas Leventhorp, esquire   reference: 2AR46r
will: 4 October 1484 [English]   probate: 20 December 1484

In the name of god Amen, the yere of oure lord god 1484 and the day of the moneth of Octobr' 24, I Nicholas leventhorpp esquyer seke in body & hole in mynde, I make my testament and laste Wylle in this maner.

Fyrst I bequeth my soule to Almyghty god, to oure lady Seint Mary and to All the Seyntes in heven; my body to be beryed in the chapel of our blissyd lady w[i]t[h]in the chirchyerd of Rikm[er]sworth.

Also I bequeth to the same chapel 13s 4d & to the parysh chirch 26s 8d. Also I bequeth to the vicary of Rikm[er]sworth my horse callyd An hoby to pray for my Soule.

Also I bequeth to the chirch of Watford 40s; to the chirch of Bushey 20s.

Also I gyf to my broder John leventhorppe 40s; also to Master doctour Cristofyr Tankyrvyle 40s.

Also alle the residue of all my godis I bequeth to my lady dame Kateryn my Wyffe to dispose as it semeth her best for my soule. Also I wyll and charge that she pay all maner of dettes to me belongyng as she wyll answer afore the face of god on the dredfull day of dome to be performyd.

The which lady my Wyffe I ordeyn my executrice.

Gevyn the yer and day afore saide byfor theyse record Master doctour Tankyrvile, John leventhorpp, Thomas leventhorpp, Thomas Thewer, Henry [*damaged*]venstey and odyr.

In witnesse wherof I have put to my signet.

Proved &c on 20 December [1484]

135. John Rolffe the elder   reference: 2AR46v
will: 23 March 1485[94]   probate: 24 May 1485

In &c. On 23 March 1485, I John Rolffe the elder of Ryk', of sound mind, make my testament &c.

First I bequeath my soul to Almighty God &c; & my body to be buried in the new aisle [*in nova Insula*] of the church of Ryk' aforesaid.

To the high altar of the same church for tithes forgotten 12d & to the mother church of St Alban 4d; to the four lights in the aforesaid [church] of Rykm[er]sworth, to each of them ?2d.[95]

The residue &c I give & bequeath to Ellen my wife & John Rolffe my son to dispose &c.

The same Ellen & John, in the presence of witnesses, I make my executors &c. Given &c.

Proved &c on 24 May in the year abovesaid [1485]; & they were released.

136. Joan Wynkeburn[96]   reference: 2AR47r
will: 20 June 1485   probate: 12 August 1485

In &c. On 20 June 1485, I Joan Wynkeburn, of whole mind, make my testament &c; [*No committal of soul*]; & my body to be buried in the parish church of the Blessed Mary of Rikmansworth next to the grave of John Wynkeborn, lately my husband.

To the high altar for tithes forgotten 3s 4d; to the fabric of the new chapel 3s 4d.

I will that John Skydmore my son have free disposal of all my goods & that he the said John share & dispose the said goods to himself, Simon & William according to the discretion of the said John Skidmore together with the said Simon & William when they shall come to their age of maturity; & if it should happen that the said Simon die before he comes to the said age, then I will that the part of the said Simon

---

[94] The date is in the 'new style' (i.e. not 23 March 1485/6) as probate was definitely granted in May 1485.

[95] Ink faded here.

[96] Widow of John, no. 132.

to remain to John & William. & if it happen that the said William die before he comes to the said age, then I will that the part of the said William shall remain to John Skidmore & Simon.

I will that William my son have all my lands & tenements in the town of Towceter in the county of Northampton after my decease, according to the will of my mother, & to the heirs of his body legitimately begotten. & if the said William should die without heirs, then when he dies I will that Simon shall have all the aforesaid lands & tenements in Towceter aforesaid for term of his life, & after the decease of the said Simon all the said lands & tenements to remain to John Skidmore my son & the heirs of his body lawfully begotten. I will that John Skidmore my son have control of all the lands & tenements in Towceter & elsewhere during the minority of William & that he repair [or, maintain] the said tenements with the rents received, according to the discretion of the said John Skidmore.

The residue of all my goods not bequeathed I give & bequeath to John my son, whom I constitute my executor that he may dispose for the health of my soul as seems best to him to do. In which will &c.

These being witnesses: Richard Nevyll, William Bukberd, John Blakwell, William Hamond, John Stevyns, Hugh Damport, John Gibbes de Wodewyk, John Tredeway & many others.

Proved & favoured &c on 12 August in the year abovesaid [1485]; & he had his acquittance.

137. Thomas Russell reference: 2AR49r
will: 10 December 1485 **probate: 20 January 1485/6**

In &c. On 10 December 1485, I Thomas Russell, of sound mind &c.

First I bequeath my soul to God &c; & my body to be buried in the chapel of the Blessed Mary *de Insula* situated in the churchyard of the parish church of Rykm[er]sworth.

To the high altar for tithes in arrears not done 5s.

The residue &c I give & bequeath to Joan my wife & William Musterd, whom I ordain & make my executors &c.

Proved on 20 January [1485/6]; & they were released.

138. Thomas Tredewey reference: 2AR50v
will: [blank] July 1486 **probate: 5 August 1486**

In &c. On [blank] July 1486, I Thomas Tredewey of Rykm[er]sworth, of sound mind &c.

[*No committal of soul or burial clause.*]

To the light of the Trinity one sheep; to the high altar 12d; to the church of St Giles of Chalfounte one sheep.

& to Thomas Davy three sheep & one cow.

To Walter my son two sheep & one cow; to Richard my son two sheep & one cow; if it should happen that Joan my wife should die before they come to their age of marriage, then I will that the aforesaid cattle [*i.e.* animals] of Walter & Richard to remain in the custody of Robert Newman, my executor, & to John Gybbes of Maplecrosse.

The residue &c I give & bequeath to Joan my wife & Robert Newman of Chalfonte St Giles, which Robert & Joan I constitute my executors that they may dispose &c. *Proved on 5 August in the year abovesaid [1486].*

139. George Wynkeburn   reference: 2AR51v
administration: 4 April 1487

On 4 April 1487 administration of the goods of George Wynkeburn, lately of Rykm[er]sworth, deceased, was granted to Thomas Grevy & Lettice his wife, relict of the said George, & master William Myller, notary.

140. Isabel Randolff   reference: 2AR52v
will: 5 April 1487   probate: 11 August 1487

In &c. On 5 April 1487 I Isabel Randolff, of sound mind, make &c.

[*No committal of soul*]; & my body to be buried in the churchyard of the parish church of the Blessed Mary of Rykm[er]sworth next to the grave of Andrew my spouse.

To the high altar for tithes forgotten 12d; & to the light of the Trinity 4d; & to the light of the Holy Cross 4d; to a suitable priest to celebrate for three years for the health of my soul and of my friends 33s 4d.

To Richard my son 40s & to Agnes my daughter 40s; & if it should fortune that the said Richard should die before then I will that the said 40s remain in the hands of my executors.

The residue &c I give & bequeath to Stephen Randolf & William his brother, whom I constitute & ordain my executors that &c.

Proved &c on 11 August in the year abovesaid [1487]; & they were released.

141. Ann Newton reference: 2AR51v
~~administration: 17 April 1487~~ probate: 18 April 1487
~~On 17 April 1487 administration of the goods of Ann Newton, lately of Ryk',~~
~~deceased, was committed to sir Thomas Hemyngforth & William Newton.~~
The testament of Ann Newton, deceased, was granted probate on 18 April in the
year above said [1487], in which she bequeathed to the mother church of St Alban
12d; to the high altar of Ryk' 20d; & administration was committed &c to Elizabeth,
wife of John Coke, her daughter, who [*plural*] were named her executors; granted by
William Lychefeld, commissary of the archdeacon.

142. Thomas Aldewen reference: 2AR54v
will: 3 April 1488 probate: 10 May 1488
In &c. On 3 April 1488, I Thomas Aldewen of Rykm[er]sworth, of sound mind &c.
[*No committal of soul or burial clause.*]
To the high altar of the same church for tithes forgotten & not done one sheep; to
the chapel of the Blessed Mary *de Insula* another sheep; to the lights of the said
church one sheep; to the mother church of St Alban 4d.
To each of my three boys one 'bullok' & six sheep; to William Ridyng one 'bullok' &
two sheep; to William Aldewyn, Roger Aldewyn & Robert Aldewyn, to each of
them, one sheep; to John Grymysdell one sheep.
The residue &c I give & bequeath to Ann my wife, whom I ordain & constitute my
executrix, that she may dispose &c.
I will that William Aldewyn & John Grymysdell be supervisors of this my last will.
Given at Ryk' &c.
These witnesses: sir Thomas Cotton, Thomas Grevye, Maurice Sare, Thomas Pygott
& others.
Proved &c on 10 May [1488]; &c & she was released.

143. Margaret Tyler, widow reference: 2AR54v
will: 7 May 1488 probate: 27 May 1488
In &c. On 7 May 1488, I Margaret Tyler, widow, in my pure widowhood &c, of
sound mind, make my testament &c.
[*No committal of soul*]; & my body to be buried in the churchyard of the Blessed
Mary in Ryk', next to the grave of my husband.
To the high altar for tithes forgotten a cloth of 'dyaper'; to the mother church of St
Alban 4d; to the church of Ryk' one large brass pot, one best basin with a ewer.

To Isabel Dorset, my daughter, one brass pan, one basin with a ewer, one bedcover & one great chest; to John Maskell one great spoon of brass, one brass pot [*and*] a bedcover with a blanket; to Joan Dorset my kinswoman one best cover, a pair of sheets with a chest; to Agnes my kinswoman one small brass pot with a pair of sheets; to Alianor my kinswoman another small brass pot with a pair of sheets; to Joan Spryng a lined tunic; to my two godsons, to each of them a pair of sheets.

The residue & I give & bequeath to Isabel Dorset my daughter & John Maskell ?my kinsman, whom I make, ordain & constitute my executors of this my last will, so that they dispose the aforesaid as seems good to them both.

Given &c. These witnesses: sir Thomas Coton vicar, John Gibbys, Philip Dorset, Thomas Warde & others.

Proved &c on 27 May in the year abovesaid [1488]; & they had their acquittance.

144. Ellen Ayleward, widow   reference: 2AR54v
will: [*damaged*] [?1488]   probate: 27 May 1488

[*damaged*] I Ellen Ayleward, widow, of Ryk', of whole mind &c.

[*No committal of soul or burial clause.*]

I bequeath to the high altar of the said church 8d & to the church of St Alban 4d.

The residue &c I give & bequeath to Christine Hede, whom I make my executrix &c.

Proved &c on 27 May [1488] &c.

145. Richard Grove   reference: 2AR54v
administration: [*damaged*; c.27 May 1488]

On [*damaged*] administration of the goods of Richard Grove of Ryk', deceased, was granted to Joan his wife &c, [*damaged*] Philip Gate vicar of Saret, canonist,[97] John Rowe & James Haydon &c.

146. Henry Baker alias Warde   reference: 2AR57r
administration: 4 December 1489

On 4 December 1489 administration of the goods of Henry Baker alias Warde, lately of Ryk', dying intestate, was committed to Joan, relict of the aforesaid Henry &c.

---

[97] The bottom of the page is damaged: the name of the vicar of Sarratt is probably Philip Gate, but as it might be Stephen (*ph'i* or *Ph'i* is visible). The list of vicars in the church sheds no light as no-one named Gate is mentioned therein. He was clearly educated as he is described as *dec't'is* (a student of the decretals or canonist).

147. Richard Over   reference: 2AR60r
will: 7 November 1490   probate: 6 November 1491

In the name of God, Amen. On 7 November 1490, I Richard Over of
Rykm[er]sworth, of sound mine & whole memory, make my testament in this
manner.

First I bequeath my soul to Almighty God, the Blessed Mary and all his saints; & my
body to be buried in the churchyard of the parish church of Rikm[er]sworth
aforesaid.

To the high altar one sheep for my tithes forgotten; to the reparation of the chapel
of the the Blessed Mary, Glorious Virgin, one sheep.

I will that Lettice my wife shall have my tenement in which I dwell called Selmyns,[98]
with all the lands, meadows, pastures and feedings, with all the appurtenances of the
tenement for the term of five years after my death peacefully, without interruption
or impediment by anyone, & my aforesaid wife shall pay, or cause to be paid,
annually to the lord the rents & services that ought to be paid for the tenement & its
appurtenances, and to do no waste in the woods or underwoods, namely, in 'le
heggerowes', and that she will mow [*damaged*][99] of the tenement, & I will that she
have sufficient, that is, 'fierbote hechebote & stakebote' to support [*damaged*] hers
[&] mine & to sufficiently repair & maintain the aforesaid tenement [*damaged*] &
after the aforesaid term of five years is complete, I will that my son William have
[the aforesaid tenement and its appurtenances] called Selmyns, holding to him & his
heirs forever.

The residue of all my goods not bequeathed, I give & bequeath to Lettice my wife,
Robert Over & Richard Cartar, whom I constitute & make my executors, that they
make dispose as seems best to them to please God & for the health of my soul.
Given &c.

These witnesses: Thomas Coton, vicar, [*2 or 3 names illeg*] Thomas Warde & many
others.

Proved on 6 November [1491]; & administration was committed to the aforenamed
executors; they were sworn in form of law & released.

---

[98] It is tempting to read this as 'Selwyns' but the letter after the l is not w. It is not like the
letter w in 'heggerowes' below.
[99] From here onwards the end of each line is faded.

148. Walter Dene[100]   reference: 2AR58v
will: 21 December 1490   probate: 25 June 1491

In &c. On 21 December 1490, I Walter Dene of Rykm[er]sworth, of sound mind &c.
[*No committal of soul*]; [*faded*] my body to be buried in the churchyard of the
Blessed Mary of Rykm[er]sworth near my parents.

To the high altar [*faded*] 3s 4d; to the reparation of the chapel of the Blessed Mary
de Insula 20d; to each of the lights of the aforesaid church [*faded*]; to each of the
parish clerks 4d.

To John Webbe my servant 20s & to Joan ?Welere my kinswoman [*faded*]
according to the discretion of my executors.

To sir Thomas Hemyngforth 33s 4d to celebrate [*faded*] for the space to the end of 9
years in the church of Rykm[er]sworth.

The residue of all my goods I give & bequeath to my [*faded*], whom [*plural*] I ordain
& constitute my executors that they may dispose it &c. Furthermore I will that
[*faded*] [sir Thomas] Hemyngforth, William Sabyn, James Fodyrley & Walter Barre
be supervisors [*faded*]

[these witnesses: …] William Syward, Thomas Warde & others.
Proved on 25 June 1491; & they were released

149. Thomas Botterfeld   reference: 2AR58v
Probate only: 19 March 1490/1

The testament of Thomas Botterfeld of Rykm[er]sworth was proved on 19 March
1490/1.

He bequeathed to the high altar 12d & to the lights of the church 12d & to the shrine
of St Alban 4d;

& he nominated his executors Emma his wife & John his son, & all his goods &c

150. John Baker   reference: 2AR58v
Probate only: 19 March 1490/1

On the same day [19 March 1490/1][101] the testament of John Baker of Ryk' was
proved.

He bequeathed to the shrine [of St Alban] 4d
& made his executors Alice his wife & William Baker his son &c.

---

[100] The beginning of each line is faded.
[101] The same day as Thomas Botterfeld's will was proved.

151. Thomas Pygot   reference: 2AR64v [*damaged*]
will: 5 May 1491   **probate: 22 September 1492**

In the name of God, Amen. On 5 May 1491, I Thomas Pygot of Rykmersworth, of sound mind & whole memory, make my testament in this manner.

First I bequeath my soul to Almighty God, the Blessed Mary & all the saints; & my body to be buried in the churchyard of the Blessed Mary of Rykmersworth beside [*my parents*] [*p….. meos*].

To the high altar of the said church for tithes forgotten & not performed one sheep; to the high altar of Watford another sheep.

To Agnes my daughter two sheep; to Denise my daughter one sheep.

I will that Robert Pygot my son have my house in which I now live under this condition: that he be a good son to his mother & that he permit his mother to remain in the said house as long as she pleases, paying to the said Robert for the house that which right demands.

The residue of my goods I give & bequeath to Alice my wife[102] & to Robert my son, whom I ordain & make my executors that they may do as seems best to them to please God & for the health of my soul.

Given &c; these witnesses: Thomas Coton [vicar], Maurice Sare & others.

Proved on 22 September 1492; & [administration] was committed &c; & they were released.

152. John Fabyan   reference: 2AR59v
will: 31 May 1491   **probate: 6 July 1491**

In &c. On the last day of May 1491, I John Fabyan of Ryk' in the county of Hertford, of sound mind &c;

[*No committal of soul*]; & my body to be buried in the churchyard &c.

To the high altar for my tithes forgotten 4d; to the light of the Blessed Mary 2 lbs of wax & two candles to be made from them.

To John Clerk 4d & to Thomas Warde 4d.

The residue I give & bequeath to Margaret my wife, whom I ordain & constitute my executrix of this my testament; in which &c.

These being witnesses: Richard Nevill, Richard Tyler, William Hamond, J' Hamond, J' Bussh, Thomas Hamond, Henry Atkyn & others.

Given &c.

Proved &c 6 July 1491; & she was released.

---

[102] Her will is no. 161.

153. George Danyell, esquire[103]   reference: 2AR62r
will: 12 October 1491   probate: 15 January 1491/2

In the name of God, Amen. On 12 October 1491, I George Danyell, esquire, of sound mind & whole memory, make my testament in this manner.

First I bequeath my soul to Almighty God, the Blessed Mary and all the saints; & my body to be buried in the aisle of St Edmund in the church of Rykmersworth.

To the high altar of the same church for my tithes forgotten & not performed 13s 4d.

To George Hatton 6s 8d; to William Hatton 6s 8d; to John Pecoke 6s 8d; to Thomas Day 13s 4d; to John Christofyr 5s; to the parish clerks, to each of them 20d.

The residue of my goods I give & bequeath to Lettice my wife & Thomas my son, whom I ordain and constitute my executors, that they may dispose of it as seems best to them to please God & profit the health of my soul.

Given &c.

These witnesses: Thomas Coton, vicar of Rykmersworth, William Hamonde, Thomas Warde & others.

Proved on 15 January in the year abovesaid [1491/2]; & administration was committed to the above named executors, sworn in form of law & they were released.

154. John Marchant   reference: 2AR60v
will: 20 October 1491   probate: 26 November 1491

In the name of God, Amen. On 20 October 1491, I John Marchant of Rykmersworth, of sound mind & whole memory, make my testament in this manner.

First I bequeath my soul to Almighty God, the Blessed Mary and all the saints; & my body to be buried in the churchyard of the church of the Blessed Mary of Rykmersworth.

To the high altar of the said church for tithes forgotten 6d; to the lights of St Edmund & St Katherine, to each of them 4d, to the shrine of St Alban 1d.

---

[103] His son John (not mentioned in the will) was a monk at St Albans; he had received his first tonsure in 1475. (H. T. Riley, ed., *Registra quorundam abbatum monasterii S. Albani: qui sæculo XVmo. floruere*, vol II, *Registra Johannis Whethamstede, Willelmi Albon et Willelmi Walingforde*, p.124) In January 1480/81 George Danyell and John Asshby received the gift of the nomination to the vicarage of Rickmansworth, and they promoted Thomas 'Cottone'. (Riley, ed., *Registra*, p.227)

The residue of all my goods I give & bequeath to Joan my wife, Walter Barr & Roger Paltoke, whom I ordain & constitute my executors that they may dispose as seems best to them to please God & for the health of my soul.

Given &c.

These witnesses: sir Thomas Coton, Thomas Warde & others.

Proved on 26 November [1491]; & administration was committed to the above named executors, sworn in form of law & they were released &c.

155. James Foderley   reference: 2AR60r
will: 30 October 1491   probate: 4 November 1491

In the name of God, Amen. On 30 October 1491, I James ~~Fodeley~~ Foderley of Rykmersworth, of sound mind & whole memory, make my testament in this manner.

First I bequeath my soul to Almighty God, the Blessed Mary & all the saints; & my body to be buried in the churchyard of Rykmersworth near [*my*] parents.

To the high altar of the said church for tithes forgotten & not done 12d & one sheep; to the reparation of the said church 3s 4d; to the light of the Blessed Mary 6d; to the light of St Katherine 4d; to the light of the Holy Trinity 8d; to the shrine of St Alban 12d.

I will that sir Thomas Hemyngforde celebrate for half a year in the aforesaid church for my soul & for the souls of my friends so that he has for his stipend according to the discretion of my supervisors & executors.

The residue of all my goods I give & bequeath to Richard & John my sons, that they may dispose as seems best to them to please God & for the health of my soul.

Furthermore I will that sir Thomas Coton, vicar of Rykmersworth, sir Thomas Hemyngforde, Thomas Thorney & John Wodwarde, bailiff of Tytenangre[104] be supervisors of this my last testament so that they oversee that my executors complete my will in all things.

Given &c.

These witnesses: John Stokker, Walter Barre, John Dene & others.

Proved on 4 November in the year abovesaid [1491]; & administration was committed to the above named executors, sworn in form of law &c & they were released.

---

[104] Tittenhanger, near St Albans.

156. John Day   reference: 2AR60v
will: 14 November 1491   **probate: 26 November 1491**

In the name of god, Amen. On 14 November 1491, I John Day of Rykmersworth, of sound mind & whole memory, make my testament in this manner.

First I bequeath my soul to Almighty God, the Blessed Mary and all the saints; & my body to be buried in the churchyard of the Blessed Mary of Rykmersworth.

To the high altar of the said church for tithes forgotten 8d; to Thomas Warde 4d.

To my three boys, to each of them two sheep.

The residue of all my goods I give & bequeath to Agnes my wife, whom I ordain & constitute my executrix, that she may dispose the said goods as seems best to her to please God & profit the health of my soul.

Given &c.

These witnesses: Thomas Coton, John Wodroffe, Robert adall[sic] & others.

Proved on 26 November [1491]; & administration was committed to Agnes named above, sworn in form of law & she was released.

157. Hugh Dampport   reference: 2AR62r
administration: 15 January 1491/2

John Thornton, archdeacon of the special jurisdiction of St Albans within the diocese of Lincoln, to sir Thomas Coton, vicar of Rykmersworth, Thomas Dampport & John Warde, administrators of Hugh Dampport, lately of Rykmersworth, greetings.[105]

Concerning all & singular the goods of the aforesaid Hugh, who died as if intestate, they are to labour in disposing the goods as seems best to them to profit the health of his soul and to please God, according to their conscience. They are to pay the debts of the said deceased and collect those that were owing to him at the time of his death; they are to faithfully do all in their power to settle his estate, trusting in God. Administration of the estate is granted to them. Sealed with the seal of his office, in the aforesaid monastery, on 15 January 1491/2.

---

[105] This is an unusual grant of administration in that it gives quite specific instructions, almost in the manner of a will.

158. Thomas Rede reference: 2AR64v
will: 10 May 1492 probate: 17 June 1492

In the name of God, Amen. On 10 May 1492, I Thomas Rede of Rykmersworth, being of sound mind & whole memory, thanks to the Almighty, make my testament in this manner.

First I bequeath my soul to Almighty God my creator & redeemer, the Blessed Mary his mother, & all the saints; & my body to be buried in the churchyard of the parish church of Rykmersworth aforesaid.

To the high altar of the same church for my tithes & oblations forgotten or owing, 4d.

I bequeath to John [illeg] my 'Murrey' coloured gown.

The residue of all my goods not bequeathed above, after the debts by me owed have been fully paid, I give & bequeath to Joan my wife & Richard my son to do with according to their own free will & I give the same goods that they may dispose & distribute [them] for my soul as seems best to please God & for the health of my soul, which Joan & Richard I make executors of this present testament.

These being witnesses: John Godfrey, John Stokker, Henry ?Manestry & others.

Proved on 17 June in the year abovesaid [1492]; & administration was committed to the executors & they were released.

159. Richard Nevell reference: 2AR64r [*very feint*]
administration: c.3 June 1492[106]

George Colte, commissary of the reverend John Thornton archdeacon [of St Albans] in the diocese [of Lincoln] to Marion Nevell, administrator of Richard Nevell lately of Rykmersworth, [grants] administration of all & singular the goods of the said Richard lately [dying] intestate […] as will seem best to her for the health of his soul [*remainder too feint to read*]

Sealed with our official seal; given at the monastery aforesaid […]

160. William Baker reference: 2AR64v [*very feint*]
administration: [*illeg*] September 1492

[…] the reverend master John Thornton, archdeacon of the exempt jurisdiction of the monastery of St Alban in the diocese of Lincoln to [the administrator] of William Baker of Rykmersworth, deceased, greeting, &c, administering all & singular the goods of him, dying intestate, & in his/her liberty, disposing for the

---

[106] A long administration, probably similar to that of Hugh Dampport, no. 157.

health of his soul as seems [best to him/her], [also] to pay the debts of the said deceased that he owed when he died ...[107] given [*illeg*] September 1492.

161. Alys Pygot   reference: 2AR65v
will: 2 October 1492 [English]   probate: 25 October 1492

In the Name of gode so be it. I Alys Pygot of Rykmersworth, the tuysday after the feste of Saint Michael the Archeangell last passed in the yere and Reigne of Kyng Henry the VII the eighth[108] [2 October 1492] in my right mynde & helth, I make my testament in this maner.

First I bequeth my soule to gode almyghty and to our lady and to all the holy company of heven; my body to be buried in the Chirch yerde of our lady of Rykmersworth aforesaid.

I bequeth to the highe Auter one sheppe; to the Roode lofte \light/ A sheppe; to syr George [*damaged*].

To Agnes my doughter A Red bollok; to Deonise my doughter a garlyd bollok; to Roger my son two shepe and two b[ushel]s whete; to Marion my daughter two shepe; to Agnes my doughter my grene gowne; to Deonyse my daughter my blewe gowne; to Roger my son a bryndlyd Bulloke and my gret brase [*damaged*], six sylver sponys, the whiche if the said Roger dey to remayne to Robert my son; to Robert my gret Brase pane.

To syr George A trentall if it may be spared and my dettes paid.[109]

To Roger [*damaged*] all tilthe that I have for to be sowen to [*i.e.* two] yere in Watford paryssh.

To John Clerke a shepe; [*damaged*]; to [*damaged*] my weddyng Rynge.

The Residue of all my goodes I geve and bequeth to Robert and Roger my sons, whom I ordeyn and make my trewe executors that they dispose for the helth of my soule as it seemeth to them the better use.

Yoven &.

Proved on 25 October the year abovesaid [1492]; & [administration] was committed &c & they were released.

---

[107] The text is probably the same as for Elizabeth & John Newell, no. 162 below.

[108] i.e. in the eighth year of the reign of Henry VII.

[109] A sum of money should be stated but has not been.

162. Elizabeth and John Newell   reference: 2AR66v
administration: 3 March 1492/3

John Thornton, doctor of sacred theology, archdeacon of the exempt jurisdiction of the monastery of St Alban in the diocese of Lincoln, Master of Arts, to the administrator of John Newell & Elizabeth his wife of Rykmersworth lately deceased, Greeting.[110]

Concerning all & singular the goods of the said John & Elizabeth, lately dying intestate & at their liberty, you are to dispose as you shall seems best to you to profit the health of their soul & do as should be done according to conscience and regarding their debts, raising, collecting and receiving that which was owed to them at the time of their death, and also paying any debts that they owed to anyone at the time of their deaths. With faithfulness & circumspection to complete your work fully, with the advice of the master & in fear of mortal ?peril. And you are admitted in form of law by us & receiving these goods you are to administer them as deputy by these presents of office; sealed; given at the aforesaid monastery on 3 March 1492/3.

163. Katherine Rydale, widow   reference: 2AR76v
will: 28 August 1494   **probate: 25 October 1494**

In the name of God, Amen. I Katherine Rydale, widow, of sound mind & whole memory, make my testament in this manner.

First I bequeath my soul to Almighty God, the Blessed ~~Mary~~ and Glorious Virgin Mary and to all the saints happily gathered in highest heaven;[111] & my body to be buried in the porch of the parish of Rykmersworth next to John Rydale, lately my spouse.

To the high altar of the said church one sheet priced 2s in money; to the mother church of St Alban 4d; to the church house of Rykmersworth aforesaid a little brass pot repaired & mended in the bottom.

The residue of all my goods not bequeathed I give & bequeath to William Sebyn & Walter Barre, whom I make & ordain my executors of this my testament that they may ordain & dispose for the health of my soul & the soul of my aforesaid spouse & all the faithful departed as seems best to them to do. I give and bequeath to my aforesaid executors for their labour that they will undertake in the execution of this testament 13s 4d.

---

[110] The administrator is not named.

[111] The Latin here is '*habrahe*' but it can only mean heaven.

And of this my testament I constitute & ordain John Assheby supervisor, that through his administration of my goods they may be disposed with greatest charity and merit.

In this testament in which is written my last will I have placed my seal.

These being witnesses: John Dean, John White & Edward Metcalf with many others. Given at Rykmersworth aforesaid on 28 August 1494.

The present testament was approved before master Thomas Newlonde, archdeacon on 25 October in the year above said [1494]; administration of the goods was committed to the executors abovenamed in this testament.

164. John Warde reference: 2AR78v
will: 1 March 1494/5 probate: 5 March 1494/5

In the name of God, Amen. On 1 March 1494/5 I John Warde of Rykmersworth, of sound mind & whole memory, make my testament in this manner.

First I bequeath my soul to Almighty God, the Blessed Mary & all the saints; & my body to be buried in the chapel of the Blessed Mary within the churchyard of the church of Rykmersworth.

To the high altar of the said church for tithes forgotten & other omissions 6s 8d; to each light in the said church 4d; to the mother church, that is to the shrine of St Alban, 12d.

To Thomas Warde my brother a gown of blue cloth; to John ~~Pher~~ Phelip another gown; to William Calley another gown.

The residue of my goods I give to master Thomas Coton & Alice my wife, whom I ordain & constitute my executors of this my last will that they may dispose the said goods as seems best to them to please God & for the health of my soul.

Given at Rykmersworth aforesaid on the year and day of the month above written.

These being witnesses: Thomas Warde, John Phelip, William Calley & others.

This present testament was approved & favoured before master Thomas Newlonde, archdeacon, on 5 March in the year above written [1494/5]; & administration of all the goods was committed to the executors named above, & they were sworn on the Holy Gospel to faithfully carry out this testament.

165. Roger Wedon   reference: 2AR80v
will: 1 July 1495   **probate: 17 July 1495**

In the name of God, Amen. On 1 July 1495, I Roger Wedon of Rykmersworth, of sound mind & whole memory, make my testament in this manner.

First I bequeath my soul to Almighty God, the Blessed Mary & all the saints; & my body to be buried in the churchyard of the Blessed Mary of Rykmersworth.

To the high altar of the said church for tithes forgotten 12d; to the light of the Holy Cross in the said church 12d; to the lights of St Edmund & St Mary de 'petie', to each of them 8d; to the light of the Holy Trinity 6d; to the reparation of the church of Rykmersworth 6s 8d; to the reparation of the chapel of the Blessed Mary *de Insula* 12d; to the mother church 12d.

To Henry my son & John his brother 12 sheep, one quarter of wheat & one quarter of barley; to George Wedon my son 12 sheep, one cow, one quarter of wheat & one quarter of barley.

I will that the said George shall have my land in Herfelde called Bakers after my decease.

The residue of all my goods I give to Joan Wedon my wife & Richard my son, whom I ordain & constitute my executors of this my last will.

I will that William my brother be my supervisor of this my testament that he may oversee that the aforesaid executors expend my said goods as seems best to them to please God & for the health of my soul.

Given at Rykmersworth aforesaid on the year, & day of the month above written. These being witnesses: sir Thomas Coton vicar of Rykmersworth, John Whitt, Robert Ovir & others.

This present testament was approved & favoured before us, master Thomas Newlonde, archdeacon of the exempt jurisdiction of the monastery of St Alban on 16 July in the year above written [1495]; & administration of all the goods was committed to the executors named above in this present testament & they were sworn on the Holy Gospel that they would well & faithfully carry out & fulfil these things.

166. Stephen Holtyng   reference: 2AR80v
will: 20 July 1495   **probate: 1 August 1495**
[*administration with transcript of will & witnesses examined*]

Examination was had of witnesses regarding the present testament by Master Hugh Lever, doctor of laws, official of the exempt jurisdiction of the monastery of St Alban in the diocese of Lincoln, through me William Spencer, notary public, on 1

August 1495, concerning and on the schedule, testament or last will of a certain Stephen Holtyng of Rykmersworth, the content & tenor of which is as follows:

In the name of God, Amen. On 20 July 1495, I Stephen Holtyng of Rykmersworth, of sound mind & whole memory, make my testament in this manner.

First I bequeath my soul to Almighty God, the Blessed Mary & all the saints; & my body to be buried in the church of the Blessed Mary of Rykmersworth near the font, facing the door of the jewel house.[112]

To the high altar of the said church for tithes forgotten one sheep or 12d; to the reparation of the church 3s 4d; to the shrine of the protomartyr Alban 6d

To Joan my wife my cart, with the plough horses with all things belonging to the cart & plough, also two cows & 30 sheep under this condition, that she shall not claim a third part of my other goods.

To Elizabeth Hosteler one heifer & six sheep; to Joan Holtyng my daughter one heifer & six sheep; to Margaret Stokke six sheep; to Ellen Wedon six sheep; to Agnes my daughter one heifer, six sheep & six silver spoons; to Marion my daughter one heifer & six sheep.

The residue of my goods I give & bequeath to sir Thomas Coton, vicar of Rykmersworth, Richard & John my sons, whom I ordain & constitute my true executors of this my last will so that they may dispose of the said goods as they best see fit to please God & for the health of my soul.

Given at Ryk' on the year & day of the month above written.

These being witnesses: William Sebene, John Dene, Richard Wilans & others.

Sir Thomas Coton, the first witness, of the age of 30 years & more, as he asserts, swearing in sacred words, speaking truly in and concerning the content in the testament of the aforesaid Stephen Holtyng, says that the contents in the same were true & [that it] contains the last will &c.

William Sebene of Rykmersworth aforesaid,[113] the second witness admitted, sworn & examined, of the age of 40 years, as he asserts, freely questioned & interrogated about & on the contents in the said schedule or testament, says that the contents were authentic & that the letters [i.e. words] that it contains are true.

John Dene of Rykmersworth, the third of the witnesses, sworn [&] examined, of the age, as he asserts, of 25 years, freely questioned on the individual contents in the said schedule or testament says that they were authentic & contained the real truth.

---

[112] Probably meaning the room where the church plate was stored.

[113] His will is no. 188.

Therefore the said Master Hugh, the official aforesaid, in so far as under the law he could & ought, pronounced concerning the validity & veracity of this testament. *This present testament was approved by Master Hugh Lever, doctor of laws, official of the exempt jurisdiction of the monastery of St Alban, on 1 August in the year above said [1495]; & administration of the goods was committed to the executors above named; & the faithful carrying out of this present testament to be done by them; they swore their corporal oath the Holy Gospel.*

167. Lettice Danyell[114] reference: 2AR82r
administration: 22 January 1495/6

Richard Runham, archdeacon of the exempt jurisdiction of the monastery of St Alban in the diocese of Lincoln, to our beloved in Christ, Thomas Danyell, of the parish of Rykmersworth within our jurisdiction, greetings. In default of authorisation of administering all & singular the goods of your mother, Lettice Danyell, late of the parish of Rykmersworth aforesaid, she, dying intestate & with freedom to dispose of them, therefore I wish that out of the goods of the said deceased you oblige the creditors of your same mother & that you make a true inventory of the goods & more that you present to us a faithful account at the time when you have been legally advised to do this & it is registered. And you with faithfulness & circumspection, in full industry, having faith in the Lord & holding ?true, we commit power to you to administer those goods by the authority of right preferred & ordained by these presents, sealed with our seal of office.

Given in the monastery aforesaid on 22 January 1495/6.

168. Margaret Adene, widow reference: 2AR83r
will: 20 April 1496 [English] **probate: 26 May 1496**

In the name of our lorde gode, Amen. In the yere of our lorde 1496 the 20th day of the Monethe of Aprell, I Margaret A Dene of Rykmersworth, Wyddowe, hole of mynde and of goode Remembraunce, in my puer Wyddowhode, make my testament in this maner of wyse.

Fyrst I bequeth my soule unto allmyghty gode, to hys blyssed moder and to all hys saintes; and my bodie to be beried in the Chirche yarde of our blyssed [Lady] of Rykmersworth beside my husband.

---

[114] *Wills at Hertford* says that this relates to Thomas Danyell. In fact, the deceased was his mother, Lettice; the registered document is a detailed grant of administration to him as she had died intestate. His father's will is no. 153.

Also I bequeth to the high auter of the said Chirche for tithis for gettyn and not at all tymes done 12d; to the Reparacion of the Chapell of our ladie of ylande 8d; to every light within the said chyrch 4d; to every auter within the same Chyrche and Chapell an autercloth.

Also I wyll that myn executours, as hastily as may conveniently be doon, they ordeyne and beye A Cope and two tuniclys of purpoll violet[115] according unto the vestment that Roger Belche and Johanne hys Wyfe lately gave to the Chyrche[116] of Rykmersworth and I will that the said Chirche shall have the saide Cope and tunicle [*sic*, singular].

To the monastery of Seint Albons 8d.

I bequethe to John Wymonde my servaunt in money 20s, A matres, a peir of blankets, a peir of shetts, A bolster and a coverlet; to Johan Hageson my servaunt A matres, a peir of Blankets, a peir of Shets, a bolster, a coverlite, a pote and a panne of Brasse, two platters, two disshes, two sawsers of pewter, A kanstyke [candlestick] and a salte seler.

The Residue of all my goods not bequeth, I putte in the disposicion of John A dene and Harry my childer, Whom I ordayn and make my executours of this my hole and laste will.

Also I wyll that Richard Carter of Rykmersworth and John Stokker of the same be supervisours of this my testament so that they supervide and see that this my will be fulfilled and that myn executours dispose my goods nat bequest to the pleasure of gode to the welthe of my soule and of my frends soulys.

Wryttyn at Rykmersworth a fore said the year of our lorde and the day of the moneth a bove writtyn.

Thes beryng witnes: sir Thomas Coton vicar, William Sebene, Harry Whitberd, Richard Waleys, Cutberd Paterson and Many other.

This present testament was approved & favoured before master Richard Runham, archdeacon, on 26 May in the year abovesaid [1496]; & administration of the goods was committed top the executors above named.

---

[115] Probably meaning purple velvet.

[116] There is no bequest of vestments in Roger Belche's will (no. 110, December 1476); if his widow Joan made a will it has not survived. It is likely that they provided St Mary's with 'the vestment' (vestments) during their lifetime. Clive Burgess gives the example of the widow Maud Spicer who donated a sumptuous suit of vestments to All Saints', Bristol, in 1496, which cost her £27. Her will, which does not mention the vestments, was made in 1504. (C. Burgess, *The Right Ordering of Souls: The parish of All Saints' Bristol on the eve of the Reformation* (Woodbridge, 2018), p.145.)

169. William Cooke   reference: 2AR83r
administration: 24 May 1496

Richard Runham, archdeacon of the exempt jurisdiction of the monastery of St Alban in the diocese of Lincoln, to our beloved in Christ, Alice Cooke, relict of William Cooke of the parish of Rykmersworth within our jurisdiction, dying intestate, greeting, &c. To you [is granted] administration of all & singular the goods of the said William & free disposition of them as seems best to you to profit his soul & to expedite that you will answer before the Lord in conscience and obtaining, raising, collecting & receiving the debts of the said deceased which were owed to him at the time of his death, and indeed to pay all the expenses & debts that the said deceased owed at the time when he passed away to anyone. And you with faithfulness and circumspection, with full industry, having faith in the Lord & holding ?true, we commit power to you, by which power from us, you, admitting & receiving administration of those goods, we ordain, make & depute you by these presents. Sealed with our seal of office.

Given in the monastery aforesaid on 24 May 1496.

170. John Felippe   reference: 2AR90v
will: 26 March 1497   probate: 12 May 1498

In the name of God, Amen. On 26 March 1497, I John Felippe of Rykmersworth, of sound mind and good memory, make my testament in this manner.

First I bequeath my soul to God Almighty, the Blessed Mary & all the saints; & my body to be buried in the churchyard of the Blessed Mary of Rykmerworth near to my parents.

To the high altar of the aforesaid church for tithes forgotten and not performed 6d; to the reparation of the chapel of the Blessed Mary *de Insula* 6d; to each of the lights in the said church 2d; to the reparation of the mother church 4d.

To Agnes my daughter two brass pots, six pairs of sheets, also 18 pieces of 'pewter', that is, six platters, six 'dishes' and six 'salvreres'; to the said Agnes one bed with all the requirements of a proper bed. I will that the said Agnes have all the appurtenances & things that appertain to a household, according to the discretion of my executors.

To George Felyppe one heifer; to William May two sheep.

The residue of my goods I give & bequeath to Margaret my wife, master Thomas Coton, my brother John Stokker[117] and Thomas Warde, whom I ordain & constitute my executors of this my last will that they may dispose of the said goods as seems best to them to please God & for the health of my soul, as they will answer before God on the day of judgement.

Given at Rykmersworth aforesaid, the year and day of the month above written.

These being witnesses: sir Thomas Hemyngforde, John Dene, John Tyler and others.

The present last will was approved by us, master Richard Runham, archdeacon, on 12 May 1498; & administration of the goods was committed to the executors above named.

171. William Sywarde   reference: 2AR90v
will: 28 March 1497   probate: 12 May 1498

In the name of God, Amen. On 28 March 1497, I William Syward of Rykmersworth, of sound mind and whole memory, make my testament in this manner.

First I bequeath my soul to Almighty God, the Blessed Mary & all his saints; & my body to be buried in the churchyard of the Blessed Mary of Rykmersworth near to my parents.

To the high altar one sheep for tithes forgotten; to the mother church 2d.

The residue of all my goods I give & bequeath to Thomas Sywarde my son, whom I ordain & constitute my executor of this my last will that he may dispose the said goods as seems best to him to please God and for the health of my soul.

Also I will that sir Thomas Coton, vicar, Thomas Creke & Walter Barre be supervisors of this testament so that they oversee that my said executor fulfils my testament aforesaid.

Given at Rykmersworth aforesaid, the year and day of the month above written.

These being witnesses: Richard Carter, John Dene, Robert Pigot and others.

The present last will was approved by us, master Richard Runham, archdeacon, on 12 May 1498; & administration of the goods was committed to the executor above named.

---

[117] *fratri meo*: see administration of Elizabeth Stokker, no. 131, where John Stokker & John Felippe (Felypp) were granted administration; perhaps they were half-brothers.

172. William Hamonde   reference: 2AR87r
will: 26 May ?1497 [English]   probate: 24 June 1497

In the name of gode Amen. The yere of our lorde 1487[?*recte* 1497][118] the 26 day of the Moneth of May, I William Hamonde of Rykmersworth, hole of mynde and good Remembraunce, make my testament and laste will in this maner of wise folowyng.

Fyrst I bequeth my soule to almygtie gode, to our blessed ladie and to all the seintes; and my bodie to be buried in the Chirche yarde of our ladie in Rykmersworth beside the buriall of my moder.

I bequeth to the auter of the seid Chirch for tithis forgotten and not at all tymes conveniently done A shepe; to the reparacion of the parish chirch of Rykmersworth A shepe; to the monasterie of Seint Albons 6d.

I will that my house in Mill ende ~~called~~ in the parish of Rykmersworth called Tokys be solde by myn executors to the most advauntage, of whiche money I will Eunice my wife have 20s and the Residue of the same money to be distributed for the welth of my soule and of my frendes.

I will that Eunice my wife shall have my \place with/ ?house with the appurtenances in Mill ende in the parish aforesaid called Hichemany where in nowe dwellith Johan Horne while she levyth and after her decesse the said place with the appurtenaunces to be solde and the money therof comyng tobe devided indeferntly betwyne John Hamonde, Thomas Hamonde and Jone Paterson my children.

The Residue of my goodes not bequethed I will and put in the distrecion of Eunice my wife and Thomas Hamonde my son as they will aunswer \to/ be disposed to the pleasure of my Saviour and to the most helth of my soule, which said Eunice and Thomas I make myn executours of this my testament and last will.

Also I will that Henry Whitberde of Rykmersworth be supervisour and overseer of this my will so that he supervide that my said executours fulfyll this my will as it is a fore rehersed.

Yeven at Rykmersworth a fore said the yere of our lorde and the day of the moneth abovewritten.

These beryng witnes: Syr Thomas Coton vicar, Richard Carter, Richard Tylson, William Elet and others.

---

[118] The year is given as M^l CCCClxxxvij. The will may have been made in 1487, but it is probably a scribal error for 1497. One of the witnesses is Richard Tylson, who also witnessed the next will, which is undated – so no clue there.

The present last will was approved by master Richard Runham, archdeacon, on 24 June in the year abovesaid [1497]; & administration of all the goods was granted to the abovenamed executors.

173. Christian More
will: [undated, ?1497] [English]

reference: 2AR89r

probate: ?29 July 1497

In the name of gode Amen &c. I Christian More in hole mynde and goode Remembraunce make my testamente in this wise manor of wise.

Fyrste and formyst I bequeth my soule to our lorde Jhesu Criste, to our ladie seint Marie and to all the company of heven; and my bodie to be beried in the Chircheierde of Rykmersworth beside my fader etc.

Fyrst and formyst I bequeth to the high auter for tithes forgotten 4d.

I bequethe to Thomas my sonne my best Coster and a peire of shettes and a brasse poote; to Margarete my dowter A sylver spone; to Agnes my doughter my greyne gowne.

And all the Residue of my goodes unbequethe I put in rewle to dispose for the weill of my soule [to] John Rolfe and Thomas Grosyn my sonne, whom I make myn executors.

And ther to beryng witnes Richard Tylson, John Adene and Richard Foderley.

This present last will was approved before master Richard Runham, archdeacon, on the unumpenultimo day of July [?29 July] 1497; & administration of the goods was committed to the executors above named.

174. Thomas Sywarde
will: 2 July 1498 [English]

reference: 2AR91r

probate: 29 July 1498

In the name of gode Amen. In the yere of our lorde gode 1498,[119] I Thomas Sywarde, leyng seke in bodie and hoole of mynde, make my Will in this wise.

Fyrst I bequeth my soule to almyghty gode and to our ladie seint marie and to all the seintes in heven; my bodie to be beried in the Chirchyarde of our ladie of Rykmersworth.

To the Shryne at seint Albons 2d; to the Roode light at Rykmersworth 2d.

To John my son assone as he comyth to age of discrecion a peyer of corall bedys; and mye oder movable goodes to Cicilie my wyfe to paye my dettes; that done the overplus to hyr and to my Children.

---

[119] Day and month given at the end of the will.

And my house I dwell In to my wyfe terme of hyr leiffe, after hyr decesse to my heyres and for lake of issue to them to the next of the blode of my said children and me, and if my said hous be solde, I will that John Forsacreley bie it afore any oder may, to paie as a noder will, And I will therbe infeffede to the use of the same Watkyne Barre, Richard Tredwey and Richard Carter and William Polart and John A dene for me and in my name to deliver to them possession and seauson according to the use as is aforesaid.

And I have made surrender of my Copie Holde in to the handes of Thomas Cotton, vicar of Rykmersworth and John A dene to the use of my wife terme of hir lyf, and after hir decesse to my heyres

And to performe this my last will I make Cicylie my wif my executor and over seer Watkyn Barre and Robert Pygot

At Rykmersworth the secunde day of July the 13th yere of the Reigne of Kyng Harry the vijth [1498].

In witnes of Thomas Creke Esquier, Thomas Cotton aforesaid vicar, Master Blewmantell, William Shawardyn, Watkyn Barre, John A dene, Robert Pygot and oder etc.

This present last will was approved and favoured by master John Kylingworth, commissary, on 29 July in the year abovesaid [1498]; & administration of the goods was committed to the executors above named & they were sworn on their corporal oath to faithfully fulfil the present will.

175a. John Assheby, gentleman

reference: 2AR95v

administration: 6 June 1499 [died in 1499]

[*will in proved in the Prerogative Court of Canterbury; see no. 175b*]

Richard Runham, archdeacon of the exempt jurisdiction of the monastery of St Alban in the diocese of Lincoln, dearly beloved in Christ, Ann[120] Assheby, relict of John Assheby, gentleman, lately of Rykmersworth, within our jurisdiction, deceased, and George Assheby, gentleman, son and heir of the same John Assheby, greetings in the everlasting Lord, for the raising, claiming, collecting and receiving and for completely disposing of all and singular the goods which belonged to the aforesaid John within our jurisdiction wherever they may be; and you are required by us by law [to act] in this matter and you must sequestrate them for paying according to right the demands of anyone to whom the said John at the time of his

---

[120] The Latin is *Agneti*; 'to Agnes', or 'to Ann'. Her name is given as Ann in her husband's will and in her own will (209). Their surname has various spellings.

death was obligated. Concerning which, in the name of the Lord, you are to undertake this burden in conscience faithfully and having faith in the Lord to carry out this out in full confidence in the Lord and we have committed full power to you; and you are empowered by us to accept and receive the aforesaid goods as administrators and disposers and we ordain and depute you by these present [writings].

Sealed with our seal of office; given in the monastery aforesaid, on 6 June 1499.

175b: John Assheby   reference: TNA, PROB 11/11/666
will: undated[121] [English]   probate: 1 July 1499

In the name of oure blesside Creator of whome procedeth all goodnes & vertue and withowte his permyttible Suffraunce & grace noo thyng canne be deduced unto perfecte end and goode conclusion, I John Assheby, knowyng my selfe corruptible And that this life is fallyng and transitory, And that I have here noo permanent Citie of Dwellyngplace, butt as a floure must vaneshe and passe hens the tyme wherof uncertayne & in noo wise distynctly knowen, have thrugh the speciall influence of the grace of god, whiles of his immensurable goodnes he hathe lente unto me Competent Witte, sufficiant discrecion & parfecte memorie delibred with my selfe to make my testament in this maner wise.

Furste I, havyng secure hoope & stedfaste assurance in thynfynite & precellyng mercy of god, beyng A bove all oder his glorious & mervelous workes by the whiche & through the merites of his glorious passionn I undoubtedly truste to be partyner of that eternall reward, perpetuall felicite And pardurable Joie, which is ordened And prepaired unto his synguler Lovers, Worshippers of his infynyte goodnes & exalters of his high name & infallible misericord, biquethe my sowle yet Encombrid with my Corruptible body unto oure blissed creatour, to the Intemerate & glorious virgyne saynte Mary, to whom I have commytted my greate truste to be my speciall advocatrice, socour and relief, And to All the holy & ioyous company of heven, Soo

---

[121] The *VCH Middlesex* states that John Ashby died in 1496. (*VCH Middlesex*, vol. 3, pp. 240-46) (http://www.british-history.ac.uk/vch/middx/vol3/pp240-246 [accessed 30 August 2020]) (no reference given for year of death). However, in the London Metropolitan Archives, there are two documents concerning an agreement about lands in Harefield between John Ashby and John Newdigate dated 24 and 25 April 1499, indicating that Ashby was alive in late April 1499. (LMA, ACC/0312/106 and 107.) The fact that administration was granted in the archdeaconry court of St Albans on 6 June 1499 (see 175a) indicates that he had died before that date.

that by their contynuall Imploracionns, suffrages & intercessions I may the soner atteyne to be with theym in blisse perpetually to endure;

And my bodie to be buried in the new Isle of the Churche of Rikm[er]sworth betwixt John Rolfe and thentre into the saide Chapell. I will that my bodie be closed in Canvas price the Elle 4d and a bove that to be coverd with lynon Cloth price the elle 8d & at the tyme of the leying of my bodie Into therthe I will that the lynon Clothe of 8d be taken of and dyvyded into four parties, & that dalte unto four pore men or women After the discrecion of my executours.

I will that At the Daie of my buriyng that I have five prestes And no Mo, with odre mynystres, to saye Diriges for me And on the Morowe every of theyme masse. And that every of theyme beyng preste have 8d, And every Clerke 4d, And every Childe Syngyng at the Diriges & masse 2d.

I bequethe unto the high aulter of the Church of Rikmersworth 3s 4d if I be there buried; or ellis the same to be unto the high aulter where it shall fortune me to be buried.

I will & bequeath unto my wife, if she remayne sole after my decease, All my goodes And Catallis for the sustenance of her & of her childrenne. And if it fortune her to Marye agayne, I will that than be fore that mariage all my goodes catallis & plate be egally devyded into two partes, that on of theym my wife to have & that oder parte to be delyverd unto my sonne & heire he to have the same to his own behofe and use

I will that at my monethis mynde there be also five prestes And noo moo to saye diriges & synge masse on the morowe, they, the clerkes And Childrenne to have for theire laboure as is a bovesaide, & that, for the pompe of the Worlde, noo Dyner be made but unto the saide prestis & clerkes And such as my wife and executours will called unto theyme, And that the same daie there be Delte unto pore men & women five loves [i.e. loaves] in the worship of the five woundes, five in the worship of the five Nailes, five in the worship of the five yerthly Joies of oure lady, seven in the worship of her seven hevenly Joies, And that asmany les Loves as wilbe made of di' [i.e. half] quarter of whete. And the same ordynaunce I will shalbe kepte at my Twelvemonethis mynde.

Of this my testament & laste will I make Anne my wife, Georg my sonne, Richarde Blounte & Jamys Edelyn my executours, And master David Philippe supervisour of the same, & I will that every of my saide executours have 6s 8d for theire laboure, & the said master David Philippe a rynge with a Dyamant.

I bequethe unto my sonne And heir my signette.

Yeven the Daie and yere A bove specified.[122]

Probate was granted to the above written testament before the lord at Lambeth on 1 July 1499 on the oath of Anne, relict, & George Assheby executors &c, And approved and favoured &c. And administration was committed to the said executors to well & faithfully and with unanimous consent &c. And to exhibit a full & faithful inventory &c before the feast of St Bartholomew the apostle next [24 August], and indeed [to render] a plain & true account &c. They were sworn on the Holy Gospel. Power being reserved of making a similar grant to Richard Blounte and James Edelyn, also executors, when they come &c.

176. Thomas Hammond   reference: 2AR96r
will: 27 July 1499   probate: 18 October 1499

In the name of God, Amen. On 27 July 1499, I Thomas Hamond of Rykmersworth, of sound mind & whole memory, make my testament in this manner.

First I bequeath my soul to Almighty God, the Blessed Mary & all the saints; & my body to be buried in the churchyard of the Blessed Mary of Rykmersworth next to my parents.

To the high altar of the said church for tithes forgotten & not performed one sheep; to the reparation of the church of Rykmersworth another sheep; to the light of St Katherine 4d; to each light in the said church 1d; to the mother church, that is, to the shrine of St Alban 4d.

The residue of all my goods I give & bequeath to Isabel my wife & to John Hamond my son, whom I ordain and constitute my executors of this my last will, that they dispose the said goods as seems best to them to please God & for the health of my soul.

I constitute William Welles of Isnamstede supervisor of this my will, that he may oversee that my aforesaid executors perform this my will in all things as aforesaid.

Given at Rykmersworth aforesaid, the year and day of the month above written.

These witnesses: Thomas Coton, vicar of Ryk', Thomas Warde, William Belche and others.

This present testament was approved and favoured by master Richard Runham, archdeacon, on 18 October in the year above said [1499]; & administration of the goods was committed by him to the executors named above in the testament.

---

[122] The registered will is undated; no witnesses are named in the registered copy.

177. John Blakwell   reference: 2AR97v
will: 2 March 1499/1500   **probate: 29 March 1500**

In the name of God, Amen. On 2 March 1499/1500, I John Blakwell of Rikm[er]sworth, of sound mind & whole memory, make my testament in this manner.

First I bequeath my soul to Almighty God, the Blessed Mary & all the saints; & my body to be buried in the churchyard of the Blessed Mary of Rikm[er]sworth aforesaid.

To the high altar of the aforesaid church for tithes forgotten & not done 8d; to the reparation of Rikm[er]sworth church 3s 4d; to each of the lights in the said church 4d; to Thomas Warde, holy water clerk, 4d.

To Margaret Whetman & Emma Osberne, my kinswomen, to each of them a sheep. To the reparation of the mother church 4d.

The residue of my goods I give & bequeath to Lettice my wife, Thomas Botervile & George Osberne, whom I ordain & make my executors of this my last will, that they dispose the said goods, not bequeathed, as seems best to them to please God & for the health of my soul.

Given at Rikm[er]sworth aforesaid in the year, day & month above written.

These being witnesses: Thomas Coton, vicar, Thomas Warde, Edward Gybbis & others.

This testament was proved by master Richard Runham, archdeacon, on 29 March 1500; & administration &c was committed to Lettice and George, executors named in the testament; they were sworn in form of law & admitted; Thomas Botervile expressly refusing to take up the burden of executing this testament.

178. Simon Rolfe   reference: 2AR100r
will: 20 July 1500   **probate: 5 December 1500**

In the name of God, Amen. On 20 July 1500, I Simon Rolfe of Rikm[er]sworth, of sound mind & good memory, make my testament in this manner.

First I bequeath my soul to Almighty God, the Blessed Mary & all the saints, and my body to be buried in the churchyard of the Blessed Mary of Rikm[er]sworth next to my parents.

To the high altar of the aforesaid church for tithes negligently paid one cloth; to the light of St Katherine 4d; to the reparation of the church 20d.

To Amice Roter one lamb.

To the mother church 4d.

The residue of my goods I give & bequeath to Lettice my wife & John Rolfe my son, whom I ordain & constitute my executors of this my last will, that they may dispose of the said goods and may seem best to them to please God & profit the health of my soul.

Given at Rikm[er]sworth aforesaid on the year and day of the month above written.

These being witnesses: Thomas Randolf, Edward Gybbis, John Gardyner & others.

This testament was proved on 5 December in the year above said [1500]; by the said master archdeacon &c; & administration &c was committed to the executors named in the same & it was accepted by them.

179. William Fylpott   reference: 2AR100r
will: 12 November 1500 [English]   probate: 5 December 1500

In the name of god Amen. In the yere of our lord 1500 the 12th day of the moneth of Novembr', I William Fylpott of Rikm[er]sworth, hole of mynde & of good remembraunce, make thus my last will & testament.

First I bequeth my soule to god, to our blessid lady and to all the holy sanctes that are in hevyn; and my body tobe buried in the chirchyard of Rikm[er]sworth.

Secondarily I bequeth unto the high wtir [*i.e.* altar] of the said chirch 4d; to the Monastery of Saint Albons my moder chirch 4d.

The Residue of my goodes I woll that Kateryn my wyfe have to pay my dettes and to dispose theim to the pleasur of god and to the moost welth of my soule, which Kateryn I ordeyn & make myn executrice of this my last will.

Yoven at Rikm[er]sworth aforesaid the yere of our lord and the day of the moneth above written.

These being witnesse: John Fox, William Colier, William Calley & diverse other.

This testament was proved on 5 December in the year above said [1500] before the said master archdeacon &c; & administration &c was committed to the executors named in the same, sworn in form of law, & it was accepted by them.

180. Richard Wynkfeld   reference: 2AR100r
will: 26 January 1501/2   probate: 14 February 1501/2

In the name of God, Amen. On 26 January 1501/2 I Richard Wynkfeld of Rikm[er]sworth, of sound mind & whole memory, make my testament in this manner.

First I bequeath my soul to Almighty God, the Blessed Mary & all the saints; & my body to be buried in the churchyard of the Blessed Mary of Rikm[er]sworth, next to my parents.

To the high altar of the said church for tithes forgotten & not done 4d; to the light of the crucifix in the said church one sheep; to the lights of St Edmund & St Katherine of the same church another sheep; to the mother church, that is, to the shrine of St Alban, 2d.

The residue of all my goods I give & bequeath to Isabel Wynkfeld my wife & to Thomas Wyknfeld my brother, whom I ordain & constitute my executors of this my last will so that they dispose my goods unbequeathed as seems best to them to please God & for the health of my soul.

Given at Rikm[er]sworth aforesaid, in the year and day of the month above written. These being witnesses: Thomas Coton, vicar, Richard Tredeway, Thomas Warde, Edward Belche & others.

This testament was proved on 14 February 1501/2 before Master John Dowman, doctor of laws, official of the exempt jurisdiction of the monastery of St Alban, and commissary general for the same; & administration &c was committed to the executors named in the same &c; & they were released &c.

181. John Stokker   reference: 2AR106r
will: 6 February 1501/2 [English]   probate: 15 March 1501/2

In the name of our lord god Amen. In the yere of our lord 1501/2 the 6 day of the moneth of February, I John Stokker of Rikm[er]sworth, hole of mynde and of good remembraunce, make my Wyll and testament in this maner of Wyse.

First I bequeth my soule to almyghty god, to our blessid lady and to all the blessid sainctes in hevyn; and my body tobe buryed within the Chirchyard of our lady of Rikm[er]sworth besyde my frendes that ar partid to the mercy of god.

To the high awter of the said Chirch of Rikm[er]sworth for tithes forgotten and negligently at summe tymes doon 16d; to the reparacion of the said chirche 20d; I will that every ~~chirch~~ light within the said chirch have to the perfourmyng of it 4d; to the light of the Holy Trinite kept in the same chirch a cowe which I lately bought of William Stokke.

Also I will that myn Executours as shortly as they conveniently may beye a good & a sufficient masse boke well written & well notyd aftir the discretion of the vicar of Rikm[er]sworth and other such as can skill of such thynges and the boke to remayne to the parissh of Rikmersworth for ever; to the reparacion of the Chapell of our lady of Iland 4d.

To the reparacions of the parissh chirches of Sarett, of Herfeld and of Ryslepe to eche of them 20d; to the monastery of Saint Albon my moder chirch 8d.

I will that Herry Philip Clement my servaunt[123] and Alice Senton eche of them have a shepe. I will that everich of my godchildren have a shepe.

The residue of my goods I geve & bequeth to Johan my wyfe and Richard Carter whom I make mine Executours of this my last will so that they dispose the said goodes to the pleasure of god and to the helth of my soule as they will answere afore god at the day of dome.

Yoven at Rikm[er]sworth the yere of our lord & the day of the moneth above Written.

These beryng witnesse: Thomas Coton vicar, William Stokke, John Grocer, John Hudson & diverse other.

This testament was proved on 15 March in the year above said [1501/2] before Master John Dowman &c & administration was committed &c to the executors named in the same testament &c.

182. John Rugmere   reference: 2AR105v
administration: 15 February 1501/2

On 15 February in the year abovesaid [1501/2], Master, official & commissary above written, [John Dowman][124] granted administration of the goods of John Rugmere, who died intestate, while he lived of Rikm[er]sworth, to Cecily, relict of the same John &c.

183. William Copshrew   reference: 2AR106v
will: 6 April 1502 [English]   probate: 9 May 1502

In the name of our lord Amen. In the yere of our lord god 1502 the 6th day of the moneth of Aprill, I William Cropshrew of Rykm[er]sworth, hole of mynde ~~of g~~ and of good remembraunce make my wille and testament in this maner.

First I bequeth my soule to almyghty god, to our blessid lady and to all theire senctes; and my body tobe buryed within the Chapell of our lady of Ilond beyng within the Chirchyard of the parissh chirche of Rykm[er]sworth.

To the high awter of the said chirch for tithes forgoten & not well payde 3s 4d.

I will that Robert Copshrew my fadere have ayen all such goodes and Catalles as ar his own such as be now in my kepyng without interruption of any body; my said Fader shall have half my crop that is now growing on the grownd of every maner of greyne.

---

[123] 'servant', singular, but this may be three men or boys.

[124] Named in the preceding record of a grant of administration.

The residue of my goodes I geve & bequeth to Robert Copshrew my fader, to Johan my wyf, to Richard Penner and to Stephyn Randolf, whom I make myn executours of this my testament and last wyll, so that they dispose the said goodes as it shalbe seen to them to the pleasur of god & moost helth to my soule.

Yeven at Rikm[er]sworth aforesaid the yere of our lord & the day of the moneth afore written.

These beryng witnesse: Thomas Coton vicar, Thomas Warde, Thomas Randolf & other.

This testament was proved on 9 May in the year aforesaid [1502] before Master John Dowman, commissary; & administration &c was committed to Robert, Johan & Richard &c; power being reserved to Stephen Randolf when he shall come &c.

184. Thomas Gray   reference: 2AR111r
will: 8 November 1502 [English] probate: 29 November 1502

In the name of our lord Amen. In the yere of our lord god 1502 the 8 day of the moneth of Novembr', I Thomas Gray of Rikm', hole of mynde & of good remembrance, make my will & testament in this maner of wyse.

First I bequeth my soule to almyghty god, to our blessid lady & to all the saintes in hevyn; & my body to be buried in the chirchyard of Rikm[er]sworth by my frendes. To the high awter of the said chirch for tithes forgoten 12d; to every light within the said chirch 2d; to the Chapell of our lady of Ilond 8d; I bequethe 8 marcs of money to the chirch of Rikm[er]sworth to beye a chales; also to the mothir chirch 4d.

Also I bequethe to John my son £5 of money & to the childe that my wyf goith withall 5 marc' if it lyve. \And if any of them decesse within age I will the survivor shall have his parte/. And if they deye the seid money to be disposed for the wele of my soule & of my frendes.

To John Gray my brodere & to John A dene to ech of theim 3s 4d.

The residue of my goodes I gyf & bequet to Johan my wyf, to John A dene & to John Gray my broder, whom I make myn Executours of this my last will so that they dispose the seid goodes as it shalbe best sene to them to the pleasur of god & to the wele of my soule.

Yoven at Rikm' the day & yere above written.

These being witnes: Thomas Coton vicar, John White, Roger Michel & other.

This testament was proved on the penultimate day of November in the year aforesaid [1502] before Master John Dowman, official, &c, & administration was committed &c to the executors named in the same testament &c.

185. William Stalon   reference: 2AR116r
will: 20 January 1502/3   probate: 9 Feb 1503/4

In the name of God, Amen. On 20 January 1502/3, I William Stalon of
Rikm[er]sworth, of sound mind & whole memory, make my testament in this
manner.

First I bequeath my soul to Almighty God, the Blessed Mary & all the saints; & my
body to be buried in the churchyard of the Blessed Mary of Rikm[er]sworth near
my parents.

To the high altar of the said church for tithes forgotten 2s; to the chapel of the
Blessed Mary *de Insula* 12d; to the reparation of the church of Rikm[er]sworth 6s
8d; to the light of the Crucifix in the said church 8d; to each of the other lights in the
said church 4d; to the reparation of the church of Watford 2s; to the reparation of
the church of Busshey 11s.[125]

To a suitable priest 30s to celebrate for the space of a quarter of a year immediately
after my decease in the church of Rikm[er]sworth for my soul & my parents' [souls].

To each of my sons a cow; to each of my godsons a sheep; to Richard Hamond my
servant 20s; to Ellen Stone a sheep; to Richard Stanborow a lamb.

The residue of my goods I give & bequeath to Agnes Stalon my wife & to Roger
Stalon my brother, whom I ordain & constitute my true executors of this my last
will that they may dispose the said goods as seems best to them to please God & for
the health of my soul.

Given at Rikm[er]sworth aforesaid on the year & day of the month above written.
These being witnesses: Thomas Coton vicar, Robert Malle, Richard Marten &
others.

*This testament was proved on 9 February 1503/4 before Richard Runham,
archdeacon, &c; & administration &c was committed to the executors named in this
testament &c.*

186. John Tredeway   reference: 2AR113r
will: 7 March 1502/3 [English]   probate: 8 April 1503

In the name of god Amen. In the yere of our lord 1502/3 the 7 daye of the moneth
of Marche, I John Tredeway of Rykm[er]sworth, hole in mynde & of good
remembraunce, make my Will and testament in this maner of wyse.

First I bequeth my soule to almyghty god, to our blessid lady & to all the sainctes;
and my body tobe buryed in the Chirchyard of our lady of Rykm[er]sworth.

---

[125] Definitely xj s, i.e 11s, perhaps a mistake for ij s, i.e. 2s.

To the hye awter of the said Chirche for tithes forgoten and at all tymes not done 8d; to every lyghte within the said chirche 4d. I will that by myn Executours ther be bought a good and an honest surples for the vicar of Rikm[er]sworth to doo god service in to the honour of the parissh.

To the parish chirche of Sarett vjs viij d to helpe to bye a masse boke.

I bequethe 3s 4d to the mendyng of the hye waye betwene lynsters & mapill crosse.

To eche of my godchildren a shepe.

To the moder chirch of Saint Albon 4d.

The residue of my goodes not bequethid I geve and bequethe to Alice my wyfe and to Richard Tredeway my broder, whom I make myn Executours of this my last will, so that they dispose the said goodes as shalbe best seen to them to the pleasur of god & most welth to my soule.

Also I will that Richard Weleis be supervisour of this my will so that he see myn Executours fulfille my will in all pointes as it is afore specified.

Yoven at Rikm[er]sworth the yere of our lord & the day of the moneth afore written These beryng witnesse: Thomas Coton vicar, William Preston, Thomas Podyfate, and other.

This testament was proved on 8 April 1503 before Master John Dowman, doctor of laws, official, &c; & administration &c was committed to the executors named in the testament.

187. Thomas Aldewen   reference: 2AR112v
will: 28 March 1503 [English]   probate: 8 April 1503

In the name of our lord god Amen. In the yere of our lord 1503 The 28 day of the moneth of Marche, I Thomas Aldewen of Rikm[er]sworth, hole in mynde and of good remembraunce, make my testament and last will in this maner of wyse.

First I bequethe my soule to almyghty god, to our blessid lady and to all their sainctes; and my body to be buryed in the chirch yard of our lady of Rikm[er]sworth.

I will that Cecily my wyf shall have all my houses & landes, as well freehold as copy, which I have in the parissh of Watford in the hamelett of hey street[126] duryng her lyfe and aftir hir decesse to the next to th heyer of me Thomas Aldewen.

To the said Cecily my wyfe all the stok longyng to my place at Heye strete which John Fysshe hath of me by yndentur. And that the said stoke with every parte therof

---

[126] Perhaps properties were in Watford high street.

be delyverd to my said wyfe in maner & fourme as it shuld have been to my self and as the said Indenturs bere wittnesse.

All my other goodes I gyf & bequeth to my said wyfe whom I make myn Executrice of this my last Wille, so that she dispose my said goodes as shalbe best sene to her to the pleasur of god & moost helth to my soule.

Yoven at Rikm[er]sworth the yere of our lord & the day of the moneth above written.

These bering witnes: Thomas Coton vicar of Rikm[er]sworth, Thomas Warde, William Preston & diverse other.

This testament was proved on 8 April 1503 before Master John Dowman, doctor of laws, official, &c, & administration &c was committed to the executors &c.

188. William Sebyn[127] reference: 2AR117v
will: 1 March 1503/4 [English] probate: 13 April 1504

In the name of god Amen. The yere of our lord 1503/4 the first day of the moneth of Marche, I William Sebyn of Rikm[er]sworth, hole of mynde & of good remembrance, make my testament and last will in this maner of wyse.

First I bequethe my soule to almyghty god, to our lady & to all the holy company of hevyn; & my body to be buried within the chirche of Rikm[er]sworth in the myddyst Aley before the Rode.

To the high awter of the said chirche for tithes forgoten 6s 8d; to the Rode light 12d; to every other light within the said chirche 12d; to the Chirche of Rikm[er]sworth a Antifoner as good as can be conveniently bought; to the Reparacion of the chapel of our lady of Ilond 12d.

I will that an honest preest shall have 23s 4d which Maister Brudenell[128] owith me to syng for my soule & all christen sowles within the chirche of Rikm[er]sworth by the space of a quarter of a yere.

To the moder chirche 3s 4d; to the high weys making 20s.

To every god child I have 4d; to William Brewed my servaunt 5 marc'; to Richard Carter & John Adene to either of them 6s 8d.

The residue of my goodes unbequthid I put in the discretion of Johan Sebyn my wyfe, of Richard Carter & of John A dene, whom I make myn Executours of this my

---

[127] One of the witnesses to the will of Stephen Holtyng (no. 166, made in 1495). At that time Sebyn stated that he was 40 years old; so he was about 48 when he made his will.

[128] Not identified; perhaps a member of the Brudenell family who lived in Chalfont St Peter. (*VCH Bucks*, vol. 3, pp.193-198)

will, so that they see the said goodes disposed as it shalbe best seen to theim to the pleasur of god & to the welth of my soule.

Written at Rikm[er]sworth in the yere of our lord & the day of the moneth above written.

These beryng witnesse: Edward Metcalfe, Robert Pereson, William Eliott & other.

This testament was proved on 13 April 1504 before us, Richard Runham, archdeacon, &c; & administration &c was committed to the executors named in the same, sworn in due form.

189. Thomas Randolf   reference: 2AR120r
will: 3 August 1504   probate: 1 September 1504

In the name of God, Amen. On 3 August 1504, I Thomas Randolf of Rikm[er]sworth, of sound mind & whole memory, make my testament in this manner.

First I bequeath my soul to Almighty God, the Blessed Mary & all the saints; & my body to be buried in the churchyard of the Blessed Mary of Rikm[er]sworth near my parents.

To the high altar of the said church for tithes forgotten 8d; to the light of the Holy Cross in the said church two sheep; to each other light in the aforesaid church 4d; to the chapel of St Mary *de Insula* 6d; to the mother church 8d.

To Hugh Randolf my son two quarters of wheat, three sheep & two oxen [*or*, bulls] and one 'hekfar'; to William Randolf my son two quarters of wheat & three sheep & one 'hekfar'; to Agnes my daughter half a quarter of wheat & one sheep; to Stephen Randolf & Edward Gybbys, to each of them 40d.

The residue of my goods I give & bequeath to John Randolf my son, Stephen Randolf & Edward Gybbys, whom I ordain & constitute my executors of this my last will, that they dispose the said goods as seems best to them to please God & for the health of my soul.

Given at Rikm' aforesaid, the year & day of the month above written.

These being witnesses: Thomas Warde, Thomas Bryton, Henry Paltok & others.

This testament was proved on 1 September in the year aforesaid [1504], before master Richard Runham, archdeacon, &c; & administration &c was committed to the executors named in the same &c.

190. John Baldewen   reference: 2AR120r
will: 20 August 1504   probate: 1 September 1504
In the name of God, Amen. On 20 August 1504, I John Baldewen of
Rikm[er]sworth, of sound mind & whole memory, make my testament in this
manner.

First I bequeath my soul to Almighty God, the Blessed Mary & all the saints; & my
body to be buried in the churchyard of the Blessed Mary of Rikm[er]sworth, next to
my parents.

To the high altar of the said church for tithes forgotten 4d; to the lights of St
Katherine & St Edmund, to each of them 2d; to the mother church 4d.

To the mending of the roads between my house & the church 12d.

The residue of all my goods I give & bequeath to Joan Baldewen my wife & to John
Baldewen my son, whom I ordain & constitute my executors of this my last will,
that they dispose the said goods as seems best to them to please God & for the health
of my soul.

I will that Roger Michell be supervisor of my will, that he oversee the said executors
perform my will in all things as it is aforesaid.

Given at Rikm[er]sworth aforesaid the year & day of the month above written.

These being witnesses: Thomas Coton vicar, Thomas Ward, John Carter & others.

This testament was proved on 1 September in the year aforesaid [1504], before
master Richard Runham, archdeacon, &c; & administration &c was committed to
the executors named in this testament &c.

191. Johan (Joan) Baldewen, widow[129]   reference: 2AR123r
will: 26 February 1504/5 [English]   probate: 8 March 1504/5
In the name of god, Amen. The yere of our lord god 1504/5, The 26th day of the
moneth of Februarye, I Johan Baldewen of Rikm[er]sworth, widow, hole of mynde
& of good remembraunce, in my pure wedowhode, make my testament & last will
in this maner.

First I bequethe my soule unto almyghty god, to our blessid lady & to all the sanctes
in hevyn; & my body to be buryed within the chirchyard of our lady of
Rikm[er]sworth by my first husbond Thomas Reed.

The duties of the chirch & my dettes content & paid, the residue of my goodes I will
be indifferently divided betwene George Rede my son and Johan Mole my doughter,

---

[129] Perhaps the widow of John (190), but she only mentions her first husband Thomas Reed.
He may have been Thomas Rede (158; died 1492): his wife was named Joan.

whom I ordeyn & make myn Executours of this my last will, so that they dispose the said goodes as it shalbe best sene to theim to the pleasur of god & to the helthe of my soule.

Yoven at Rykm[er]sworth in the yere of our lord & the day of the moneth abovewritten.

These beryng witnes: Thomas Coton vicar of Rikm[er]sworth, Thomas Warde parish Clerk of the seid town, Richard Carter & other.

This testament was proved on 8 March in the year above said [1504/5], before the Reverend in Christ prior & lord, Master Thomas [the] Abbot [Thomas Ramryge], &c; & administration was committed &c to the executors named in the same &c.

192. John Lyghthasill   reference: 2AR124v
will: 5 May 1505   probate: 12 May 1505

In the name of God, Amen. On 5 May 1505, I John Lyghthasill of Rikm[er]sworth, of sound mind & whole memory, make my testament in this manner.

First I bequeath my soul to Almighty God, the Blessed Mary & all the saints; & my body to be buried in the churchyard of the Blessed Mary of Rikm[er]sworth.

To the high altar of the said church for tithes forgotten 12d; to the mother church 4d.

The residue of all my goods I give & bequeath to Joan Lyghthasill my wife, John & Cuthbert Lyghthasill my sons, whom I ordain & constitute my executors of this my last will, that they may settle my debts & dispose the said goods as seems best to them to please God & to profit the health of my soul, as they would wish to answer for before the High Judge on the day of judgement.

Given at Rikm[er]sworth aforesaid the year & day of the month above written.

These being witnesses: Thomas Coton vicar, John White, Robert Over & others.

This testament was proved on 12 May in the year aforesaid [1505], before Master John Stonywell, professor of sacred theology, archdeacon, &c, & administration was committed &c to the executors named in the same &c.

193. Mawde (Maud) Bullok, widow[130]   reference: 2AR130v
will: 4 March 1505/6 [English]   probate: 15 October 1506

In the name of our lord god, Amen. In the yere of our lord 1505/6, the 4th day of the moneth of March, I Mawde Bullok of Rikm[er]sworth Widowe, in my pure

---

[130] See the Introduction, pp. xliv–xlv a brief discussion of a letter sent by the pope to three bishops in London regarding an alleged defamation by Maud and two of her relatives.

Widowhode, hole of mynde & of good remembraunce, make my testament & last Wyll in this maner of Wyse.

First I bequeth my soule to almyghty god, to our blessid lady & to all ther sainctes; and my body to be buryed within the chirch of our lady in Rikm[er]worth aforesaid. To the high auter of the said chirch for tithes forgoten 3s 4d; to every light within the said chirch 8d.

Also I bequethe to Johanne london my servaunt a Matres with a bolster, a pair of shetes, a pair of blankettes, a keverlyte, a stayned cloth with Jhesus for a testour, a brasse pott of two galons, a brasse panne of six galons.

The residue of my goodes, my dettes payde, I yeve & bequeath to William Yong my godson, Whom I ordeyn & make myn Executour of this my last Wyll and that the said William dispose the said goodes as shalbe best seme to hym to the pleasur of god & to the helth of my soule.

Yoven at Rikm[er]sworth aforesaid in the yere of our lord & day of the moneth above Written.

Theyse beryng Witnesse: M[aster] Thomas Coton vicar of Rikm[er]sworth, John A Dene Bayly, Edward Metcaf, Thomas Seybene, William Calley & diverse other.

This testament was approved on 15 October 1506 by master John Albon, archdeacon, &c; & administration was committed &c to the executors named in the same &c.

194. John Frere reference: 2AR129r
will: 30 June 1506 [English] probate: 4 July 1506

In the name of God, Amen. In the yere of our lord god 1506 The last day of the moneth of Juyn, I John Frere of Rikm[er]sworth, hole of mynde & of good remembraunce, make my testament & last wille in this maner wyse.

First I bequeth my soule to almyghty god, to our blessid lady saint Mary & to all the saints in hevyn; And my body to be buried within the chirchyard of our lady Rikm[er]sworth besyde my children.

To the high awter of the said chirch of Rikm[er]sworth for tithes forgoten 16d; to the Rode lighte there 4d; and to every other lyght in the said chirch 2d; to the Monastery of Saint Albon as my moder chirch 4d.

I bequeth toward the makyng of a new vestyary in Rikm[er]sworth 7s.

To fyve of my broder William children, to eche of theim 12d; to eche of my broder Thomas Children other 12d; to every of my Godchildren 4d; to every of Richard Randolfes children 4d; to Thomas Frere my son & to William his broder to either of theim £5 of money.

The residue of my goods I geve & bequethe to Elisabeth Frere my wyfe & to Thomas my son, whom I make myn Executours of this my last will, so that they dispose the seid goodes as it shalbe best seen to theim to the pleasur of god & to the welle of my soule.

Also I will that Thomas Frere my broder, Walter Barre myn unkle, John Adene & Richard Carter ben supervisours of this my Will, so that they supervide that my said Executours fulfille my Will in every thyng as it is afore specified.

Yoven at Rikm[er]sworth the day & yere afore rehersid.

These beryng Witnes: sir Thomas Coton vicar, Thomas Warde, William Elyott and other

This testament was proved on 4 July in the year aforesaid [1506], by master John Killyngworth, archdeacon, &c; & administration was committed &c to the executors named in the same testament &c.

195. Roger Michaell   reference: 2AR132r
will: 7 February 1506/7   probate: 27 March 1507

In the name of God, Amen. On 7 February 1506/7, I Roger Michaell of Rikm[er]sworth, of sound mind & healthy memory, make my testament in this manner.

First I bequeath my soul to Almighty God, the Blessed Mary & all the saints; & my body to be buried in the churchyard of the Blessed Mary of Rikm[er]sworth.

To the high altar of the said church for tithes forgotten & not done 8d; to each light in the said church 2d; to the mother church 4d.

The residue of all my goods I give & bequeath to Joan Mychaell my wife, John Mylward & Thomas Hamond, whom I ordain & constitute my executors of this my last will, that they dispose of the said goods as seems best to them to please God.

Given at Rikm[er]sworth aforesaid on the year & day of the month above written.

These witnesses: William Elyott, John Gray, Thomas Warde & others.

This testament was proved on 27 March 1507 before master John Albon, archdeacon, &c; & administration was committed &c to the executors named in the same &c.

196. William Stokke   reference: 2AR132r
will: 27 February 1506/7   probate: 27 March 1507

In the name of God, Amen. On the penultimate day of February 1506/7, I William Stokke of Rykm[er]sworth, of sound mind & whole memory, make my testament in this manner.

First I bequeath my soul to Almighty God, the Blessed Mary & all the saints; & my body to be buried in the churchyard of the Blessed Mary of Rikm[er]sworth.

To the high altar of the said church for tithes forgotten 4d; to each light in the aforesaid church 2d; to the mother church 4d.

The residue of my goods I give & bequeath to Margaret Stokke my wife, Thomas Mylsham & Richard Fodirley, whom I ordain & constitute my executors of this my last will, that they may dispose of the said goods as seems best to them to please God & for the health of my soul.

Given at Rikm[er]sworth aforesaid on the year & day of the month above written. These witnesses: Thomas Warde, William Calley & others.

This testament was proved on 27 March 1507 before master John Albon, archdeacon, &c; & administration was committed &c to the executors named in the same &c.

197. Edward Metcalfe   reference: 2AR132v
will: 12 March 1506/7 [English]   probate: 27 March 1507

In the name of God, Amen. In the yere of our lord 1506/7, the 12th day of the moneth of March, I Edward Metcalfe of Rikm[er]sworth, hole of mynde & of good remembraunce, make my last Will & testament in this maner.

First I bequeth my soule to almyghty god, to our blessid lady saint Mary & to all the holy company of heven; & my body to be buryed within the parissh chirch of Rikm[er]sworth, before the Image of saint Christofer.

To the high awter of the said Chirch for forgotten tithes 20d; to every lyght within the said Chirch 4d; toward the makyng of a new store house in the same chirche 6s 8d.

I will that an honest preest shall syng for my soule & for all cristen soules in the chirche of Rikm[er]sworth by the space of a quarter of a yere as hastely after my decesse as it convenyently may be doon; and the said preest to have for his labour as right requireth.

To the reparacion of the Chapell of our lady of llond 8d; to the moder chirche 4d; to the mendyng the high ways about Rikm[er]sworth where moost nede requireth 3s 4d.

To Thomas Lamvale my cosyn my best gown & my best dowblett; to John A dene 6s 8d; to Cecily my doughter in law a bed with all thynges apperteynyng unto the same, a brasse pot & six peces of pewter.

The residue to of my goodes I yeve & bequeth to Jone Metcalfe my wyfe, to Richard my son, to Thomas Lamvale & to John A dene, whom I make myn executours of this my last Wyll, so that they dispose the said goodes as will best seen unto theim to the pleasur of god & to the helth of my soule.

Yoven at Rikm[er]sworth the yere of our lord god & day of the moneth above written.

These beryng witnesse: Thomas Warde, Robert Person, Thomas Hamond, John Grocer & divers others

This testament was proved on 27 March 1507 before master John Albon, archdeacon, &c; & administration &c was committed &c to Joan, relict and executrix named in the same testament; John A Dene at present wholly refusing to take on the burden of execution; power being reserved to the other executors when they come.

198. William Elyot   reference: 2AR132v
will: 19 April 1507   probate: 22 April 1507

In the name of God, Amen. On 19 April 1507, I William Elyot of Rikm[er]sworth, of sound mind & healthy memory, make my testament in this manner.

First I bequeath my soul to Almighty God, the Blessed Mary & all the saints; & my body to be buried in the churchyard of the Blessed Mary of Rikm[er]sworth.

To the high altar of the said church for tithes forgotten 4d; to each of the lights of the said church 1d; to the mother church 4d.

The residue of my goods I give & bequeath to Joan Eliott my wife & Walter Barre, whom I ordain & constitute my executors of this my last will, that they may dispose the said goods as seems best to them to please God & for the health of my soul.

Given at Rikm[er]sworth aforesaid on the year & day of the month above written.

These being witnesses: Thomas Coton vicar, John A dene, Robert Rollis, Richard Fodirley, John A Dale & others.

This testament was proved 22 April 1507 before master John Albon, archdeacon, &c; & administration was committed &c to the executors named in the same testament &c.

199. Richard Randolf   reference: 2AR133r
administration: 19 June 1507

On 19 June 1507 administration of the goods of Richard Randolf of Rikm[er]sworth, dying intestate, was granted by master John Albon, archdeacon, to Margaret Randolf, relict of the same Richard.

200. John Badcok   reference: 2AR133v
administration: 17 July 1507
On 17 July in the year aforesaid [1507] administration of the goods of John Badcok of Rikm[er]sworth, dying intestate, was committed to Joan, relict of the same John.

201. John Besowthe   reference: 2AR137v
administration: 27 April 1508
On 27 April in the year aforesaid [1508] was committed by us, John Albon, archdeacon &c, administration of the goods of John Besowthe of Rikm', dying intestate, to Alice his relict.

202. John Gybbys   reference: 2AR142r
will: 16 December 1509   probate: 24 January 1509/10
In the name of God, Amen. On 16 December 1509, I John Gybbys of Rykm[er]sworth, of sound mind & whole memory, make my testament in this manner.
First I bequeath my soul to Almighty God, the blessed Mary, and all the saints; and my body to be buried in the churchyard of the Blessed Mary of Rikm[er]sworth next to my parents.
To the high altar of the said church for tithes forgotten & negligently done 12d; to each of the lights in the said church 4d; to the construction of the new vestry [*fabrice novi vestiarij*] in the said church 3s 4d; to the mother church, the monastery of Saint Alban, 6d.
To Cecily & Joan Gybbys my kinswomen, to each of them six sheep; to William Gybbys my son 20 sheep, five quarters of wheat and five quarters of oats.
The residue of my goods I give and bequeath to Joan Gybbys my wife and John Gybbys my son, whom I ordain and constitute my executors of this my last will, that they may dispose of the said goods as seems best to them to please God & for the health of my soul, as they would answer for on the day of Judgement.
Given at Rikm[er]sworth aforesaid on the year & day of the month above written.
These witnesses: John A Dene, Richard Carter, Richard Foderley, Richard Tylson and others
This present testament was approved on 14 January in the year aforesaid [1509/10], by master John Maynard, archdeacon, &c; & administration &c was committed to the executors named in the same, &c.

203. John Durrant alias Estbury, husbandman[131]

reference: 2AR142v

will: 10 March 1510/11   probate: 4 May 1511

In the name of God, Amen. On 10 March 1510/11, I John Durrant, otherwise called John Estbury, of Rykm[er]sworth in the county of Hertford, 'husbandman', being of sound mind & good memory, make my testament in this manner.

First I give and bequeath my soul to Almighty God, the Blessed Mary his mother, and all the saints; and my body to be buried in the churchyard of the Blessed Mary of Rikm[er]sworth next to my parents.

To the rector of the said church for tithes forgotten 20d; to the building [*edificationi*] of the said church being done in this year 6s 8d, which the wardens of the said church will receive from Margaret Stoke.

To the light of the Trinity of the said church 4d; to the light of St Mary the mother of our Lord Jesus Christ 4d; to the light of St Anthony in the said church 4d; to the light of St Katherine in the said church 4d; to the light of St Mary Magdalene in the same church 4d; to the mother church 4d.

To my wife Agnes all her own goods which she had before the day of the marriage between us was celebrated; to John Durrant my son all his own goods; to John my son 26s 8d and two 3-year-old heifers; to John Alyn my servant one 2-year old heifer.

The residue of all my goods and give & bequeath to Agnes my wife and John Durrant my son that they will order & dispose it for the health of my soul, as seems best to them to do to please God & profit my soul.

And the same Agnes and John I ordain, make & constitute my executors by these presents that they may faithfully execute my present testament and accomplish it effectively.

These witnesses: Roger Gonner, John Danyell, Richard Foderley, Robert Pereson, Henry Edlyn & Nicholas Baker, and others

This present testament was approved on 4 May in the year abovesaid [1511], by master John Maynard, archdeacon, &c; & administration &c was committed to the executors named in this testament, &c.

---

[131] The last Latin will. His alias suggests that he was a tenant of the manor of Eastbury, which lay just in Watford parish. See *VCH Herts*, vol. 2, p.463.

204. Jone Stokker, late wife of John   reference: 2AR151v
will: 16 January 1512/13 [English]   probate: 10 February 1512/13

In the name of our lord God, Amen. In the yere of our said lord god 1512/13, the 16 day of the moneth of January, I Jone Stokker, late wyfe unto John Stokker of Rykm[er]sworth, in my pure wedowhode, hole of mynde & of good remembraunce, make my last wyll & testament in this maner wyse folowyng.

First I bequeth my soule unto almyghty God, to our blessid lady saint Mary, & to all ther sayntes; And my body tobe buryed within the chapell of saint Kateryn within the parissh chirch of Rikm[er]sworth.

To the hye awter of Ryk' for tithes forgoten & negligently doon 12d; to the rode lyghte of the said chirch 8d; to the other lyghte[132] within the said chirch of Rikm[er]' 4d; to the reparacion of the chapell of our Lady of Ilond a shepe callid an Ewe; to the Monasterie of Saint Albon my moder chirch 8d.

I will that myn Executours, with thadvyse of the discrete of the parissh, see that the new wyndowe that now is unglasid in saint Kateryn chapell be honestly glasid as hastely as it may be convenyently at my charge.

I will that a crosse of silver by the discretion of myn executours and the sadde of the parissh be bowte to the value of 20 markes and the saide crosse to remayne to the parissh of Rikm[er]sworth for ever.

I will that an honest preest, which can syng in the quer' and also can do such thynges as ar convenient to a discrete preest to doo, be hyred by myn executours & the discrete of the parissh immediatly after my decesse to sing in the parissh chirch of Rikmersworth at the awter of saint Kateryn for my soule & my husbandes & all cristen sowles by the space of two yeres Immediatly sewing. And the said preest to have yerly for his stipend & wages 9 markes.

I will that six shepe to be yeven to six of my godchyldren such as myn executor thynk ther unto have moost need; every other of my godchyldren to have 4d.

To the fynysshyng of the new werk in the chyrch of Rykm[er]sworth 6s 8d.

I wyll that my Cosyn Herry Felippe to have a bollok; to Cecily Bukmaster my servaunt a cowe, a shepe, a matresse, a bolster, a pair of shetes, a blankett, a coverlite, a potte & a pan of brass, a plater & a dissh of pewter. I will George Hamonde have a bullok; to Edward Bukmaster a shepe.

I will that a stone of marbill be bowte by myn executours tobe leyde on my husband John Stokker & me with a knowlage on the same who they ar that ar buryed ther

---

[132] Most likely meaning 'other lights'.

under.[133]

I have made a surrendere into the handes of John a Dene, Bayly to my lord of Saint Albons of his lordship of Rik', of all my landes & tenementes beyng & lyeng in the parissh & lordship of Rikm[er]sworth aforesaid to the use and behoif of John Hede my son in law & of Margarete his wyfe my doughter, they paying for the said tenementes & londes with thappurtenaunces £25 of lawfull mony of England, and the said mony to fulfille this my wyll, and the residue with other my goodes to be disposid for the wele of my sowle, my frendes and all cristen sowles.

The residue of my goodes not bequeathed, I yeve & bequethe to John Hede & Richard Carter, whom I make myn Executours of this my last & hole Wyll so that they dispose my said goodes unbequethid as it shalbe best seen to theim to the pleasure of god & moost helth for my sowle as they will answer afore god at the dredefull day of Jugement. And the said John Hede & Richard Carter either of theim to have for their laboures 6s 8d.

Also I will that the vicar of Rikm[er]sworth & Thomas Creke Esquyre be supervisours of this my wyll, so that they supervide & see that my said Executours fulfill this my wyll in every point as it is aforespecified.

Yoven at Rikm[er]sworth the yere of our lord & day of the moneth afore rehersid. These beryng witnesse: John A dene, Roger Gunner, Robert Rolles, Richard Foderley, Thomas Hamond, John A dale, John Milward, John White & diverse other

This present testament was approved on 10 February in the year abovesaid [1512/13], by master Richard Runham, prior & archdeacon, &c, & administration was committed to the executors named in this testament, sworn in due form &c.

205. John Barbour   reference: 2AR154r
administration: 23 September 1513

On 23 September 1513 Master Archdeacon committed administration of the goods of John Barbour of Rikm[er]sworth, dying intestate, to Agnes, relict of the same John, & to John Long, citizen & 'Salter' of London.

---

[133] Indicating that she had had her husband buried in the place where she also wished to be buried. In his will (181), written in 1502, he had requested burial in the churchyard.

206. Herry Paltok   reference: 2AR155v
will: 14 November 1513 [English]   probate: 18 February 1513/14

In the name of god, Amen. In the yere of our lord god 1513 the 14th day of the moneth of Novembr', I Herry Paltok of the paryssh of Rykm[er]sworth, hole of mynde & in good remembraunce, make my testament & last wyll in this maner wyse.

First I bequethe my soule to almyghty god, to our lady saint Mary & to all their saintes; & my body to be buried within the chirch yard of our lady of Rykm[er]sworth.

Also I bequethe to the high awter of the said chirch for tithes forgoten & negingently doon 4d; to the Monastery of Saint Albon my modir chirche 4d.

To Elyn paltok my doughter a hecfare, a potte & a ketill of brasse, a shete & a towel; to George Paltock my son another hecfare.

The residue of my goodes I geve & bequethe unto Margarete Paltok my wyfe & to Walter Barre, whom I make myn executours of this my last will.

Yoven the yere of our lord & the day of the moneth above written.

Theyse beryng witnesse: M[aster] Thomas Coton vicar, John White, John Randolf & diverse other.

This testament was approved on 18 February in the year abovesaid [1513/14], by master Richard Runham, prior & archdeacon, &c; & administration was committed &c to Margaret, executrix in &c; Walter Barre for the present expressly refusing to take up the burden of executor of the said testament.[134]

207. Walter Barre   reference: 2AR159r
will: 16 November 1513 [English]   probate: 11 December 1514

In the name of god Amen. The yere of our said lord god 1513 the 16th day of the moneth of Novembr', I Walter Barre of Rikm[er]sworth, hole in mynde & of good remembrans make my last wyll & testament in this maner.

First I bequethe my soule to almyghty god, to our blessid lady saint Mary & to all the saintes; & my body to be buried within the chirchyard of our lady of Rikm[er]sworth besyde my frendes.

I bequethe to the hye awter of the said chirch for tithes forgotten & negligently doon 2s; to the rode lyghte 12d & to every other lyghte within the said chirch of Rikm[er]sworth 4d; to the reparacion of the said chirch 2s; to the reparacion of our lady chapell of Ilond 8d; to the Monastery of Saint Albon my moder chirch 8d.

---

[134] Perhaps Barre was ill, as he made his own will just two days after Herry Paltok.

To Margarete my doughter six sponys of silver, my secunde brasse potte, a federbed & a bolster; to Robert Palmer a gown; to Thomas Gray half a dekyr of over lethir;[135] to Johan Osbern two candelstykes, two platers, two disshes, two sawcers of peauter & a pan.

The residue of my goodes I geve & bequethe unto Kateryn Barre my wyfe, whom I make myn Executrice, to dispose the said goodes as it shalbe best sene to her to the pleasur of god & to the wele of my sowle.

These beryng Witnesse: M[aster] Thomas Coton vicar, John A Dene, Nicholas Sothewyk, John Clerk and other.

Yoven at Rikm[er]sworth aforesaid the yere of our lord & day of the moneth above specified.

This testament was approved by the venerable Master William Throkmarton, doctor of laws, official, &c on 11 December 1514 &c; & administration was committed to the executrix named in the same &c.

208. John Belche   reference: 2AR155v
administration: 16 February 1513/14
On 16 February 1513/14 Master Richard Runham, prior & archdeacon of the monastery, committed administration of the goods of John Belche of Rikm[er]sworth, dying intestate, to John Braunche of Rikm[er]sworth, he being sworn in form of law &c.

209. Anne Asshby, widow[136]   reference: 2AR159r
will: 21 October 1514 [English]   **probate: 1 March 1514/15**
In the name of god Amen. The yere of our said lord god 1514 the 21st day of the

---

[135] Suggesting that Walter Barre was a tanner, and also Thomas Gray.

[136] Her husband John's probate documents are no. 175a and 175b. In the early seventeenth century John Weever saw her monument in the church, although the inscription that he recorded is something of a mystery. He says that at Rickmansworth 'In the chappell or buriall place of the ancestors of the *Ashbeys* now living, this Inscription. Here lieth *Anne Ashby* wyf of *Iohn Ashby* of Herfeld Esqwyre dawghter of Thomas Peyton of Iselham[*sic*] Esqwyre; who dyed 22. Oct. 1503. On whose sowl Iesu have mercy. Amen.' Anne's will was granted probate in March 1515. Although the Peyton family was prominent in Isleham (Cambs), the *VCH Cambs* (vol. 10, 'Isleham manors', pp.427-437) does not record anyone named Thomas Peyton dying in 1503. So the date does not refer to her father, nor to her husband, who had died in 1499. (J. Weever, *Ancient funerall monuments within the united monarchie of Great Britaine, Ireland, and the islands adiacent* (London, 1631), p.590)

moneth of Octobr', I Anne Asshby of Rykm[er]sworth widow, in my pure wedewhode, sikke in body but hole in mynde & of good remembraunce, make my last wyll & testament in maner folowyng.

First I bequethe my soule to almyghty god, to our blessid lady saint Marye & to all the saintes that ar in hevyn; And my body tobe buryed within the parissh chirch of Rykm[er]sworth afore the ymage of saint Kateryn in the new Ile of the said chirch. To the high awter of the said chirch of Rikm[er]sworth for tithes & oblacions forgotten & negligently doon 3s 4d; to the rode lyght & to the lyghte of saint Kateryn within the said chirch to eyther of theim 3s 4d; to every other lyghte within the said chirch 8d; to the reparacion of the chapell of our lady of Ilond 6s 8d.

I will that be myn executour be bought a pyx of silver & gylt for the sacrament to be put there in to the valew of £5 & to remayne to the chirch of Rykm[er]sworth; also a paire of cruetes of silver to the valew of 40s & to remayne also to the said chirch.

To every of my godchyldren 4d; to Robert Catour my chylde whom I have brought up of my charyte 20s to bynde hym prentyse withall.

To the vicar of Rykm[er]sworth my beedes of white ambre gawdid with silver & gilt & corall.

To Emme A dene a cofer wherein is seven paire of shetes with such tabull clothes & toweles as are within the same cofer, also a silver salte with a cover, a goblett of silver & four silver sponys of the secund sorte; to my son George Ashby a stondyng cuppe of silver & gylt with a cover; to William Ashby my son my best salte, a silver pece with a cover & six silver sponys of the best sorte; to Anne, doughter to my said son William, two sylver sponys; to Anne A dene my doughter my gylte Salt, a goblett of silver with a cover, a pece of silver & six sponys of the best sorte; to Jone & Anne, doughters to my said doughter Anne, to either of theim two silver sponys; to Anne daughter, to my son George, a pece of silver without a cover.

And I make George Ashby my son my sole executour, to whom I commytte the disposicion of the residue of all my goodes & cattalles after his discretion for the welth of my soule.

Yoven at Rykm[er]sworth the day & yere aforesaid

These beryng witnesse: M[aster] Thomas Coton vicar, John A dale, John Clerke & other.

And written with the hand of the said vicar of Ryk'.

This testament was approved on 1 March in the year aforesaid [1514/15], by the venerable Master William Throgmarton, doctor of laws, official, &c, & administration &c was committed to the executor named in this testament &c.

210. William Rydyng reference: 2AR161v
administration: 11 January 1515/16
On 11 January 1515/16 administration of the goods of William Rydyng of
Rykm[er]sworth, dying intestate, was committed to John Horne of Rykm[er]sworth
aforesaid, he having been sworn on the Holy Gospel &c.

211. Keteryne Barre, widow reference: 2AR163r
will: 17 July 1516 [English] probate: 9 August 1516
In the name of god, Amen. In the yere of our said lord god 1516, the 17th day of the
moneth of July, I Keteryne Barre of Rikm[er]sworth, Wedow,[137] in my pure
Wedowhode, hole in mynde & of good remembraunce, make my last will &
testament in this maner wyse folowing.
First I bequethe my soule to almyghty god, to our lady saint Mary & to all the
sainctes; my body tobe buried within the chirch yard of our lady of Rykm[er]sworth
beside my husband.
I bequethe to the high awter of the said chirch for tithes & offerynges forgoten 8d; to
every lighte within the said chirch 2d.
I wyll that John Gray my son[138] be myn Executour to pay my dettes & to dispose the
residue of my goodes to the pleasur of god & to the welth of my soule.
These beryng witnes: M[aster] Thomas Coton vicar, John White parissh clerk &
diverse other.
yoven the day & yere above rehersed.
*This testament was proved on the oath of the aforesaid vicar and parish clerk & of
the executor before Master John Incent, doctor of laws, official; & approved by him
&c on 9 August in the year aforesaid [1516]; & administration was committed &c to
the executor named in this testament &c.*

212: John Gray reference: 2AR148r & 164r[139]
will: 28 October 1517 [English] probate: 28 November 1517
In the name of our lord god, Amen. In the yere of our said lord god 1517 the 28th
day of the moneth of Octobr', I John Gray of Rykm[er]sworth, hole in mynde & of
good remembraunce, make my testament & last will in this maner.

---

[137] Her husband's will is no. 207.

[138] Most likely her son by an earlier marriage; perhaps the same John Gray as no. 212.

[139] The wills on folio 148r are out of chronological sequence. This will is repeated exactly on
fol. 164r, with the same probate date, so that version has not been included separately.

First I bequethe my souile to almyghty god, to our lady saint Mary & to all their sainctes; And my body tobe buried in the chirchyard of our lady in Rikm[er]sworth bysdye my frendes.

I bequethe to the high awter of the said chirch for tithes forgoten & negligently doon 12d; to every lyght within the said chirch 2d; to my moder chirch of saint Albans 2d.

To eche of my chylder a pair of shetes.

The residue of my goodes I geve & bequethe to Anne Gray my wyff, whom I make myn Executrice of this my last wylle & to dispose the said goodes to the pleasur of god & to the welth of my soule as it shalbe best seme her to doo.

Yoven at Rikm[er]sworth the yere of our lord & the day of the moneth above written.

Also I will that John A Dale be supervisour of this my wyll, to supervide that my said Executrice fulfill my wyll in every thyng as it is afore specified.

These beryng witnesse sir Herry Taylour preest, John White parissh clerk, William Grocer & other.

This testament was approved on 28 November in the year above written [1517], by us, Thomas Kyngesbury, bachelor of sacred theology & laws &c, archdeacon, &c; & administration was committed &c to the executrix.

213. Robert Goldhurst, husbandman   reference: 2AR166r
will: 10 April 1518 [English]   probate: 7 May 1518

In dei nomine, Amen. the 10th day of the moneth of Aprill the 9th yere of the reign of Kyng Henry VIII, in the yere of our lord god 1518, I Robert Goldhurst of Rikm[er]sworth in the countie of Hertf', husbondman, hole in mynde, order & make my last wyll in maner & fourme folowing.

First I bequethe my soule to almyghty god & to our lady saint Mary & to all the holy company of heven; And my body tobe buryed in the chirchyard of Rykm[er]sworth.

I bequethe to the high awter of Rikm[er]sworth for my tythes & oblacions forgoten 3s 4d; to saint Albans shrine 6d; to the parissh church of Stanmer the more (Great Stanmore, Middx) to the high awter 10s; to the Churchwardens of the same town for the behoif of the hole paryssh 3s 4d; to the high awter of Busshey 12d.

I will that Henry my son shalhave my new lease purchased of the Monastery of Saint Alban when tyme comyth to his own behoif duryng his lyff, And after his decesse to remayne to the next of his kyn duryng the said lease as the Indenturs doth appere. Ad[sic] to this I wold that William Baldwen shuld kepe my lease to the behoif of my chylde. I wold that Maryon my wyff shuld occupy my ferme duryng my old lease to her moost awauntage. I wold that Henry my son shold yeve unto his broder Thomas 20s of money, to be paide to the said Thomas the third yere after the entryng of his lease. I bequethe to the residue of my children eche of theim 20s, Which that I wold my son Henry shuld content & truely pay to theim at their full, beyng 21 yere of age. I bequethe to Thomas, John, Robert, William, Richard & William[*sic*], my children, eche of them five shepe.

The residue of all my goodes, my dettes payde, I yeve unto Maryon my wyff & Henry my son, Which I ordeyn & make myn Executours to dispose for the welth of my soule as they thynke best.

And William Baldwen I make my supervisour & for his labour I bequeth hym 20s.

I bequethe to the churchwardens of Rikm[er]sworth for the reparacion of the church 6s 8d.

To this my last wyll I have sette my seale the day & yere abovesaid.

These beryng witnesse: Richard Foderley, John Whyte & John Colyns.

This testament was approved on 7 May in the year aforesaid [1518], by Master Thomas Kyngesbury, archdeacon, &c; & administration &c was committed to the executors named in the same testament &c.

214. Edward Gybbys   reference: 2AR172v
will: 21 February 1518/19 [English]   probate: 12 March 1518/19

In the name of our lord god Amen. In the yere of our said lord god 1518/19, the 21st day of the moneth of February, I Edward Gybbys of Rykm[er]sworth, hole of mynde & of good remembrance, make my testament & last will in this maner folowyng.

First I bequethe my soule to almyghty God, to our lady saint Mary & to all the sainctes; And my body tobe buryed within the chapell of our lady of the Ilond beyng within the chirchyard of the parissh chirch of Rykm[er]sworth, to the reparacion of the which chapell I bequethe 3s 4d.

To the hygh awter of my parissh chirch of Rykm[er]sworth for oblacions & tithes forgoten & negligently doon 10s; to every lyght within the said chirche 4d; to the chirch of Rikm[er]sworth 4 marc' of money to by an ornament or tobe bestowid to the profyte of the said chirch after the discretion of myn Executours.

To John Gybbe my son £4 of money & two oxen; to William my son other £4 of money & two oxen, Which said William I make oon of myn Executours & he to have for his labour 10s; to Nicholas my son & to Henry his brother to either of them 5 marc' of money; to Alice my doughter 5 marc' of money. And if so it is that any of my foresaid childer decesse or [*i.e.* before] that the said money be paid to theim, I will that the said money be equally divided among theim that ar lyvyng. To every of my godchilder 4d.

I will that a tenement of myn, with thappurtenanuces, callid lokers which is Frehold, after the decesse of my wyfe, shall remayne to Henry Gybbys my son.

The residue of my goodes not bequethid I yeve & bequethe to Mawde Gybbe my wyffe, whom I make Also myn Executrice; she to have the said goodes to fynde her & dispose theim as it shall best be seen to her after her discretion.

I will that George Wynkborn be supervisour of this my last will, to supervide that this my wyll be fulfilled in every poynt as it is aforespecifyed and the said George to have for his labour 3s 4d.

Yoven the yere of our lord & the day of the moneth abovewritten.

These beryng wytnes: M[aster] Thomas Coton, John Randolf, John Rolf, John Henre and other.

This testament was approved on 12 March in the year above written [1518/19], by Master Thomas Kyngesbury, archdeacon, &c, administration was committed to the executors named in the same &c.

215. William Atkyns   reference: 2 AR 178v
administration: 3 March 1520/1

On 3 March [1520/21] administration of the goods of William Atkyns of Ryk', dying intestate, was committed by Henry Ampthyll &c, commissary, to Isabel Atkyns, relict of the said William &c.

216. Isabell Hammond, widow   reference: 2AR183r
will: 18 September 1522 [English]   probate: 11 November 1522

In the name of god, Amen. The yere of our said lord god 1522 & the 18th day of the moneth of Septembr', I Isabell Hamond of the parissh of Rykm[er]sworth, Wedow, in my pure Wedowhode, hole in mynde & of good remembraunce, make my last will & testament in maner & fourme folowyng.

First I bequethe my soule to almyghty god, to our lady saint Mary & to all the sainctes that are in hevyn; And my body tobe buryed within the churchyard of our lady of Rykm[er]sworth.

I bequethe to the hygh awter of the said church for tithes forgoten a shepe; to the reparacion of the said church of Rykm[er]sworth 6s 8d; to every lyghte within the said church 2d.

I will immediatly after my decesse that frere John within the church of Rykm[er]sworth syng a trentall of masses for my soule, my frendes & all christen sowles & to have for his stipend & labour 10s.

To Emme my daughter a cowe; to Alice my daughter a cowe, a bullok & my best gyrdyll.

The residue of my goodes not bequeathed I geve & bequethe to Richard Belche my son in law & to Johan his wyf my doughter, which Richard & Johan I make myn Executours, they to dispose the said goodes as it shal please theim to the pleasur of god & the welth of my soule.

Also I will that John A ?dene[140] be supervisour of this my will.

These beyng witnesse: M[aster] Thomas Coton vicar, John Henry, George Belche & other.

This testament was approved on 11 November in the year aforesaid [1522], by Master Thomas Kyngesbury, archdeacon, &c; & administration was committed to the executors named in this testament &c.

217. Richard Wedon

reference: 2AR186r

will: 20 April 1523 [English]   **probate: 22 February 1523/4**

In the name of god, Amen, the yere of our lord god 1523 the 20th day of the moneth of Aprill, I Richard Wedon of Rikm[er]sworth, hole in mynde & of good remembrance, make my testament & last Wyll in this maner folowyng.

First I bequethe my soule to almyghty god, to our blessid lady & to all the sainctes; And my body to be buryed in the churchyard of our lady of Rykm[er]sworth.

To the high awter of the said church for tithes forgoten & negligently doon I bequethe 4d; to every lyghte within the said church 2d; to the brotherhed of our lady & saint Kateryn within the church of Rykm[er]sworth I bequethe a yong kowe.

To Henry Wedon my son a quarter of whete & a quarter of barly; to every of my four doughters 3s 4d in money.

And where it is so I had bequeathed to Richard Wedon my son a quarter of whete, an other quarter of barly, two kene & ten shepe, the said Richard now decessed, I will that John Wedon, son of Henry Wedon, have five of the said ten shepe and the other five to remayne to myn Executours and the residue both whete barly & two kene tobe indifferently divided among my other children now lyvyng.

The residue of my goodes I yeve & bequethe to Elyn Wedon my wyf & to John Weden my son, whom I make myn Executours.

Yoven the day & moneth above written.

These beyng witnes: M[aster] Thomas Coton vicar, John A dene, Philip Wedon,

---

[140] The will is damaged here but this seems the likely reading.

Richard Blakemore, G Belche & mo.

This testament was approved on 22 February in the year above written [1523/4], by Master Thomas Kyngesbury, archdeacon, &c; & administration was committed &c to John Wedon &c; power having been reserved of committing similar administration &c [to the other executor]

218. Robert Fawcett   reference: 2AR187r
will: 2 March 1523/4 [English] probate: 4 April 1524

In the name of god Amen, the yere of our lord god 1523/4, the second day of the moneth of March, I Robert Fawcett of Rikm[er]sworth, hole in mynde ~~of of good~~ & of good remembraunce, make my testament & last will in maner & fourme folowyng.

First I bequethe my soule to almyghty god, to our blessid lady & to all the sainctes; & my body tobe buryed within the church yard of our lady of Rikm[er]sworth.

Also I bequethe to the hygh awter there for tythes forgoten 12d; to my moder church of saint Albon 4d.

The residue of my goodes I gyff unto Margery Fawcett my wyff to kepe & to bryng up my thre children, which Margery I make myn Executrice.

These beyng witness: M[aster] Thomas Coton, John a dale, John Atkyn, John Colenson & other.

This testament was approved on 4 April 1524, by Master Thomas Kyngesbury, archdeacon, &c; & administration &c was committed &c to the executrix &c.

219. William Dolte   reference: 2AR190r
will: 26 June 1524 [English] probate: 16 July 1524

In dei nomine, Amen. In the yere of our lord Jhesu Criste 1524 the 16th yere of Kyng Henry the VIII the 26th day of the moneth of Juyn, I William Dolte of the paroch of Rykm[er]sworth, within the countie of Hertf', beyng of hole mynde & good memorye, make my testament in this maner folowyng.

First I bequeth my soule to almyghty god, to the blessid lady saint Marye & to all the holy cumpany of hevyn; And my body tobe buried in the paroch church of Rik[mer]sworth aforesaid.

I bequethe to the hie awter of the same church 6s 8d; to the mother church of saint Albon 8d; to the reparacions of the paroch church of Rikm[er]sworth 3s 4d; to the mayntenaunce of every lighte in the same church 4d; to the fraternite of our lady & saint Kateryne within the said church 2s.

To everyoone of my doughters here named, Elisabeth, Elyne, Agnes & Letice, in money worth 40s to be putt in to the use of cattell as shortly as may be after the benyvolence & discretion of theire mother, the cholderne to have the incresse of the same.

I will & bequeth to Agnes Dolte my wyffe for terme of her lyffe all such interest, title, right, covenauntes & premysys that I have in an howse & landes of Richard Wylleys of Rikm[er]sworth above written sometyme called Canons, For which howse & landes I the said William Dolte have covenauntyd to geve to the said Richard Wylleys £23 and have paide of the same £17 6s 8d to the said Richard Willeys, And after the decesse of my said wyffe Agnes Dolte I will that my son Thomas Dolte shalhave the said Interest, title, right, covenauntes & premyse of the said howse & landes, And if it be that, by any crafte, disceipte or otherwyse for lacke of a sufficient surrender & Astate of the said house & landes after the use above rehersed, my wyffe or the said Thomas shuld be defrauded, then I will that the said Thomas shalhave all such money as I have paide for it or shalbe payde as is above rehersed. And if the said Thomas by any means be dispoyntyd of the said landes or money then I will that he shalhave in money or catell to the value of 40s to be putt in use to his profytte as shortly as can be.

I the said William Dolte will that Agnes my wyffe shalhave the Indenture of my howse that I dwell in as long as she shalbeable to occupie it. And if it so be that she be nott able to occupie it, then I will that Richard Gybbes shalhave such parte as she is not able to occupie and to help her & to maynten her in itt, payng for all such as he shall occupie after then rate as she shuld paye.

I will that myn Executours ioyntly together shalhave myn Indenture of Westmyll in the paroch of Rykm[er]sworth, gevyng to John Rolfe reasonably for such costs & charges as he can prove that he hath been at for the same.

I will that myn Executours shall paye all such money as I owe to paye to Richard Wyllcys & his wyffe for such covenauntes as I have made with the said Richard & his wiffe for the howse & landes above written, with all the costs & charges that shall perteyne to the makyng sure of the said howse & landes to my said wiffe & Thomas Dolte my son in maner & fourme as is above written.

The residue of my goodes above not bequethid I geve & bequethe to Agnes Dolte my wyfe.

I make the said Agnes my wyffe & Robert Dolte my son my veray & lawfull Executours of this my present testament & last will, and William Ewar of Flawden Supervisour of the same.

Gevyn at Rikm[er]sworth aforesaid the yere & day abeve written.

Hijs testibus: M[aster] Thomas Cotton, M[aster] Thomas Herytage, Richard Gybbes, John Rolffe, Richard Miller & many other.
This testament was proved before Master John Eggerton &c, commissary, on 16 July in the year aforesaid [1524]; & administration was committed &c to the executors.

220. Robert Randolf
reference: 2AR195r
will: 22 November 1525 [English]   probate: 23 January 1525/6

In the name of our lord god, Amen. In the yere of our said lord 1525 & the 22nd day of the moneth of Novembr', I Robert Randolf of Rykm[er]sworth, hole of mynde & of good remembrance, make my testament & last Wyll in maner & fourme folowyng.

First I bequethe my soule to almyghty god, to our lady saint Mary & to all the sainctes that are in hevyn; And my body tobe buryed Within the churchyard of our lady of Rykm[er]sworth among my frendes.

And to the high awter of the said church for tithes & other forgoten & neglygently done I bequethe 8d; to four lyghts Within the said church to eche of theim 8d; to every of my god childer 2d; to my moder church 4d.

The Residue of my goods I geve to John Randolfe my son, Whom I make myn Executour.

Also I Will that Stevyn Randolfe my cosyn be supervisour of this my Will.

yoven the yere & day above Written

These beryng Wytnes: Richard Blakeamor, George Bee, John Gardyner & other

This testament was proved on 23 January in the year aforesaid [1525/6], before Master John Eggerton, commissary &c, & administration &c was committed to the executor named in this testament &c.

221. Robert Pereson
reference: 2ARl95r
will: 13 January 1525/6 [English]   probate: 19 February 1525/6

In the name of our lord god, Amen. The yere of our said lord god 1525/6, the 13th day of the moneth of Januarye, I Robert Pereson of Rykm[er]sworth, hole of mynde & of good remembraunce, make my last Will & testament in maner & fourme folowyng.

First I bequethe my soule to almighty god & to his blessid modir Mary & to all the holy cumpany in hevyn; and my body tobe buryed in the churchyard of Rykm[er]sworthe.

I bequethe to the hygh awter of the said church for my tithes forgoten & negligently doon 12d; to every lyghte that is kepte yerely in the said church 2d; to the brotherhed & gylde of saint Kateryn within the said church 3s 4d; to my modir church the Monastery of Saint Albons 4d.

I will that Symon Bysshop my servaunt have, after the decesse of my Wyffe, all the stuff of my shop such as apperteynyth to my crafte & occupacion.[141]

The residue of all my goodes I yeve & bequethe to Isabell Pereson my Wyff, Whom I make myn Executrice.

Yoven at Rykm[er]sworth the yere & day aboveWritten.

These beryng Witnes: George Wyngburn, Richard decon, John ~~harvy~~ Henry & other.

Also I Will that Henry Wedon be Supervisour of this my Wyll, to Whom I yeve 12d.

This testament was approved on 19 February in the year aforesaid [1525/6], by Master Thomas Kyngesbury, archdeacon, &c; & administration was committed &c to the executrix named in this testament &c.

222. Thomas Goldstone reference: 2AR195r
will: 26 January 1525/6 [English] **probate: 19 February 1525/6**

In dei nomine, Amen. The 26 day of the moneth of January the yere of our lord god 1525/6, I Thomas Goldstone of the parissh of Rykm[er]sworth, With a good hole mynde & memorye, make my last Wyll & testament in maner folowyng.

First I bequethe my soule to almyghty god & to his blessid moder Mary & to all the holy cumpany in hevyn; & my body tobe buryed in the church of the foresaid parissh of Rykm[er]sworth before the auter of saint Nicholas.

I bequethe to the high awter of the said church for my tithes negligently forgoten 4d; to everych of the lyghts that ar kept yerely in the said church 2d; to my moder church 8d.

To my moder 3s 4d; to my broder John Goldstone my best bras pott; to my broder Alyn Goldstone my swerd & my buclare; to my broder William Goldstone my best capp, my bow & my shaffts.

I Wyll to an honest preest to syng for my soule oon trentall in the church of Rykm[er]sworth 10s; to the bretherhed in the same church 12d.

The residue of my goods I yeve to Johan my Wyf Whom I make myn Executrice.

These beyng Witnes: George Wyngbourn, John henre & William Edynbras.

---

[141] No indication of what that occupation was.

This testament was proved on 19 February in the year aforesaid [1525/6], before Master Thomas Kyngesbury, archdeacon, &c; & administration was committed &c to the executrix named in this testament &c.

223. William Belche, husbandman   reference: 2AR196v
will: 3 February 1525/6 [English]   probate: 12 May 1526

In the name of god, Amen. the third day of Februar' in the yere of our lord god 1525/6, & in the 16th yere of the reign of Kyng Henry the VIII, I William Belche of the town of Rykm[er]sworth in the Countie of Hertf', husbondman, hole of mynde & of good memory, ordeyn & make my testament & last will in this maner.

First I bequethe my soule to almyghty god & to our blessid lady saint Mary & to all the holy company of hevyn; And my body tobe buryed in the churchyard of Rykm[er]sworth nye to my frendes.

To the high awter of Rykm[er]sworth for my tithes forgoten 12d; to my mother church of Saint Albons 4d; to the rode lyght of Rykm[er]sworth church 8d; to our lady chapell 4d; to saynt Kateryn lyght 2d; to saint Edmundes lyght 2d; to the Trinite lyght 4d; to saint Antony lyght 2d; to saint Nicholas lyght 2d; to the lyght of our lady of Pitie 2d; to St George lyght 2d; to saint Clement lyght 2d; to the Fraternite of the brotherhed of our lady & saint Kateryn founded within the paryssh of Rykm[er]sworth 6s 8d, to thentent that the brethern & sustren therof do pray for my soule.

The residue truly of all & singular my goodes & catalles whatsomever they be, after my dettes payde, myn expenses funerall maide & done, & this my present testament fulfilled, I hooly yeve & bequeth to Elysabeth my doughter, wyff to John Twychett. And of this my present testament I ordeyn & make myn Executours Elisabeth Twychett my doughter & William Baldewyn, to dispose for my soule as they think best, & John Twychett my sonelaw overseare.

I bequethe to William Baldewyn for his labour 6s 8d.

In witnes wherof to this my present testament I have sett my seale.

These bering witness: William Creke gent', Richard Puderley & other &c.

Proved on 12 May 1526, before Master John Eggerton, commissary, &c; & administration &c was committed to the executors named in this testament.

224. John Whyte   reference: 2AR196v
will: 7 April 1526 [English]   probate: [c. 22 May 1526]

In dei nomine Amen. The 7th day of Aprill the yere of our lord god 1526, I John Whyte of the parish of Rykm[er]sworth, with good hole mynde & memory, make my last Wyll & testament in this maner folowyng.

First I bequeth my soule to almyghty god & to his blessid moder saint Marye & to all the holy company of hevyn; my body tobe buryed in the chapell of our lady of Ilond stondyng in the churchyard of Rykm[er]sworth.

To the hygh awter of the same church 12d; to every lyghte that is kept yerely in the said church 2d; to the cathedrall church of saint Alban 8d.

The residue of all my goodes I bequeth unto my son Thomas Whyte, whom I make my sole Executour, to acquyte my dettes & to bestowe it for the welth of my soule. And I will that the said Thomas gyve unto Agnes my wyff such parte of my said goods as he thynk it most expedient for her.

These beryng witnes: George Wyngburn, John A Dene, John a Dale, with many others

This testament was proved before Master Thomas Kyngesbury, archdeacon, &c; & administration was committed &c to the executors named in this testament &c.[142]

225. George Wynkborn, gentleman   reference: 2AR197v–198r
will: 16 October 1526 [English]   probate: 27 November 1526

In the name of god Amen. the 16th day of the moneth of Octobr' the yere of our lord god [1526],[143] I George Wynkborn of Rykm[er]sworth Gentilman, in the jurisdiccion of Saint Alban, hole of my[nd and] in good memory, make my testament & last Will in this maner & fourme folowyng.

First I beq[uethe] my soule to almyghty god & to his blessid modir Mary & to all the holy company in hevyn; & [my body] to be buryed in the church of our lady of Rykm[er]sworth next the buryall of my fader.

To the high awter in the said church for my tithes & offeryngs forgotten & negligently payd 2s; to the moder church of Saint Alban 12d; to every lyghte in the church of Rykm[er]sworth that the Wardeyns of the same church be charged With to make 4d; to the lyghte of Saint George Within the said church 8d; to the

---

[142] The date of probate is not stated; the preceding will recorded in the register was proved on 22 May 1526.

[143] The register is damaged and some words are missing from this will; the likely words have been supplied in [ ].

fraternite & broderhed of our blessid lady & of saint Kateryn in Rykm[er]sworth aforesaid two Ewes & two lambes of the best among [*fol. 198r*] all my shepe.

The Residue of my goods nott yeven nor bequethed I yeve & bequethe [to Eme] Wynkborn my Wyffe she to pay my detts & bryng up my children unto such season they will [---] to doo service & help theirselfs.

And the said Eme & William Norton of Ryslyp togydir I ord[ain con]stitute & make myne Executours of this my testament & last Will.

Also I Wyll that the said William Norton, if it lyke hym to take the labour upon hym & tobe frendly to my Wyff & children, to have for his labour 6s 8d.

Also I will & graunt that Robert Rollys yoman of the crown, Henry Gunner & John Alexander or Alisaunder now feffid & seased in my free londs & tenements, Rents & services, sette, lying & being aswell in the paressh of Rykm[er]sworth as in the parissh of Watford in the countie of Hertford called Croxleys Julyans lond & dellys with thappurtenaunces to stond still feffid & seasid in my said londs & tenements, With the premissis, to the use of Eme Wynkborn my Wiffe, for the terme of her lyff naturall, tobe hold of the chief lord of that fee by the rents & services due & of ryght customed; And after the decesse of the said Eme, then I Wyll that my said lands & tenements, with thappertenaunces & premisses, to remayne to John Wyknborn & to his heyres of his body lawfully begotten, tobe hold of the chief lords in maner & fourme as it is afore rehersed. And if it fortune the said John my son to be Without heyres, or his heyres happen to dye, Then I Wyll that my said lands & tenements, with the premisses, to remayne to George my son & to his heyres of his body lawfully begotten; and for lak of such heyres of the said George, then I Will that the said lands & tenements, With thappurtenaunces & premisses, to remayne to William my son & to his heyres lawfully begotten; And for lakke of hym & his heyres, Then I Will that all the said londs & tenements, rents & services, With thappurtenaunces & premisses, to remayne & turne ayen to the next ryghtfull heyre of me the said George Wynkborn & to their heyres for evermore.

Also I Will & graunt by these presents that all such covenaunts, bargayns & graunts as be made betwene me the said George and John Hayward before the date of this my last Wyll to stond styll in strength & vertu duryng his termys.

Also I Will in lyke maner that all such bargayns & graunts as I have made to Henry Stanborow stand styll in full strength & vertu duryng his termys.

Yoven at Rykm[er]sworth the day & yere aboveWritten,

These beryng Witnes, not oonly of this my last Will but also of the possession takyng in my londs to the perfourming of my Wyll as it is aforespecified: M[aster] Thomas Coton vicar of Rykm[er]sworth, Robert Rollys, William Herde, John

Heyward, Robert Hutton, Richard Decon, John A Dale, Robert A Dale, John Coke, William Madows, Thomas Lampton, Cuthbert Lyghthasell, William Edynbrace & diverse other.

This testament was proved before Master Thomas Kyngsbury, archdeacon, &c on 27 November in the year aforesaid [1526]; & administration &c was committed to Emma, executrix &c; power being reserved of committing administration to the other executor when he shall come.

226. Richard Tredeway   reference: 2AR201r
will: 22 June 1527 [English]   probate: 17 September 1527

In the name of our lord god, Amen. In the yere of our lord god 1527 & the 22nd day of the moneth of Juyn, I Richard Tredeway of the parissh of Rykm[er]sworth, hole in mynde & of good remembraunce, make my testament & last wyll in maner and fourme folowyng.

First I bequethe my soule to almyghty god, to our blessid lady saint Mary & to all the sainctes that are in hevyn; And my body tobe buryed within the churchyard of our lady of rykm[er]sworth by my frendes.

To the hygh Awter of the said church for tithes forgoten & negligently doon 3s 4d; to my moder church 12d; to every lyghte within the church of Rykm[es]sworth 4d; to the reparacion of the chapel of our lady of Ilond 12d; to the brederhed in Rykm[er]sworth a shepe.

To every of my god childer 4d; to Elisabeth Tredeway my wyff all such stuff of houshold as she brought to me, four kene & twenty shepe.

The residue of my goodes I geve & bequethe to Water Tredeway my son, whom I make myn Executour, to dispose the said goodes for the welth of my soule.

Also I will that Thomas Holte my son in lawe be supervisour of this my Wyll.

These beryng witnes: M[aster] Thomas Coton, sir Richard Porter, John Henry, Andrew Braunche & other.

This testament was proved on 17 September in the year aforesaid [1527], before Master John Eggerton, bachelor of canon law (decretals), commissary, &c; & administration &c was committed to the executrix &c.

227. John Grosser
will: 13 December 1527 [English]

reference: 2AR202v

probate: 12 February 1527/8

In the name of our lord god, Amen. the yere of our seid lord 1527 the 13 day of Decembr', I John Grosser of Rikm[er]sworth &c make my testament in this maner.

First I bequeth my soule to god; my body to be buryed in the churchyard of Rykm[er]sworth.

To the high awter 4d; to Saint Albans shryne 2d.[144]

The residue of my goodes I geve to Denys my Wyff &c.

This testament was proved on 12 February in the year aforesaid [1527/8], before Master Thomas Burley, bachelor of canon law (decretals), commissary, &c; & administration &c was committed to the executrix &c.

228. Richard Belche
will: 13 March 1527/8 [English]

reference: 2AR204v

probate: 24 April 1528

In the name of God, Amen. The 13th day of Marche in the yere of our lord god 1527/8, I Richard Belche dwelling in the paryssh of Rykm[er]sworth, with a good hole mynde & memorye, ordeyn & make my last wyll & testament in this maner folowyng.

First I bequethe my soule to almyghty god, to our blessid lady & to all the holy company of hevyn; my body tobe buryed in the churchyard of the said paryssh of Rykm[er]sworth.

To the hygh awter in the said church I bequethe 12d; to the mayntenaunce of the lyghte before saint Kateryn two busshells of whete; to every lyghte that is kept yerely within the said church 2d.

To Johan my wyff all my houshold stuff, oon fylde of whete called long fylde, five acres of ~~wh~~ wootes, half of all my barley that is or shalbe sowyn this yere, oon horse, four kyen, ten yowys with ten lambys, four hogges; to my moder a cowe, a hog, a busshell of whete & a busshell of malt; to my broder George all my horssys not before bequethyd and my carte with the pertenances to the same.

---

[144] Margaret Aston commented on the brevity of Grosser's will, the fact that he made no bequests to lights in the church, and perhaps crucially the commendation of his soul only to God, rather than Almighty God, the blessed Mary and all the saints. On their own these points do not necessarily mean anything. However, in 1521 John Grosar (his name is spelled variously) had given evidence during Bishop Longland's proceedings against heretics, and admitted having had a book of the Gospels in English. The omissions in his will are, therefore, suggestive, if not incriminating. (Aston, 'Troubles of churchwardens', pp.540-1)

The residue of all my goodes I gyve & bequethe to my said broder George & to John Knyght, whom I ordeyn & make myn Executours, to dispose my said goods for the welth of my soule as they think best.

Also I will that sir Richard Porter be overseerr of this my last wyll.

These beryng witnes: John Henre, John Davyd & John Gybb.

This testament was proved on 24 April 1528 before Master Thomas Burley, commissary, &c; & administration was committed &c.

229. John Grover   reference: 2AR204v
will: 11 April 1528 [English]   probate: 24 April 1528

In the name of God, Amen. The 11th day of Aprill the yere of our lord god 1528, I John Grover of the paryssh of Rykm[er]worth, with good hole mynde & memorye, ordeyn & make my last will & testament in this maner folowyng.

Fyrst I bequethe my soule to almyghty god, to our lady saint Mary & to all the holy company of hevyn; my body tobe buryed in the churchyard of Rykm[er]sworth.

To the high awter of the said church for tithes forgoten oon shepe; to the reparacions of the ~~said church~~ chappell of our blessid lady of Eyland oon shepe; to the shrine of the blessid martir saint Albon 2d.

I give & bequeth to Agnes my wyff all my houshold stuff, oon quarter of whete, a quarter of barley, two kyen and £6 13s 4d of lawfull money of England, of the which £6 13s 4d I will & charge my fader Robert Grover to paye or cause tobe payde unto Agnes my said wyff or to her Assignes at the feest of the Holy archangel saint Myghell next folowyng after this present date ~~nexte folowyng~~ above written 20s, And at the feest of the nativite of saint John Baptist next ensuing 46s 8d. And at the feest of saint John Baptist then next folowyng £3 6s 8d for the full contentacion of the foresaid sum \of/ £6 13s 4d. And then the foresaid Robert Grover tobe discharged of the said sum.

The Residue of all my goods I gyve & bequethe to my said fader Robert Grover, whom I make my hol Executour of this my said wyll, so that he dispose the said goodes to the pleasur of god & to the welth of my soule.

Yoven the day & yere above written.

These beryng witness: Edmund Twechyn, John Henre & other.

This testament was proved on 24 April in the year aforesaid [1528], before Master Thomas Burley &c; & administration &c was committed to the executor named in the same.

141

230. Robert Grover[145]   reference: 2AR206v

will: 2 May 1528 [English]   probate: 1 June 1528

In the name of God, Amen, the secund day of May the yere of our lord god 1528, I Robert Grover of the parissh of Rykmersworth, with good hole mynde & memorye, make my testament & last wyll in maner folowyng.

First I bequethe my soule to almyghty god, to his blessid moder Mary, & to all the holy company of hevyn; my body tobe buryed in the churchyard of the foresaid paryssh of Rykm[er]sworth.

To the high aulter of the same church for my tythes negligently forgoten oon shepe; to the chapell of our blessid lady of Eyland oon shepe; to the maintenance of saint Nicholas lyghte an Ewe & a lambe; to every lyghte that is yerely kept within the said church 2d; to the shryne of the holy martir saint Alban 4d.

I bequethe to Agnes my wyff all such houshold stuff that she brought to me at the tyme of our mariage, oon crofte of whete called boy crofte, oon acre of whete liyng at mede gate, two acres of barly, two kyne of colour brendid & ten ewys with their lambys. To my son John Grover[146] ten shepe & a bullock; to my son William ten shepe, a bullock, half a quarter of whete, an ewe & a lamb; to everych of my servauntes an ewe & a lambe; to everych of my son Richardes children a lamb; to Edmund Twchyn a busshell of whete & a busshell of malt.

To sir Richard Porter 3s 4d. I will to an honest preest to say 30 masses for the helth of my soule & all soules 10s.

The Residue of all my goodes I yeve & bequethe to Roger Grover & Thomas my sonnys, whom I ordeyn & make myn Executours, to dispose my said goodes for the welth of my soule as they thynke best & to perfourme this my last wyll & testament.

I will & desire the said Roger & Thomas myn Executours to perfourme the wyll or testament of my sone John, that is, that they, as it apperyth in his wyll, at certayn days & tymes assigned to give or pay unto Agnes Grover lately the wyffe of the said John Grover or to hir assignes £6 13s 4d, a quarter of whete, a quarter of barly & two kyen.

This will made the day & yere above written.

These beryng witnes: John Henre, George Hatton, Edmund Twychen.

---

[145] Father of John Grover (229).

[146] It appears that he had two sons named John. John Grover, son of Robert (no mention of elder/younger), had died by 24 April 1528 (no. 229). His will is mentioned by Robert. John's widow, Agnes (231), also made a bequest to John Grover.

I will that all such land that I hold by Indentur of Master Whitton to my son Richard, so that he pay or cause to be payde to John Gardiner of Whit end £3 10s 4d.

I will that my foresaid Executours Roger & Thomas or their Assignes holde & kepe the ferme that I have taken of Master Creke by endentur.

This testament was proved on 1 June 1528 before Master Thomas Burley, commissary; & administration &c was committed to Thomas Grover, executor named in the testament &c.

231. Agnes Grover, widow[147]   reference: 2AR205v
will: 2 May 1528 [English]   **probate: 18 July 1528**

In the name of God, Amen. The secund day of May the yere of our lord god 1528, I Agnes Grover, widow, dwelyng in the parissh of Rikm[er]sworth, with good hole mynde & memory, make my last will & testament in this maner folowyng.

First I bequethe my soule to allmyghty god, to his blessid moder Mary & to all the holy company of hevyn; And my body tobe buried in the churchyard of the said parissh of Rikm[er]sworth.

To the high aulter of the same church 4d; to the chapel of our blessid lady of Ilond 4d; and my best keychur to the shrine of the holy martir saint Albon 2d[sic].

To my moder my best gowne & 3s 4d; to my moder in law my bed that I lye on, my best kyrtell & 3s 4d.

To Edmund Twechyn & to his wyff to goo in pilgrimage to our blessid lady of Walsyngham 20s.

To my sister Johan my second gowne, my crimson kyrtell, a pan, a pair of shetes & 3s 4d; to everych of my sisters children 3s 4d; to everych of theim that bereth me to church 3s 4d; to Thomesyn Twchyn my best petycote, my worst gowne, a pair of shetes, a kerchur, a smok, a naprun, a blankett & 3s 4d; to John Grover 3s 4d; to Thomas Grover 3s 4d.

To the mayntenaunce of saint Nicholas lyght in the church aforesaid 12d; to oon honest preist to syng a trentall of masses for the helth of my sowle, my husbondes & all christen soules 10s.

To Roger Grover a coffer; to William Grover a coffer.

I will that all the costes & charges that shalbe done for me at the day of my buryall & my legacye tobe levelyd & fulfilled with parte of the goodes & monay that restith in the handes & custodie of my fader in law Robert Grover, the which at certain days

---

[147] Widow of John Grover (229) and daughter-in-law of Robert Grover (230).

assgnyd as it apperith in the will of John Grover my husband, lately departed unto the mercy of god, is bound to contente & pay unto me or my Assignes; and with the overplus of the said goodes & monay that remayneth in the custodie of the foresaid Robert Grover, I will that therbe bestowed of it every yere 6s 8d to kepe an obit for our sowlys unto the tyme that the hole sum cum up or spent to the said use, the which sum apperith in the will of my said husbond John Grover.

I will that oon of my kyen be solde to help bryng me in the arthe.

The residue of all my goods not bequeathed, I do will it unto my brother Richard Robyns, whom I ordeyn & make myn Executor, to dispose it for the welth of my soule, to whom I geve for his labour 6s 8d.

I will that Roger Grover be overseer of this my last will, that it be perfourmed & doon in maner & fourme as is above written, to whom I geve for his labour 3s 4d. Thes beryng witness: John Henre, Edmund Twechyn.

This testament was proved on 18 July in the year aforesaid [1528], before Master Thomas Burley, commissary, &c; & administration &c was committed to the executor named in this testament &c.

232. Roger Gunner   reference: 2AR219r
will: 31 August 1528 [English]   probate: 21 February 1531/2

In the name of god, Amen. The last day of August in the yere of our lord 1528 & the 20th yere of the reign of king Henry the VIII, I Roger Gunner, being in good & hole mynde, laude & praysyng be unto almyghty god, make & ordeyn this my present testament conteynyng therin my last wyll, as well of all my goodes and catelles movabyll & unmovabyll whatsoever thay be, as of all my londes & tenementes, medes, lasues & pastures with thappurtenances sett & lying in the paryssh of Istylworth in the Countie of Myddelsex or in any other place.

First & principally I recommende my soule unto almyghty god, my maker & redemer, & to his moost blessid moder & virgin our lady saint Mary & to all his sainctes of hevyn; and my body tobe buryed in the churchyard of Rykm[er]sworth. I bequethe to the hygh awter of the same church for tithes & oblacions negligently witholden or forgoten if any such be, in discharge of my soule 2s; to the Roode lyghte of the same church 3s 4d; to saint Kateryns lyghte 20d; to saint Anthonys lyght 12d; to the Trinitie lyght 12d; to my moder church of saint Albons 2s.

All such londes & tenementes that I have bowght of John Kyng, my wyffes broder, after his decesse, I wyll that my wyff have for terme of her lyff, And after her decesse to Remayne to Harry Gunner my son and to his heyres of his body lawfully begotten. Also I bequethe to Harry Gunner my son the third part of all my movabill goodes & catalles.

Also I wyll that my wyff have my lease of the parsonage of Rykm[er]sworth for terme of her lyff, if she doo nott marye. And if it fortune her to marye ayene after my decesse, then I wyll the Harry Gunner my son have my lease to hym and to his Assignes immediatly.

Also I make Johan my wyffe and Harry Gunner my son myn Executours.

This testament was proved on 21 February 1531/2 before Master Thomas Kyng,[148] master of arts, official, &c; & administration was committed to the executors &c.

233. John A Dene, yeoman[149]   reference: 2AR209v
will: 5 May 1529 [English]   probate: 18 May 1529

In the name of god Amen. The 5th day of May in the yere of our lord god 1529, I John A Dene of Rykm[er]sworth in the countie of Hertford, yoman, of hole mynde & good remembraunce, laud & praysyng be to almyghty god, make & ordeyn this my present testament & last wyll in this maner wyse.

First I recommende my soule unto almyghty god & to our blessid lady saint Mary & to all the holy company of hevyn; & my body tobe buryed in the churchyard of Rykm[er]sworth, next to my frendes.

To the high awter of the said church for all maner of tithes negligently forgoten in discharging of my conscience 12d; to saint Albans shrine 4d.

I bequethe to the reysyng of the organs with in the said church of Rykm[er]sworth 6s 8d.[150]

To the Roode lyghte & saint Kateryns lyghte eyther of theim 4d; to the brotherhed of our lady & saint St Kateryn within the same church 3s 4d; to the lyghtes of saint Cristofer & saint Anthony within the said church eyther of theim 2d.

To Thomas A Dene my son my shop with all the Implementes beyng within the same; to the said Thomas the chamber over the hall with a fetherbed & a mattres, with all the hanginges in the same chamber as it is now at this present day, after the

---

[148] Master Thomas Kyng, MA, was not the same man as master Thomas Kyngesbury; both were among the men who granted probate to wills during this period.

[149] He was actually a blacksmith. He was one of the witnesses to the will of Stephen Holtyng (no. 166, made in 1495). At that time (A) Dene stated that he was 25 years old, so when he made his own will he was about 59.

[150] This relates to the new organ (or, as often described at that time, the pair of organs) needed after the arson attack in 1522.

decesse of Alice my wyfe; to Thomas a fetherbed with all that belongyth to the same & a brass pan.

The residue of all my goodes not bequeathed, aftyr my dettes payde, I will that Alice my wyff and George my son do dispose for the welth of my soule & all cristen soules as they thynke moost exp[edient] tobe done.

Whych Alice & George I make myn Executours.

And I wyll that Thomas Spenser & John Edwardes be overseers of this my last wyll.

These beyng witness: M[aster] Thomas Coton vicar of Rykm[er]sworth, William Belamy & other

This testament was proved on 18 May in the year abovesaid [1529], before Master Thomas Burley, commissary, &c; & administration was committed &c to the executors named in the same &c.

234. John Hede   reference: 2AR213v–214r
will: 15 May 1530 [English]   probate: 25 August 1530

In dei nomine Amen. The yere of our lord god 1530 the 15th day of the moneth of May, I John Hede of the parissh of Rykm[er]sworth, hole in mynde & of good remembrance, make my last Will & testament in maner & fourme folowyng.

First I bequethe my soule to almyghty god, to our lady saint Mary & to all the sainctes in hevyn; And my body tobe buryed in the Ile of saint Kateryn within the church of Rykm[er]sworth beside my wyff.

I bequethe to the high alter of the said church for tythes forgotten 20d; to the shryne of the holy martir saint Alban 12d.

To the church of Rykm[er]sworth £20 of laufull money of England; I will that my supervisours bestowe the said £20 in bookes for the said church of Rykm[er]sworth.

I gyve to the reparacions of the highway called Waleys lane 40s.

I bequethe to the maintenance of every lyght within the church of Rykm[er]sworth 4d; to the maintenance of the Trinite light in the said church two kyen.

To every of my god children 4d; to every of my servantes a lambe; to Guy Aylward a kowe & a gown.

I will that a preest shall syng [*fol. 214r*] for my soule, all my frendes soules & for all cristen soules the space of a yere.

I will that John Mylward & Richard Fotherley shalbe supervisours of this my last will and eyther of theim to have for his labour 6s 8d.

I will that John Alen have and hold my landes callid Stockers for the space of three yeres next folowyng this present date, And he to paye \yerely/ £6 13s 4d duryng the said terme to myn assignes as it is covenanted betwene hym & me before sufficient recorde.

I will that Edmund Aldewyn have my myll lying in Bachworth unto the feest of saint Myghell tharchangell next comyng & two yeres folowyng, he payng yerely £10 duryng the said terme to Jone Hede my wyffe as it is covenanted & agryd betwene hym & me, And after the terme of the said yeres, I will that Jone my wyffe shall selle it to keep an obite yerely for me & for all my frendes.

I will that the foresaid John Mylward & Richard Fotherley, Supervisours, do sell my house & my landes called Stockers of the which I have gevyn a surrender to the use of my last will to John Case gentilman[151] dwelling in London, gevyng therefore as an other man will.

I will that the foresaid £20 to the church of Rykm[er]sworth be payde of the money that shall come of the said landes callid Stockers when it is solde, And also the foresaid 40s to the reparacions of Waleys lane to be payde of the same money of Stockers

And the residue of the money of the said landes & all my goodes I geve & bequethe (my dettes payde) to Jone my wyffe, the which I make myn Executrice, to bestow it yerely for my soule health & all cristen soules as she knowith was doone in my tyme.

Witnes hereof: Richard Decon, John Twichett, John Henry, Robert Atkyn, John Burford & John Colyn with other.

This testament was proved on 25 August 1530, before Master Thomas Kyngesbury, archdeacon; & administration was committed to the executrix &c.

235. Stevyn Randalff   reference: 2AR216r
will: 23 March 1530/1 [English]   probate: 30 May 1531

In the name of god Amen. The 23rd day of the moneth of Marche the yere of our lord god one thousand fyve hundred & thirty [1530/1], I Stevyn Randalff of the parissh of Rykm[er]sworth, With good mynde & hoole memory, make my last Will & testament in this maner & fourme folowyng.

First I bequethe my soule to almyghty god, to oure blessid lady & to all the holy company of hevyn; And my body tobe buried in the churchyard of the said parissh of Rykm[er]sworth.

I bequethe to the high awter there in the honour of the holy sacrament 4d; to the shryne of the holy martir saint Alban 4d; to the mayntenance of saint Kateryn lyght

---

[151] Possibly the man whose will is no. 241.

in the said church of Rykm[er]sworth 4d; to the roode lyght there 4d; to the reparacion of the chapell of oure blessid Lady of Ilond 4d.

I will unto John Monke as moch wull as will make fyve yardes of cloth; to John Monke my Wyvis godson a shepe.

I will that Robert my yongest son have half of all my lands within the parissh of Rykm[er]sworth, With my nether house that he now dwellith in, the space of a yere next ensuyng aftir the feest of Saint Mighell tharchangell next folowing after the date above written, he givyng unto Andrewe my eldest son for the said terme 40s. The Residue of all my goods I give & bequeth unto Johan my Wyf, Whom I make myn Executrice, With Andrew my eldest son, & I will that he see that this my last Will be fullfillid & perfourmyd in every point, to Whom I give for his labour 6s 8d.

theys beryng Witnesse: John Buttirfeld, Roger Fuller & John Man

This testament was proved on 30 May 1531 before Master Thomas Kyngesbury, archdeacon, &c; & administration was committed to the executors &c.

236. John Haydon reference: 2AR216v
will: 30 March 1531 [English] probate: 6 June 1531

In dei nomine Amen. I John Haydon of the parissh of Rykm[er]sworth, the 30th day of March the yere of our lord god 1531, make my last Wyll and testament in this maner & fourme folowyng.

First I bequethe my soule to almyghty god; my body tobe buryed in the churchyard of the parissh of Rykm[er]sworth.

To the high awter of the said church in the honour of the holy sacrament 12d; to the shryne of the holy martir saint Albon 2d.

To Thomas my eldest son a bullok; to Richard my son six bullokes & two quarters of Whete; to Johan my daughter a bullok; to Dorothe my daughter a Cowe or else 11s of lawfull money of England.

The Residue of all my goodes I geve & bequethe to Letice my Wyff, Whom I make myn Executrice.

I ordeyn & make John Rowtt oversear of this my last Wyll, to whom I bequethe for his labour 3s 4d.

These bering Witnesse: Henry Gonner, George Belche, John Knyght.

This testament was proved on 6 June 1531 before Master Thomas Kyngesbury, archdeacon, &c; & administration &c was committed to the executrix named in this testament &c.

237. Agnes Wedon, widow reference: 2AR217v
will: 23 October 1531 [English] probate: 18 November 1531

In dei nomine Amen. The 23rd day of Octobr' the yere of our lord god 1531, I
Agnes Wedon, wydow, of the parissh of Rykm[er]sworth, good of mynde & hole of
memory, do make my last wyll & testament in this maner & fourme folowing.

First I bequethe my soule to almyghty god, to our blessid lady & to all the holy
company of hevyn; my body tobe buried in the churchyard of the said parissh of
Rykm[er]sworth.

To the high awter there 20d; to the maintenance of the brotherhed there 20d; to the
shrine of the holy martir saint Alban 8d.

I bequethe to my son Barthilmew a kowe, two bullokes, of shepe 16, a horse & six
pair of shetes; to my daughter Ann[*damaged*] a kowe, two bullokes, of shepe 12, a
horse, a mattres & six pair of shetes; to Elisabeth Peper two kyen, my second best
gown & my kyrtell; to Sibill Peper a bullok of this yeres; to Katheryn Elys a bullok of
this yeres.

To the awter in the Chapell of our lady of Ilond a shete; to the mayntenance of the
roode lyght in the church of Watford 20d; to the brotherhed there 20d; and to the
reparacion of the torches there 12d; and to our lady Chapell there 12d.[152]

I bequethe to oon honest preest to syng 30 masses for the welth of my soule & all
cristen soules.

The Residue of all my goodes I gyve & bequethe to John my son, whom I ordeyn &
make my sole executor to bestow it for the welth of my soule as he thynketh best.

I wyll that William Samson be overseer of this my last wyll, that it may be fulfilled &
perfourmyd in every point, to whom I gyve for his labor 3s 4d.

These beryng wytnes: sir Richard Portar, Robert Ipswyche, Thomas Boterfeld &
John Ewer.

This testament was proved on 18 November in the year aforesaid [1531], before
master Thomas Newnham, sub-prior of the monastery of St Albans & official of the
exempt jurisdiction of the same monastery, &c; & administration &c was
committed to John, executor named in the same testament &c.

---

[152] These latter three bequests are probably also to St Mary's, Watford.

238. Thomas Melsam   reference: 2AR219r
will: 16 February 1531/2 [English]   **probate: 9 March 1531/2**

In the name of god, Amen, the 16 day of the moneth of February the yere of our lord god 1531/2, I Thomas Melsam of the parissh of Rykm[er]sworth, good of mynde & hole of memory, doo make my last wyll & testament in this maner & fourme folowyng.

First I bequethe my soule to almyghty god, to our blessid lady & to all the holy company of hevyn; and my bodie tobe buried in the churchyard of the said parissh of Rykm[er]sworth.

I bequethe to the high awter there in the honour of the holy sacrament 12d; to the maintenance of everyly[sic] lyght that is yerely kept in the said church 2d; to the reparacion of the chapell of our blessid lady of eyland 8d; to the shrine of the holy martir saint Alban 2d.

The residue of all my goodes I doo yeve & bequethe unto Alice my wyff, whom I doo ordeyn & make my sole Executrice, And after the decesse of the said Alice my wyff, I will the said goodes then departid amongyst my children as she thynkith best.

These beryng witnesse: John Nores, sir Richard Porter preest.

This testament was proved on 9 March 1531/2, before Master Thomas Kyng, official &c; & administration &c was committed to the executrix named in the same &c.

239. Margaret Eglestone   reference: 2AR219r
probate: 12 March 1531/2

The testament of Margaret Eglestone of Rykm[er]sworth was proved on 12 March 1531/2 in the presence of Master Thomas Kyng, official &c; And administration was committed &c to sir Richard Porter, chaplain, executor named in the said testament, who was sworn in form of law & he was admitted by the same [man].

240. John Holtyng the elder   reference: 2AR231v
will: 1 February 1534/5 [English]   **probate: 27 February 1534/5**

In the name of god Amen, the yere of our lord god 1534/5, the fyrst day of February, I John Holtyng thelder, here in the parissh of Rykm[er]sworth in the countie of Hertf', in good & hole mynde, make & ordeyn this my last will in maner & fourme folowyng.

First I bequethe my sowle unto almyghty god, to our lady saint Mary & to the cumpany of all sainctes; & my body to be buried in the church or churchyard of our lady of Rykm[er]sworth.

To the reparacion of my moder church of Saint Albans 4d; to the high aulter of my parissh church of Rykm[er]sworth 8d.

To my son John Holtyng after my decesse all my londes frehold & copyhold callid Harry Smythes & Waterdell & all that belongith to theim, paying yerely to Margrett my Wyff duryng her lyff 6s 8d.

To Jone Dynes, my doughters daughter, oon bullok of the yongest that I have; and to Margrett Stains oon shepe & a lambe; to Richard Whytt my servant two shepe & a lambe; to my doughter Isabell Cokes four shepe; and to my doughter Cicely Richardes two busshelles of whete; to Jone Reyd my servant one shepe & a lambe; to John Holtyng my son a blak table & one fourme & a chest & a bedstede & the bourdes about the shed.

To Margrett my Wyff all the residue of my houshold stuff; & all my goodes not bequethid as catell withall other movable I gyve to John Holtyng my son & to Margrett my Wyff, to be equally dividid betwixt theim, Whom I do make myn exec'tours.

Witnes: the vicar of Rykm[er]sworth sir William Man; witnes also William Herd, Thomas Spenser, Robert Richardes.

This testament was proved on 27 February in the year abovesaid [1534/5], before Master Thomas Kyngesbury, archdeacon, &c; & administration &c was committed to John Holtyng executor &c; power being reserved of committing similar administration to Margaret, executrix, when she shall come &c.

241. John Case the elder   reference: 2AR233v-234r
will: 13 June 1535 [English]   probate: 28 July 1535

In dei nomine Amen. The 13th day of Juyn in the yere of our lord god 1535, I John Case the elder, of good & hole mynde, to god,[153] make & ordeyn this my last will & testament in maner & fourme folowyng.

First I bequethe my soule to allmyghty god, to our lady saint Mary & to the cumpany of all holy saintes; And my body tobe buryed within the parissh church of Rykm[er]sworth.

To my parissh church of Rykm[er]sworth 6s 8d; to the parissh church of Redburn 6s 8d; to the parissh church of Bardfeld in Essex 6s 8d; to the parissh Church of Wylsdon 3s 4d; and to the high aulter in the same church of our lady of Wylsdon 3s 4d;[154] to my moder church of Saint Alban 12d.

---

[153] Perhaps 'praise be' has been omitted?

[154] There was a very popular shrine of Our Lady at Willesden (Middx; now Brent).

To Mercy my daughter in law my standyng cup & my standyng maser with the covers & a pin[155] coverd with blew chamlett & the clasps of silver; to Agnes Sewell my servaunt a gown furd with cony & a yeres wages after my decesse & a silver spone; to Elyn my servaunt a brass pott by estimacion not a gallon, a pewter salt, two candelstickes, a pewter pott, a pair of shetes of tow, a silver spon & in money 6s 8d. An old federbed that my maydens do ly on With the bolster & the coverys belongyng to the same bed.[156] To Joyse my servaunt oon shete of flex, a nother of tow, a candelstik, two sawcers, two potengers, a silver spon & a ryall of gold.

To the brethered of our lady & saint Kateryn 3s 4d.

I will that three trentalles of masses be saide for my soule, my father & my mother & all cristen soules at my buriall & immediatly folowyng as shortly as may be possibill.

I bequethe to John Case my son two fetherbeddes, bolsters, pelowes, hangynges & all that belonges to them & two pair of fyne shetes, a silver salt, a colar of silver & a roose of gold.

I have four yardes of brode cloth, the Which I will shalbe solde & the money distributed for my soule health.

And my house that Thomas Thomson dwellith in I Wyll it [*fol. 234r*] shalbe solde, And 40s of the money I bequethe to Elisabeth the Wyff of Robert Tod[*damaged*] Carpentar, the residue tobe distributid for my soule.

The Residue of my goodes ne gyven nor bequethid I bequethe to John Case my son and to John a Dale, whom I make and ordeyn myn Executours for to distribute them for my soule helth by thadvice of the vicar, whom I make oversear.

Thes Wytnes: sir William Man, vicar of Rykm[er]sworth, George Herd, William Groser, John Colynson, Thomas Frydey, John Woods & John Wood parissh clerk.

This testament was proved on 28 July 1535, before Master Thomas Kyngesbury, archdeacon, &c; & administration &c was committed to the executors named in the same.

---

[155] The word is hard to see but it looks like 'pin'.

[156] The legatee of this 'feather bed' has been omitted; or perhaps it was another bequest to his servant Elyn.

242. John Alen   reference: 3AR1r[157]
will: 23 November 1535 [English]   **probate: 24 August 1537**

In dei nomine Amen. In the yere of our lorde god 1535 the 23rd Day of Novembre, In the 27th yere of the reigne of King Henry the VIII, I John Alen, hole of mynde and good remembraunce, made this my last wyll in this wise.

First I bequeith my sowle to allmyghty god, and to our lady saynt Mary, and to all the holy company in heven; my body to buryed[*sic*] in the churchyard of Rickm[er]sworthe.

To Saynt Albans shryne 2d; to the hyghe alture of Ryckm[er]sworthe 2d.

I wyll that myn executours gyve 10s at leysour to a preist to saye a trentall of Masses for my sowle, my frends sowelles and all christen sowles.

I wyll that Joan my wiff have all suche stuffe of houshold as I now have whiche were hers afore our maryage.

The residewe of all my gooddes, my debtes paid, I wyll that Joan my wyff have thone half, the other half to be devyded among my children.

I wyll that Joan my my[*sic*] wyffe be my executrix and John Danyell overseer of this my last wyll to be fulfilled.

Wyttenes: sir William Man vicar, John Danyell, Richard Sotherley, John Sotherley,[158] Richard Marten with other.

This testament was proved by Master Thomas Kingisbury, bachelor of sacred theology, archdeacon of the monastery of St Alban, on 24 August 1537, and in the 28th of the reign of our illustrious lord Henry VIII, by the grace of God king of England and France, defender of the faith and supreme head of the English church, there visitor and commissary; & administration &c was committed to Joan, relict and executrix named in the same testament; & she was admitted by the same &c; saving all rights whatsoever &c.

[*margin*]: Robert Garret, clerk, registrar of testaments.[159]

---

[157] Also recorded in HALS, 4AR1r.

[158] Definitely Richard and John Sotherley, not Fotherley; could be a scribal error.

[159] This is the only time that the probate clause is so detailed, and the only time that the probate clerk identifies himself: perhaps because it is the first will in a new register.

243. Henry Evelyn, husbandman[160]   reference: 2AR237v–238r
will: 18 March 1535/6 [English]   probate: 25 September 1536

In the name of god Amen, the yere of our lord god 1535/6, the 18 day of March, I Henry Evelyn of Rykm[er]sworth in the countie of Hertf', husbandman, of good & hole mynde, make & ordeyn this my last wyll in maner & fourme folowyng.

First I gyve & bequeth my soule to almyghty god, to the cumpany of our lady Saint Mary the mother of Crist & of all the saincts; And my body tobe buried in the parissh church or churchyard of Rykm[er]sworth.

I bequethe to my mother church of saint Albon 2d; to the high aulter of my parissh church of Rykm[er]sworth 3s 4d; to the parissh church of Stanmer (Stanmore) 3s 4d; to the brotherhed of our lady and saint Kateryn in the said parissh church 6s 8d; and to every lyght kept & mayntened within the said church 4d.

To William Evelyn my son & to his heires all my land that is freehold, paying yerely to Alice my Wyff duryng her life 20s by the yere, tobe payde quarterly by equall porcions for the house that she standith in state of duryng hir lyfe.

I bequeth to my son John Evelyn my copyhold land called ?Eygaps & that that was mother Atkyns; and Alice my wyfe to have one of theim duryng her lyfe whether that she will chose.

I bequeth to John Guds[161] & to my doughter his wyfe my copyhold land within the parissh of Chalfunt.

I bequeth to the mendyng of the hyghway where moost neid is betwixt my house & my parissh church 20s.

To Robert Wattes my servaunt oon cowe; to Maud Gybs oon cowe beside that she hath delyverd & all the stuff that was Asshleys[162] & 40s of lawful money; to Jone Buttirfild oon bolok; and to every godchild that I have that will call for it 4d; I bequeth to my doughter Jone Gybs oon cow, five shepe with their lambs & 40s in money; to my daughter Alice Martin 40s wherof she hath received vid[elicit] 6s 8d; to my daughter Isabell Godfrey oon cow.

To William my son all my cart horses with their harnes & all my stuff belongyng to husbandry & all my corn sown & not sown, also my new cupburd & my great pott & my grete cawdron & three silver sponys. To Alice my wife my bald gelding & 20 sheep with their lambs & all my beyse[163] & houshold stuff not bequeathed, except

---

[160] A churchwarden in the 1520s.

[161] Definitely 'Guds' rather than 'Gybs' (see below), presumably a scribal error.

[162] Perhaps referring to the manor of Ashleys, rather than a person.

[163] Meaning 'beasts' rather than 'bees'.

my best fetherbed, the which I will [*fol. 238r*] remayn to William my son after the decesse of my wyff. I will that such tabulls, fourmys, trestils with such other thyngs as my wyff hath no neid of shall remayn with William my son, whom I ordeyn & make my sole executour.

And I bequeth to John Wood the parissh clerk 12d.

I bequeth to Andrew Randall 3s 4d; to John Roffe 3s 4d; whom I make overseers of this my Wyll.

this wytnes: the vicar, John Knyght, Andrew Randall, John Wood and other.

This testament was proved on 25 September 1536 before Master Thomas Kyngesbury, by royal authority,[164] archdeacon, &c; & administration &c was committed to the executrix named in the same &c.

244. Henry Wedon, husbandman[165] reference: 2AR238r
will: 14 July 1536 [English] probate: 2 October 1536

In the name of God amen, the 14th day of July in the yere of our lord god 1536, I Henry Wedon of Rykm[er]sworth, husbandman, of good & hole mynde, to god,[166] make & ordeyn this my last wyll in fourme & maner folowyng.

First I gyve & bequethe my soule to almyghty god, to the cumpany of our blessed lady & of all sainctes; & my body to be buried within the churchyard of Rykm[er]sworth.

To my mother church of saint [*Alban*] 4d; to my parissh church 6s 8d; to the gyldyng of the Rood within the said church 6s 8d; to the high aulter 8d.

I wyll that Thomas my son shall have my houses & all my t[*damaged: ?tenements*] after the decesse of Alice my wyff.

Also I will that all my movable goods shalbe equally dyvided betwixt Alice my wyff & Thomas my son.

And Alice my wyffe tobe my soole executrice.

And [*John*] Knyght & Thomas Castylman to be overseers of this my last wyll tobe fulfillyd & eyther of them to have for their labour 6s 8d.

Theis Wyttnes: sir William Man vicar, John Knyght, Thomas Castylman & John Wod.

I bequethe to George Grover 40s.

---

[164] Acknowledging Henry VIII as head of the Church.

[165] Another of the churchwardens in 1520s, This will and the next are damaged on the right-hand side; likely missing words supplied in italics in [ ].

[166] Perhaps 'praise be' omitted? Not damaged here.

This testament was approved on 2 October in the year aforesaid [1536], by Master Thomas Kyngesbury, by royal authority, archdeacon, &c; & administration was committed to the executrix named in the same &c.

245. Roger Baker
reference: 2AR238r
will: 28 August 1536 [English]   **probate: 30 September 1536**

In dei nomine, Amen. The yere of our lord god 1536, the 28th day of the moneth of August, in the yere of the reign of our soverayn lord Kyng Henry the VIII, I Roger Baker, Hole of mynde & in [*good*] remembrance, make my testament conteynyng my last wyll, in this wyse.

First I bequethe [*my soul*] to almyghty god & to all the company of heven; And my body tobe buried in the churchyard of [Rykmersworth].

To Thomas my son a fetherbed, a bolster & a coverlid; to my eldest son John a [*?gown*] with yellow lynyng, a jackett & a paire of hosen.

To thamendyng & reparacion of the way in Wa[*damaged*] 20s.[167]

The Rewsidue of my goods movable I gyve to Elen my wyff, whom I make sole Executrice of [*this*] my testament.

And Thomas Spenser, Thomas Baker & John Knyght overseers.

Wyttnes: Thomas Baker my son, John Knyght, Cristofer Brewton, John Wod, Richard ?Eton, John Wod the clerk & other mor.

This testament was approved on 30 September 1536, by Master Thomas Kyngesbury, by royal authority, archdeacon, &c; & administration &c was committed to the executrix named in the same &c.

246. Richard Wylson
reference: 3AR3r[168]
will: 19 July 1537 [English]   **probate: 30 September 1537**

In dei nomine Amen. In the yere of our lorde god 1537 the 19th day of Julij, I Richard Wylson of Ryckm[er]sworthe, hole of mynd and perfecte remembraunce, ordeyn and make my last wyll and testament in forme folowyng.

First I bequeithe my sowle to Allmyghty god, to our lady saynt Mary and to all the holy company of heven; my body to be buryed within the churche yerde of our blessed lady of Ryckm[er]sworthe.

To my mother churche of saynt Alban 4d; I bequeithe 13s 4d to be gyven to pore people to pray for my soule within the parishe of Ryckm[er]sworthe; to the highe

---

[167] Perhaps Walys Lane; see Thomas Spenser's will (249).
[168] Also recorded in HALS, 4AR4v-5r.

Altare of my parishe churche 6d; 20s to be gyven to pore people within the parishe of Watford; to the highe Altare in Watford churche 6d.

To \my/ eldest sonne Blase £3 6s 8d; to John my sonne £3 6s 8d; to my three dawghters, Alice, Dorothe and Margaret, to be delyvered equally amonges them £20 by equall porcions. And [if] it shall fortune one or mor of them to departe to god, that then their parte or partes shall remayne to the other that shall lyve.

I wyll that John my sonne shall have the house that I doe duell yn, the whiche I dyd bye of Blakemore, when he shall come to lawfull aige.

I wyll that Magdaleyn my wyffe shall have my \lease/ wyff of a ferme called Haroldes lyenge within the paryshe of Watford and to sell it if she have neade for to performe my wyll.

I wyll that Wyllyam Baldwyn shalbe myn executour with my wyff, and he to have 6s 8d for his paynes taking.

I wyll that John Rolff thelder be over\seer/ of thys my last wyll to be performed, and he to have for his labo[ur] 6s 8d.

Thes wytnes: John Roff the elder, Richard Roff, James White, with other

This testament was approved before Master Thomas Kyngisbury, archdeacon, &c on the last day of September in the year aforesaid [1537] &c; & administration &c was committed to Magdalene Wylson, relict, and William Baldwyn executors &c, saving &c.

247. William Spone

will: 1 October 1538 [English]

reference: 3AR15v

probate: c.17 August 1539[169]

In the name of god amen. I William Spone, beyng in good remembraunce and good memory, makyng my last wyll.

fyrst I bequeath my soule to allmyghty god and all the company of heven; and my body to be buryed in the parishe churche of Rykm[er]sworth before the Roode.

I make my Wyff Johan my hole executrix, and John Parmer and Thomas Spenser my oversears.

I bequeathe all my goodds moveable and unmoveable unto the sayd Joan my Wyff, whom I make my hole executrix. I bequeathe to my oversears to every of them 6s 8d.

---

[169] Probate clause undated; the probate date of the preceding will in register was 17 August 1539; *Wills at Hertford* index says probate year was 1539. Also recorded in HALS, 4AR26v, where the probate clause is also undated.

I wyll to John Parmer my office and the lease concernyng my baylywycke of the More, paying to Joan my Wyff 20 markes of true and lawfull money at suche days as ~~he and~~ my executrix and he shall agre.

This Wyll and last testament was made and wrytten, theys men beryng wyttnes, Hugh Byrde, Richard Sotherley, William Goold, John Gowld, by me sir John Rolff, beyng the vicars deputie, the first day of Octobre, In the 30th yere of King Henry VIII.

This present testament was proved before William Est, archdeacon; & administration &c was committed, saving &c [undated].

248. Thomas Spenser, baker   reference: 3AR15v–16v[170]
will: 22 August 1539 [English]   probate: 6 October 1539

In dei nomine amen. the 22nd day of August In the yere of our lorde god 1539, And in the reigne of king henry the VIII 31st, I Thomas Spenser of Rykm[er]sworthe in the Countie of Hertford, baker, beyng hole of mynd and in good memory, laude be unto almyghty god my maker and redemer and to the most gloryous virgyn his mother, make and ordeyn this my present testament in maner and forme folowyng that is to say.

First I bequeythe and commend my soule to allmyghty god and to the glorious Virgyn his mother saynt Mary and to all the holy company in heven;[171] and my body to be buryed within the church [*fol. 16r*] yerde of our lady in Ryckm[er]sworth.

To my mother churche of Saynt Alban 4d; to the Highe Altar of my paryshe churche for my tythes and oblacions by me necligently forgoten or With holde in discharge of my soule and conscience 2s; to the Rode light maynteyned in the said churche to the honour of allmyghty god 4d; to the mayntenaunce of the fraternite of our lady and saynt Katheryn in the said churche 6s 8d.

I bequeith to noyous repayring in Walys Lane 20s.

I wyll that Master Shawe of the Quenys college in oxford[172] \shall/ to have to synge for my soule and all chrysten soules by the space of one quarter of a yere 33s 4d; and

---

[170] Also recorded in HALS, 4AR27r-28r.

[171] Spenser was one of the men 'detected' by John Grosar/Grosser in 1521 during Bishop Longland's heresy trials, but, unlike Grosser (227), Spenser committed his soul in the traditional manner. (Aston, 'Troubles of churchwardens', p.540) Spenser was also one of the witnesses in the church court case against George Belche relating to the funds of the guild of St Mary. (Aston, pp.530-32)

[172] Margaret Aston identified 'Master Shawe' as Lancelot Shaw, who had become a fellow of Queen's College in 1534 and was to be provost of the college during Elizabeth's reign.

if he doo hit not hymselff then I wyll that he commytte hit to som of his bretheryn suche as he thynkthe wyll truly doo the same.

I bequeythe to be distribut to the pore and most nedy people at my buryall 20s.

To Roger Spenser my sonne £5 sterling and a sylver salt parcell gylt with a cuver weying 11 oz a quarter [blank];[173] to the same Roger my best fetherbed with a brysell tyke, withe the bolster, the bedd and bolstar weyng 10 stones 2 powndes £8 to the stone; to the same Roger a sylver pott with a cover parcell gylte weyng 10 oz halff quarter [blank], And a half dosen of sylver spones with mayden hedds gylt weyng 11 oz a quarter [blank]; to the sayd Roger a Seler and a testour, the best cuveryng, A payer of Whyte fustyan blankets, two payer of flexen shetes good and hole, with the curteyns now to the same bedd belonging; to the same Roger my two best gownes; to the same Roger my best brasse pott, my best brasse panne, my best charger of pewter, two of my best platters, two of the pewter disches, two of the best sawcers and too poryngers.

To the same Roger £33 6s 8d apon this condicion: that if Anne my Wyff doo clayme at any tyme duryng her lyff any Interest tytle or clayme of dowry of or in any of my landes, meases, tenements, meads, pasturs, commyns or Wooddes or underwooddes, with their appurtenaunces, set, lyeng and and beyng in the Counties of Middelsex and buckyngham, then I wyll that she shall pay unto the same Roger the said £33 6s 8d Withowt any delay. And if she suffre the said Roger to enyoye the foresaid landes and tenementes, I wyll that she shall not pay the said £33 6s 8d, nor noo parcell therof to the said Roger

Also I wyll that if my sonne Roger [do sell][174] any of the said landes, meases, tenementes, with there appurtenaunces, or any parcell therof, then I wyll that it shalbe lawful to Anne my Wyff to clayme her dowre in suche parcelles as he doythe sell at her pleasur, Any thing in this my last wyll to the contrary not withstandyng and withowt payeng of the foresaid £33 6s 8d to the said Roger.

I bequeithe to George my sonne £6 13s 4d sterling.

I bequeithe to Charles Spenser my sonne, after the decesse of Anne my wyff, a standyng cupp called a maser with a bounde of sylver duble gylt and a fote of sylver parcell gylt weyng 10 oz and a half; to the said Charles, after the decesse of Anne my wyff, all the Implements of my bakhowse, that is to saye, Troves, bordes, brake and a

---

(Aston, 'Troubles of churchwardens, pp.540-1.) His connection with Thomas Spenser is unknown.

[173] The space has been left for the value per ounce, and elsewhere.

[174] This has been omitted but is in the version in register 4AR.

furnyshe sett with a panne, the coborde, the table and forme in the hall, A cownter in the Ware shoppe, a brasen morter. All whiche I wyll that Anne my wyff shall occupye duryng her lyff, but I wyll that at noo tyme she shall remove them owt of the house; to the said Charles £3 6s 8d sterling.

I bequeithe to my sonne William Spenser £3 6s 8d sterling; to the same William, after the decesse of Anne my wyff, A sylver goblett parcell [*fol. 16v*] gylt waying 10 unc' and a half @ 4d.[175]

I bequeythe all my landes and tenementes whiche I holde frely by deade with ther appurtenauncs sett lying and beying only in the parishe of Rickm[er]sworthe to thuse of Anne my wyff, and after her decesse to remayne to the use of John Spenser and his heyrs for ever; to the same John Spencer 40s in money sterling.

I wyll that if any of \my/ sayd sonnes dye befor that they receyve their legacyes, then I wyll that it shalbe equally devyded amongst them that survye[*sic*].

I bequeith to my foure dawgthers, that is to say Alice, Margaret, Brydgett and Johan, to every of them £5 sterling; *viz* for the dawghters £20 to be payd at the daye of their mariges or before if their be cause resonable / ~~Also~~ Also I wyll that if any of my sayd dawghters happen to dye before they receyve their moneye, then I wyll that it shalbe equally devyded among my dawghters survyving.

The resydewe of all my gooddes, catalles and debtes, after my debtes payd, my funerall charges done, and theas my legacyes performed and fulfilled, I gyve and bequeythe to Anne my wyff to her owne propre use.

And of the execution of this my testament and last wyll I make and ordeyn Anne my wyff my soole executrix

And for the oversight of thexecution of this my last wyll and testament I make and ordeyn John Case and Henry Gunner overseers, And I bequeith to eche of them 6s 8d for their labours.

Wyttenesse of this my testament and last will: Master doctour Norbury,[176] William Grocer, Roger Spenser and William Homonger

The same testament was proved before William Est, archdeacon; & administration &c was given to the executrix named in the same testament, saving the rights of whosoever, on 6 October 1539.

---

[175] Perhaps at 4d per ounce?

[176] Margaret Aston suggested that 'Master doctour Norbury' was Robert Norbury, the Benedictine monk who was admitted Bachelor of Theology at Oxford in 1523; again his connection with Spenser is unknown. (Aston, 'Troubles of churchwardens', p.541, n.56)

Appendix 1

1307 Lay Subsidy returns for the vill of Rikemersworth

Reference: TNA, E179/120/8, membrane 37.

See also, J. Brooker and S. Flood, eds, *Hertfordshire Lay Subsidy Rolls 1307 and 1334* (Hertfordshire Record Society, vol. XIV, 1998), pp.146-148.

The text has been laid out in two columns as in the original. Three placenames were given in the margin (see footnotes). As Mickelfield was only a small manor it seems likely that the names of taxpayers elsewhere in the vill recommence (at least) with Ralph le Reve and continue in the second column.

There are 67 taxpayers in total. Comparing the surnames here with those in the 1524 returns (Appendix 2) it is noticeable that some recur two centuries later.

William Bernard[177]	3s 7¼d	Edmund ate Hid	2s 5d
Thomas de Flaunden	2s	Peter ate More	18d
William Blaket	5s 6d	Amice Bithewod	16d
John ate Crouch	17¼d	William Dauwe	10d
John Tukke	18¾d	Richard Camm ·	9d
William Parsun	9d	Roger de Lexen	7d
Roger Custance	7½d	Alan Morel	7d
Nicholas Starie	7d	Roger le Rouwe	10½d
John Ulting	8¾d	Hugh le Reve	13d
Henry ate Dene	10	John Wallekyn	9d
John Gilbe	9¼d	Walter Turevill	7½d
Thomas Giles	11d	Robert Jon	8¾d
Thomas Walkyn	15d	Ralph Alme	12d
Robert ate Gate	7d	John ate Hach	12d
Richard le Drivere	7½d	Ralph de Wedon[178]	16¼d
Simon Vincent	12d	William Pope	7½d
Geoffrey Spyr	8d	Robert Bolu'	10d
William de Langele	2s 6d	William ate Fern	13d
Henry Sekersteyn	7d	Roger Stonhard	12d

---

[177] Rikemersworth written in the margin here, in larger letters than the personal names.
[178] In Brooker & Flood's transcript Ralph de Wedon has been omitted in error, and his assessment of 16¼d assigned to John ate Hach, instead of 12d.

Adam de Cane	9½d	Henry Graung	10d
John Osemund[179]	12d	John le Helder	9d
William Cote	7d	William Southe	7½d
Robert Shepherd [*Bercario*]	12½d	John Julian	15d
Alexander Broman	10¼d	Walter ate Delle	12½d
John Crips	9d	Simon ate Waterdelle	6½d
William Elys	14½d	Henry ate Forde	7½d
Richard ate Ford[180]	6½d	Simon ate Nattuk	12d
Thomas de Mikelfeld	15d	John le Blount	9½d
Ralph ate Fortnye	6½d	Ralph Torold	9d
Nicholas de Whethamstud	3s 8¼d	Robert de Asshele	2s ¼d
Ralph le Reve	16d	Simon ate More	8d
John ate Mor'	6¾d	Geoffrey de Boterfeld	9½d
John Aignel	2s	John de Snelleshale	2s 1¼d
Walter ate Mor'	12d		

Total [*correct*]	76s 5d

---

[179] Crokesl' written in the margin here, in smaller letters than the personal names.
[180] Mikelfeld written in the margin here, again in smaller letters.

Appendix 2

Lay Subsidy return, 1524

Reference: TNA, E179/120/114, subsidy granted by parliament on 21 May 1523.

This tax was known as a lay subsidy because it was imposed on the laity not the clergy (who were taxed differently). It was based on individual assessments of people's landed wealth, ownership of goods or wages. Liability was determined by a series of scales laid down in the statute, which had a minimum threshold. Payments were to be made in three annual instalments.

The definition of landed wealth for these purposes was based on the person's income from their land, not its capital value, so copyholders and leaseholders were not taxed on land.

Taxable goods were clearly defined. The assessment was made on coins and on 'plate stocke and merchaundyse, all maner of cornes & blades severed from the grownde householde stuf and of all other goodes movable ...'.

For the 1523 subsidy only people who fell below the qualification for land or goods might be taxed on wages: the threshold was 20s (£1) *per annum*. (Subsidies were not levied on wages again.)[181]

This is the assessment of individuals for the first collection. Estimated date of document: between 26 February and 17 June 1524. The 4th column indicates the taxation category: L = land; G = goods; W = wages.

	Assessment	To pay	on
Rickmansworth			
George Wyngborne	£10	10s	L
Robert Rolles	£6	3s	G
Roger Gonner	£26 13s 4d	£1 6s 8d	G
Henry Gonner, his son	60s	1s 6d	G
Reygnold Mylsham, servant	20s	4d	W
Thomas Lauraunce, servant	20s	4d	W
Thomas Gee, servant	20s	4d	W
John Mylward	£20	20s	G

---

[181] See R. Hoyle, *Tudor Taxation Records: a guide for users* (London, 1994), pp.12-14.

John A Dene	£10	5s	G
Thomas Mylsham	£10	5s	G
Thomas Spenser	£13 6s 8d	6s 8d	G
Richard Decon	£5	2s 6d	G
William Hucheson	£13 6s 8d	6s 8d	G
Robert Pereson	60s	1s 6d	G
John Randoll of Sheperdes	£10	5s	G
[*unnamed*], his servant	£1 6s 8d	4d	W
?Scybbys Harman, alyen born	40s	2s	G
Richard [*blank*], servant	20s	4d	W
John A Dale	60s	1s 6d	G
[*blank*] Golde, servant	40s	1s	G
John Kyng	60s	3s	L
William Holt	60s	1s 6d	G
Thomas Castylman	40s	1s	G
William Hedynbrace	40s	1s	G
[*blank*] Atkyn, servant	20s	4d	W
John Knyght	£4	2s	G
Robert Faucett	£3 6s 8d	1s 8d	G
John Atkyn, servant	20s	4d	W
John Colynson, servant	20s	4d	W
William Grocer	40s	1s	G
William Creke	40s	1s	G
John Eve	40s	1s	G
John Grocer	40s	1s	G
William Myller, 'bocher' (butcher)	£4	2s	G
[*blank*] Canon	40s	1s	G
Thomas Barbour	40s	1s	G
John Henry, clerk	40s	1s	G
Thomas Denys	40s	1s	G
John Horne, the younger	40s	1s	G
Richard Whyte, fuller	60s	1s 6d	G
John Horne, the elder	40s	1s	G
Robert Bentley	£1 6s 8d	4d	W
Raff Hyll	£1 6s 8d	4d	W
Thomas Sydney	40s	1s	G
Thomas A Dene	40s	1s	G

William Robynson, servant	20s	4d	W
John Whyte, clerk	40s	1s	G
John Moyer	40s	1s	G
George Bee	£6	3s	G
William [blank], servant	20s	4d	W
Moder (Mother) Tylson	£4	2s	G
Richard Blackamore	£6 13s 4d	3s 4d	G
Richard Wylson	£5	2s 6d	G
[unnamed], his servant	£1 13s 4d	4d	W
John Gardener	£2 13s 4d	1s 4d	G
Thomas Whyte	60s	1s 6d	G
Robert A Lane	£3 6s 8d	1s 8d	G
Henry Wedon	£5	2s 6d	G
Moder (Mother) Atkyn	40s	1s	G
Henry Bulbroke	40s	1s	G
[unnamed], his servant	20s	4d	W
John Davy	40s	1s	G
William ?Brude, in the custody of William Herde	£3 6s 8d	1s 8d	G
Symond Browne	20s	4d	W
John Cooper	40s	1s	G
William ?Colte	£8	4s	G
Richard [blank], his servant	20s	4d	W
Thomas ?Colte, servant	20s	4d	W
John Gybbe, servant	20s	4d	W
John Hayward	£8	4s	G
Thomas Atkyn, servant	20s	4d	W
Richard Whylys	40s	1s	G

West Hyde

Henry A Wedon of Westwykes	£20	20s	G
Thomas A Wedon, his son	40s	1s	G
Raff Whyte, servant	20s	4d	W
John Fyssher, servant	20s	4d	W
Henry Evelyn	£22	22s	G
William Evelyn, his son	40s	1s	G
John Evelyn, his son	40s	1s	G

John A Wedon, of long lane	£6 13s 4d	3s 4d	G
Stephyn Randoll	£7	3s 6d	G
John Randoll, his son	£4	2s	G
Robert Randoll, his son	20s	4d	G
Walter Tredewey	£6	3s	G
Moder (Mother) Hargate	40s	1s	G
John Heydon of Westhyde	£6 13s 4d	3s 4d	G
John Clark, servant	20s	4d	W
John Rolff	40s	1s	G
John Randoll of Pynchefeldes	£5	2s 6d	G
John Alyn	£6	3s	G
John Whyte	£5	2s 6d	G
John Tredewey	£6	3s	G
Thomas Carter	60s	3s	L

Chorleywood

Richard Tredewey	£20	20s	G
William Tredewey, his son	20s	4d	W
John Butterfield	20s	1s	L
Andrew Braunche	40s	1s	G
Richard Butterfield	40s	2s	L
Robert Braunche	40s	1s	G
John A Wedon	40s	1s	G
Richard Belche	£4	2s	G
John Gybbe of Heryngarste	£8	4s	G
Richard Gybbe, his son	20s	4d	G
Thomas ?Downe	£5	2s 6d	G
Richard Roys	60s	1s 6d	G
Stephyn Roys	40s	1s	W
John [*blank*], servant	£1 6s 8d	4d	W
Thomas [*blank*], servant	£1 6s 8d	4d	W
George Belche	£12	6s	G
William Belche	20s	1s	L

Croxley

William Baldewyn	£20	20s	G
William Pereson, servant	£1 13s 4d	4d	W

John Holtyng the younger	40s	1s	G
Richard Bybbesworth	£4	2s	G
Thomas Paltok	40s	1s	G
John Norrys	60s	1s 6d	G
Thomas Dukke	40s	1s	G
Thomas Butterfeld	40s	1s	G
Thomas Langton	40s	1s	G
William A Wedon	£4	2s	G
Henry Stanborowe	£2 6s 8d	1s 8d	G
Richard Gybbe	£7	3s 6d	G
John Holtyng the elder	£6	3s	G
Hugh Stanys	40s	1s	G
Andrew Randoll	40s	1s	G
John Heydon of Mekylfeld grene	£13 6s 8d	6s 8d	G
Edward [blank], servant	20s	4d	W

Batchworth

John Hede	£20	20s	G
Jamys [blank], his servant	20s	4d	W
Alyce Golde remaynyng in the handes of the said John Hede	£6	3s	G
Johanne Goold in goodes remaynyng in the handes of the said John Hede	£4	2s	G
Richard Foderley	16s 8d	3s 4d	L
Margerie Fraunceys in goodes remaynyng in the hands of the said Richard	£4	2s	G
John Foderley	£6 13s 4d	3s 4d	G
John Cokdell	60s	1s 6d	G
Nicholas Baker	60s	1s 6d	G
Roger Baker	40s	1s	G
John Twyches	40s	1s	G
Richard Marten	60s	1s 6d	G
Thomas Marten, servant	40s	1s	W
John Martyn, servant	40s	1s	W
John Burford	10s	1s 6d	G
Edmonde Aldwyn	£5	2s 6d	G

John Blythe	20s	4d	W
William Woode	20s	4d	G
Henry Smyth	£4	2s	G
John Estbery	60s	1s 6d	G
In box of Our Lady fraternyte	£10	5s	
In box of the Trynyte	£1 10s 4d	4d	
In box of Seynt Kateryn	20s	4d	
In box of Seynt Antony	20s 6d	4d	
[*total to be collected*] [*correct*]		£19 12s	

Appendix 3

The Rickmansworth Indulgence (1522)

Reference: British Library, General Reference Collection, C.18.e.2 (96)

Be it knowen to all crysten people which ioyeth in theyr hartes of the power of god shewed by his owne precyous body in fourme of brede in the chyrche of Rykmersworthe where wretched & cursed people cruelly & wylfully set fyre upon all the ymages & on the canape that the blessyd sacrament was in & to make the fyre more cruell they put towe with baner staves bytwene the sparres & brases of the chaunsell thrughe the whiche fyre the sayd chaunsell was brent & the pyx was molten & the blessyd body of our lorde Jhesu cryst in forme of brede was founde upon the hyghe awter & nothynge perysshed. Also they brake into the vestry & put fyre amonge all the ornamentes & Jewelles & brent the sayd vestry & all that was therin. Also in the rode lofte they wrapped towe aboute the blessyd rode & about apayre of organs & melted all the wexe in the sayd lofte conteynynge in weyght xiiii score [280] pounde where as the flambynge fyre was in the sayd lofte about the blessyd ymage of Jhesu cryst nother the sayd ymage nor the towe about it was nothynge hurte thrughe the might & power of our savyour Jhesu cryst. Also to maynteyne theyr cruell opynyons they wente unto the fonte & brake it open & dyspoyled the water that was hallowed therin & cast it a brode in the chyrche flore in dyspyte of the sacrament of baptyme. And for as moche as the substancyall men of the sayd parysshe hath invewed the kynges grace how honourably god was served in the sayd chyrche in tyme past; & also that it pleased hym to shere his grete might and power.

Wherfore my lorde Cardynall and legate de latere hath graunted C. [100] dayes of pardon releasynge of theyr penaunce in purgatory to all them that gyve ony parte of theyr goodes to the restorynge of the said chyrche [*damaged*]

Also my lorde of Lyncolne hath graunted xl [40] dayes [*damaged*]

(Previously published in Margaret Aston, 'Iconoclasm at Rickmansworth, 1522: Troubles of Churchwardens', *Journal of Ecclesiastical History*, vol. 40, 4 (1989), pp.524–552, p.552.)

Appendix 4

Archdeacons and other officials (with their stated role) who granted probate

The dates, taken from the probate clauses to the wills published here, indicate when the men were known to be active. The probate clauses between March 1447 and December 1482 are very brief and provide no names.

Archdeacons

William Alnewyke	February 1426 to May 1428
John Peyton	February 1436
William Albon, doctor of canon law	March 1447
Thomas Newlonde[182]	December 1482
John Rothebury	August 1483
John Thornton, doctor of sacred theology	January 1492 to March 1493
Thomas Newlonde	October 1494 to July 1495
Richard Runham[183]	January 1496 to September 1504
John Stonywell, professor of sacred theology	May 1505
John Killingworth[184]	July 1506
John Albon	October 1506 to April 1508
John Maynard	January 1510 to May 1510
Richard Runham, prior	February 1513 to February 1514
Thomas Kyngesbury, bachelor of sacred theology & laws	November 1517 to September 1537
William Est	August 1539 to October 1539

Other officials

Croxley manor court

Brother Simon Wyndsore	cellarer	May 1409
Brother Michael Cheyne	cellarer	September 1416

---

[182] Served again in the mid 1490s.
[183] Probably the same man as Richard Runham, prior, below.
[184] He had been commissary in July 1498.

Archdeaconry court

Hugh Lever, doctor of laws	official	August 1495
John Killingworth	commissary	July 1498
John Dowman, doctor of laws	official	February 1502 to April 1503
Thomas Ramryge	abbot	March 1505
William Throkmarton, doctor of laws	official	December 1514 to March 1515
John Incent, doctor of laws	official	August 1516
Henry Ampthyll	commissary	March 1521
John Eggerton, bachelor of canon law	commissary	July 1524 to September 1527
Thomas Burley, bachelor of canon law	commissary	February 1528 to May 1529
Thomas Newnham	sub-prior & official	November 1531
Thomas Kyng, master of arts	official	February 1532 to March 1532

Glossary

The modern spelling has been given, followed by the original spelling used in the English wills. Relevant will numbers are supplied in brackets.

Sources
The main source is the *Oxford English Dictionary*, online version, but these other sources have been noted where applicable:

Duffy   E. Duffy, *The Stripping of the Altars: Traditional Religion in England, c.1400-c.1580* (1992)

MED   *Middle English Dictionary* (in progress, 1956-) online at: https://quod.lib.umich.edu/m/middle-english-dictionary/dictionary

Purvis   J. S. Purvis, *Dictionary of Ecclesiastical Terms* (1962)

Yaxley   D. Yaxley, ed., *A Researcher's Glossary of words found in historical documents of East Anglia* (2003)

abut: to adjoin, border on, referring to land.

accounts, executor's: statement of expenses and receipts connected with the administration of testator's estate.

acquit: discharge executors from further action.

acre: measure of land area, 4840 square yards, approx. 0.4 hectare.

administration: the management and disposal of the estate of a deceased person.

age, full: 21 years (boys), 14 years (girls).

age of inheritance: for lands, 21 years; for goods, 14 years; unless otherwise stated.

aisle (aley, isle): part of church built alongside and parallel to nave or chancel, from which it is separated by pillars and arches.

altar: stone table at which mass was celebrated.

andiron (aundyerne): fire-dog; bar of metal on feet in the fireplace, on which logs were placed.

anniversary: an obit; the commemoration of the deceased a year after death, and in subsequent years, taking the form of a re-enactment of the funeral ceremony, that is, (at its fullest) the evening service of *placebo*, preceded by the ringing of bells, with the morning service of *dirige* followed by requiem mass the next day.

antiphon: musical composition based on scriptural text and sung.

antiphoner (antifoner): service book containing music for the antiphons and other parts of divine service.

appurtenances (thappurtenances): a minor property, right, or privilege, belonging to another more important, and passing in possession with it.

arable: tilled land, as distinct from meadow and pasture.

archdeacon: ordained ecclesiastical dignitary next under bishop in church hierarchy, responsible for part of diocese called archdeaconry; he exercised jurisdiction on the bishop's behalf in his archdeaconry.

attorney: legal representative, not necessarily a lawyer.

bailiff: manorial official; the agent or steward of landlord.

bakehouse: building or room in which baking is being, or has been, carried out.

bark: bark, especially oak-bark; used in tanning.

basin: a circular vessel of greater width than depth, with sloping or curving sides, used for holding water and other liquids.

basilard (baselard): dagger (fashionable). (*MED*)

bawdkynne: rich embroidered cloth originally made with a warp of gold thread and a woof of silk, then any rich brocade.

beads: usually, especially when 'a pair of beads', a rosary; *see* **paternoster.**

beam: *see* **candlebeam.**

bed: usually denotes bedding, rather than a complete bed in the modern sense; a typical 'bed' consisted of a mattress, a pair of sheets, a pair of blankets and a cover.

blanket: kind of woollen cloth, often white or undyed. (*MED*)

brake (248): bracken, which was used as fuel. Here it is included in the 'implements' in the bakehouse of Thomas Spenser.

boards (and trestles): surface of wood, used with trestles to form a table.

bound: 1) strapped with metal, as in the case of domestic vessels; 2) obliged, either morally (e.g. to pray for souls or pay debts), or by written bond (to pay money or fulfil certain conditions).

brass: alloy of copper with tin or zinc (Latin *eneus*).

brindled (brendyld) (79): the *OED* has 'brinded/brended' meaning 'of a tawny or brownish colour, marked with bars or streaks of a different hue' dating from 1430, but variants of 'brindled', in a separate entry, date only from 1678; William Gybbs's will, written in 1466, clearly has the English word 'brendyld' more than 200 years earlier.

broadcloth (brode cloth): woollen cloth woven on a broadloom; the measurements of a broadcloth were laid down by an Act of 1483–4 (I Rich.III c.8: *Statutes of the Realm*, ii, 485): 2 yards (approx. 1.83 metre) wide and 24 yards (22 m.) long.

brysell tyke (248): as a tick was the case for a mattress and bristles were the stiff hairs that grow on the back and sides of the hog and wild boar; perhaps this was a robust mattress. (not in *OED*)

buckler, 'buclare': a small round shield

bullock: bull-calf (*MED*), but used of both sexes.

burette (Latin *burettum*) (53): a protective burette called 'un **salet**' (*see* **salet**).

candle: generic term for all cylinders of wax incorporating wicks, but often used of the smallest type; *cf* **torch**.

candlebeam: literally, a beam on which candles and lights were placed in a church, usually in front of an image.

canvas: coarse fabric made from flax or hemp. (*MED*)

cap (135): a helmet or headpiece. (*OED* first mention is 1530)

carucate: a measure of land, varying with the nature of the soil, etc., being as much as could be tilled with one plough (with its team of 8 oxen) in a year; a plough-land.

cauldron (cawdron): kettle or pot for heating water or cooking. (*MED*)

celebrate: perform a religious rite, especially celebrate mass.

cellarer: the monk responsible for the supply of food, drink and fuel for a religious community and its guests; the manor of Croxley belonged to the cellarer of St Albans Abbey.

celure: canopy of bed.

chalice: a goblet of precious metal to contain the wine at mass; communion cup.

chamlet: beautiful fine cloth from the east, a blend of silk and other fibres.

chancel: the east end of a parish church, separated from the nave by screens and by the chancel arch; the choir was usually situated in the chancel.

chapel: a building containing an altar, either within a church, or free-standing.

chaplain: usually, an unbeneficed priest; **parish chaplain:** priest serving the cure on behalf of the incumbent, but not officially instituted.

charger: large serving-dish or plate.

chattels (sometimes 'cattels'): property of any kind, goods, treasure, money, land etc (*MED*); 'cattels' may refer to cattle/animals but may be other chattels.

chest: large, strong box.

chief lord of the fee: major landlord in the feudal pyramid, holding his land (fee) directly of the crown.

clerk: cleric (used of a **priest**, as today), *but see also* **parish clerk**.

cloak: loose outer garment. (*MED*)

close: piece of land appropriated to private use, such as meadow or field, usually hedged or fenced. (*MED*)

coffer: trunk, chest or case of any size. (*MED*)

commendation of soul: the commending, by the testator at the beginning of a will, of his or her soul to God, etc.

commissary: one who had a commission, either temporary or permanent, usually from a bishop or archdeacon, to carry out some particular duty or duties.

coney, cony: rabbit. The rabbit was introduced into England in early Norman times; coney/cony was the usual medieval name for the animal; the fur was used for clothes and bedclothes.

cope: a full-length, hooded cloak of rich fabric, fastened at breast, worn by clergy especially in processions and at choir services.

copy (noun): copy of court roll; *see* next entry.

copy (adjective), **copyhold:** of customary, or bond land, held by copy of court roll, whereby the tenant, a **copyholder**, has, as his title-deed, a copy of the entry in the court roll of his admittance to the property.

coral (corall): red coral, an arborescent species, found in the Red Sea and Mediterranean, prized from times of antiquity for ornamental purposes, and often classed among precious stones.

coster: a hanging for a bed, table, wall of a room, etc.

cottage: holding consisting of a cottage and the land belonging to it. (*MED*)

court book: the record of a manorial court.

cover: usually refers to bed-cover, but also used for the covers of vessels, especially silver.

coverlet: bed-cover.

croft: small piece of ground used for farming purposes (usually enclosed; often adjoining a house). (*MED*)

cruets: vessels to hold the wine and water for mass.

curate: technically, any member of clergy who has the cure of souls, not necessarily an assistant as implied today; often used by testator of priest in whose special care he has been, or his confessor.

curtains: the hangings about a bed, *not* at windows.

custom: rules operating within a manor, built up over time, and often embodied in a written 'custumal'.

customary: subject to manorial custom, e.g. bond land, copyhold land.

default of heirs: lack of direct heirs of the person being referred to.

diaper: fabric having repeated patterns of figures or geometrical designs; garment or cloth of this fabric. (*MED*)

dicker (dekyr): a quantity of ten hides or skins.

dirige: origin of the English word 'dirge'; the matins of the office of the dead, said in church after the corpse had been brought in and before the requiem mass; so called from the antiphon with which it began, *Dīrige, Domine, deus meus, in cōnspectū tuō viam meam* (Guide, O Lord my God, my way by your sight).

distrain: to seize goods to force someone to do something.

divine service: literally, any religious service, but usually implying the celebration of mass.

doublet: man's tight-fitting garment, covering the body from the neck to the hips or thighs. (*MED*)

dower (dowry): the portion of a deceased's property in which his widow could claim a life-interest, normally a third of the total.

ell (elle): a measure of length (usually of fabric) varying in different countries. The English ell = 45 ins.

emend: repair or make good; can be used of new, as well as old, work.

enfeoff: to put into the hands of **feoffee(s)** (*qv*).

esquire: originally a shield-bearer to a knight (Latin *armiger*, i.e. armour-bearer); a man belonging to the higher order of English gentry, immediately below a knight.

estate: a legal interest in land.

ewer: a pitcher with a wide spout, used to bring water; often paired with a basin.

executor: one who is given the task of executing, or carrying into effect, the provisions of a will and/or testament; the feminine form is **executrix**.

exequies: funeral rites; funeral ceremony.

fabric: the construction and maintenance (of a church).

farm (verb): let out for rent; **farm** (noun): that which was let out for rent ('farmed'), or the rent itself.

farmer (7): lessee of a manor (*see* farm).

feast: a saint's day, or a day celebrating events in the earthly life of Christ and the early church.

featherbed: bed, i.e. mattress, filled with feathers.

fee: land held of a superior lord; *see* **chief lord of the fee**.

feoffee: one to whom property was entrusted (enfeoffed) (225, 'feffid') and who then held the estate or interest in the property on behalf of the original grantor or **feoffor**.

field: usually referred to open-field land, divided into furlongs and strips; *cf* **close**.

firebote (fierbote) (147): firewood, esp. that which a tenant is entitled to take from a landlord's estate for fuel; (hence) the right or privilege of a tenant to take such wood.

fishery: a fishing site; the right to fish in a particular place.

five earthly joys of Our Lady (175b): Duffy (pp.257–8) says that the 'usual' five English five joys of Our Lady were the Annunciation, the Nativity, the Resurrection, the Ascension and her own Coronation in Heaven. No. 175b also mentions **seven heavenly joys of Our Lady:** these are not discussed by Duffy. According to 'CatholicsOnline', the seven joys of Our Lady are: the Annunciation, the Visitation, the birth of Our Lord Jesus, the Adoration of the Magi, the finding of the Child Jesus in the Temple, the Appearance of Christ to Mary after the Resurrection, and the Assumption and Coronation of Mary as Queen of Heaven (https://francismary.org/the-seven-joys-of-our-lady-the-franciscan-crown/)

five nails (175b): perhaps a devotion or meditation on five nails used to crucify Christ (Duffy does not mention this, and one of the wounds was a sword thrust in the side).

five wounds (of Christ): a votive, or special, mass, commemorating the wounds to hands, feet and side of Christ at his crucifixion; it was very popular in the late Middle Ages, being regarded as having particular benefit for souls in purgatory. (*See* Duffy, pp.243–6.)

flax (flex): cloth made of flax; linen.

form: a long seat without a back, a bench.

fraternity: brotherhood, guild.

free: of land, exempt from customary services or exactions (*MED*); *cf* **bond**.

frend(e): some kind of trimmed garment. (*MED*)

furnace (furnyshe): an oven, hearth or fireplace, kiln, furnace, etc.

furred: trimmed or lined with fur.

fustian: kind of cloth, made from cotton, flax or wool. (*MED*)

garled (garlyd bollok) (161): spotted, speckled (of cattle). The *OED* gives 1506 as the earliest example; will 161 was written in 1492.

gallon: liquid measure of 8 pints, approx. 4.55 litres.

gaud (gawde): one of the large beads of the rosary, representing a *paternoster;* (*see* **beads.**

gauded (gawded): with beads.

gentleman: a substantial property-holder whose income was generally derived from rents and profits of farming (in the modern sense).

guild: a religious and social confraternity, brotherhood or association, formed for the mutual aid and protection of its members.

girdle (gyrdyll): belt worn round waist, to secure or confine the garments.

good: property; could include land.

gown: an outer garment, robe. (*MED*)

harnessed (harnesshid): decorated

hearse (hers): metal or wooden structure for supporting cloths, candles, statues, etc., placed over the corpse in church during a funeral.

hedgebote (hechebote) (147): wood or thorns for the repair of fences; the right of the tenant or commoner to take such material from the landlord's estate, or the common (same as heybote, *OED*).

heifer (hekfyr): commonly used of a young cow that has not had a calf but, technically, a cow prior to having a second calf.

heriot: payment, usually the best beast, payable to the lord of the manor by the heir of a deceased **copyholder.**

high altar: the chief altar of a church, but often used in medieval wills to mean the incumbent, or priest serving the cure, to whom were due offerings and tithes.

highway, *often* **king's highway:** (Latin *via regia*) a major road.

hoby (my horse callyd An hoby) (134): a small or middle-sized horse; an ambling or pacing horse; a pony.

hog: castrated male sheep aged one year, i.e., between its first and second shearing, but *may* be a pig.

holy water carrier: priest's assistant, usually the **parish clerk,** who carried the holy (blessed) water at **mass** and other religious services and ceremonies, and also sprinkled parishioners' houses after mass; also called **holy water clerk.**

honest: (Latin *honestus*) 1) honourable, respectable; 2) suitable, competent. (*MED*)

hood: hood, either attached to outer garment, or worn as a separate head-covering. (*MED*)

hose: close-fitting garment resembling tights worn by men and boys; joined hose (*MED*); often termed a pair of hose.

husbandman: small-scale farmer (in the modern sense), with a landholding capable of supporting a family and producing a modest surplus, relying mostly on family labour.

image: representation of holy subject by statue or painted picture.

indented: in the form of an **indenture**, i.e. a deed between parties; two or more copies were written on the same sheet, and then separated by being indented or serrated for identification and security.

intemerate (175b): inviolate, undefiled, unblemished.

inventory: list of goods, chattels and possessions, especially those of the deceased, as required by ecclesiastical courts of executors and administrators.

issue: children or lineal descendants.

issues: the product of any source of income; proceeds from livestock, land, rents, services, fines, etc. (*MED*)

jack (jakke): short, close-fitting, sleeveless jacket, often of quilted leather, sometimes plated; a coat of mail; in bequests often paired with a **sallet** (*qv*), thus providing the beneficiary with some very basic armour.

jacket (jaket, jackett): an outer garment for the upper body, often relatively short in length.

kercher, kerchief (kerchur, keychur): a cloth to cover the head.

kettle: vessel, usually metal, for boiling water and cooking; until the eighteenth century it was a pot or cauldron, sometimes covered, and without a spout. (Yaxley)

kine (kene, kyen): archaic plural of cow.

kirtle (kyrtell): garment for women or girls, often outer garment, sometimes worn over smock. (*MED*)

lasues (232): *see* **leasow**.

laver (lavour): water-pitcher, ewer. (*MED*)

leasow: pasture; pasturage; meadow-land.

legal age: *see* **age**.

lessee: one to whom something is let or leased.

let (noun): hindrance, obstacle; **let** (verb): to hinder, obstruct.

light: lighting in church, here usually a candle, but sometimes a taper or torch.

malt: barley or other grain prepared for brewing by steeping, germinating and kiln-drying.

maltman: the men so designated might have been maltsters, i.e., they made malt from barley for the brewing of ale, it is likely that they were traders in malt because supplying the medieval London market with malt was a specialism of Hertfordshire. (See Introduction, p. xlii.)

manor: an administrative unit held by a landlord – 'the lord' – who himself held it of a superior lord, often the king; only rarely did the term refer to the actual manor house.

mantle: a loose sleeveless cloak.

marble stone: stone used for paving the floors of churches and for grave-slabs; rarely actually marble, more usually limestone, and, later, slate.

mark: a unit of account (not a coin) equal to two thirds of £1, i.e. 13s 4d.

mass: the service of Holy Eucharist, the chief service of the medieval church, which could be said or sung.

mass book (missal): mass-book, containing everything necessary for the priest at the altar when saying or singing mass.

Master: title used of a man who was an MA or had gained a higher university degree (Latin: *Magister* abbreviated to *M*); occasionally the vicar of Rickmansworth was designated M when named as a witness; here this has been shown as M[aster].

master: used of a man of higher social standing, e.g. some of the archdeacons. Here the difference is designated by the Latin word *dominus* which has been translated as 'master' in the probate clause.

mazer: originally a drinking bowl of maple-wood, but often used of similar bowls made of metal.

mead (mede): meadow

measure (of grain): the Latin (*modium*) is non-specific, but perhaps a bushel.

mercer: a merchant, a dealer in textiles (*MED*); perhaps implying membership of the Mercers' Company of London.

messuage (mease) (248): a house-site and the land belonging to it; *cf* **tenement**.

misericord (175b): mercy.

missal: *see* **mass book**

morrow: the day after.

mortuary: the traditional death-gift or burial payment due to the incumbent on behalf of a deceased parishioner, usually the second-best animal (after the heriot had been claimed by the manorial lord).

motley (motlay): diversified in colour, variegated, particoloured.

murrey: dark red or purple-red colour. (*MED*)

napron: an apron

noble: gold coin, usually equivalent of 6s 8d. (*MED*)

notary: person legally authorized to record an action or attest the accuracy of a copied document.

nuncupative: of wills, given orally on the death-bed, and later written in the third person.

obit: *see* **anniversary.**

obsequies: funeral rites.

official, archdeacon's: officer appointed by archdeacon and empowered, among other duties, to prove wills within the archdeaconry.

ornament: the accessory or furnishing of the church and its worship.

overleather (over lethir) (207): leather suitable for the uppers of shoes.

overseer: supervisor, (*qv*).

pair: often means a set, rather than just two, e.g. of beads, a string of beads (rosary).

pan (pane, panne): a cooking vessel, shallower than a kettle, but often of considerable size.

pardurable (175b): everlasting; eternal; existing without end or for all time.

parents: often means, as well as actual parents, forebears, ancestors and kinsmen.

parish clerk: the pre-Reformation parish clerk was an assistant to the parish priest.

paternoster: the large bead in a rosary, usually occurring every eleventh bead; so called from the practice of saying a *Paternoster* ('Our Father') at each large bead, and an *Ave* ('Hail Mary') at each small one.

pavement: a hard covering laid on the ground, in a building, formed of stones, bricks, tiles, or similar materials fitted closely together.

pelowe: pillow

pewter: alloy of tin with various other ingredients, chiefly copper and lead.

Pity, Our Lady of: the *Pietà*, an image showing Mary grieving over the dead Christ.

platter: flat dish.

porringer (potenger): small basin or similar vessel of metal, earthenware or wood.

posnet: small cooking-pot with a handle and three feet.

pot: cooking-pot, with legs, to stand over fire.

potell: a measure holding 2 quarts (4 pints, i.e. half a gallon). (Yaxley)

power reserved: part of the probate sentence was the grant of **administration** where the executors present in court were named and 'power reserved' to those not present, that is, power was reserved to the court to make grant of administration to the other executor(s) when they came to 'take it up'.

precellyng (175b): pre-eminent, excellent.

priest: cleric ordained to celebrate mass, hear confessions and administer all other sacraments except confirmation and ordination.

prior: head of a priory or friary, or deputy to the abbot in an abbey.

probate: the approval, in an ecclesiastical court by an official appointed for the purpose, of will and/or testament submitted to him by executors; **probate sentence:** the certificate of that approval entered on the will by the clerk to the proving authority, usually including the **administration**.

pyx: small container of metal, ivory or wood to hold the consecrated host, suspended over the altar and covered with a pyx-cloth; occasionally the pyx had an ornate wooden canopy.

quarter: dry measure for grain, etc., of 8 bushels; unit of weight, a quarter of a hundredweight, or 28 pounds.

re-enter; enter: take over property when another party had been holding it.

remain: (as in expression 'to remain to . . .') the route specified by a testator for the eventual descent of estate or interest.

renounce: decline (to act as executor).

reparation: upkeep, maintenance.

residue: remainder of testator's possessions not hitherto disposed of.

reversion: return of estate or property to its ultimate owner(s) after certain specified conditions.

rial (ryall of gold) (241): a gold coin formerly current in England, originally of the value of ten shillings, first issued by Edward IV in 1465; also called rose noble.

rood: the crucifix, either a carving or a picture, with figures of the Virgin Mary and St John the Evangelist, one on each side, which stood on or was suspended above the roodloft

roose of gold (241): perhaps a gold rose, but may be a rose noble (*see* **rial**).

russet: coarse woollen cloth of reddish-brown, grey or neutral colour, formerly used for the dress of peasants and country-folk.

sallet (salet): in medieval armour, a light globular headpiece, either with or without a vizor, and without a crest, the lower part curving outwards behind.

salt: saltcellar (usually silver).

sanctus bell: rung at the elevation of the host in the mass. There was a small bell in the church and a large one in the steeple which was rung at the elevation of the host so that those who could not attend daily mass and were working in the fields or at home could participate by kneeling at the sound of the bell. (Purvis)

saucer: a receptacle, usually of metal, for holding the condiments at a meal; a dish or deep plate in which salt or sauces were placed upon the table.

seal: wax imprint, formed by metal (etc.) stamp, with which a document was authenicated.

seisin (seauson, 174): possession (of land)

seler: (168), a salt-cellar; (248) 'a Seler and a testour', *see* **celure**.

sepulchre: the Easter sepulchre, sepulchre of Our Lord, etc., a structure, either temporary or permanent, on the north side of the chancel. On Good Friday a host (consecrated wafer) was placed in the sepulchre and there remained, with 'watchers' in attendance and decorated with lights and hangings; on Easter Sunday morning the host was removed with great ceremony; the lights, burning night and day, attracted gifts from the devout. (*See* Duffy, pp.29–34.)

shaft (135): the long slender rod forming the body of a lance or spear, or of an arrow; here of arrows, since a bow is mentioned.

shop: usually a 'workshop', but in no. 81, it refers to a mercer's retail shop.

shrine: place to which pilgrims came, to pray to and venerate a saint or other holy person, often incorporating an elaborate tomb.

sir: courtesy title (Latin *dominus*) given to priests not having a master's degree from a university (*see* **Master**); not to be confused with the same title given to a knight, which would be written as Sir.

slough (slowgh): a muddy place or large pothole in a road.

smock (smoke): a woman's undergarment, a shift or chemise.

spit: long iron rod on which meat was roasted over the fire.

stakebote (147): perhaps wood or timber which a tenant is entitled to cut for making and repairing stakes for ?fences (not in *OED*). (*See* **hedgebote**.)

standing cup: a cup with a stem and a foot.

stock: the assets, both possessions and money, of a gild, etc.

stone: unit of weight equivalent to 14 pounds, an eighth of a hundredweight and half a quarter.

stuff: foodstuffs, grain, etc (*MED*); also household stuff.

supervisor: one appointed by a testator to oversee the proper carrying out of the terms of a will by the executors; also called the **overseer**.

surplice (surplus): a loose linen clerical garment, reaching right down to the feet, with very large sleeves cut so that the openings hung down vertically, and ample material gathered in at the neck.

surrender: in feudal tenure, the giving up of his right to hold a bond tenement by a tenant; the surrender was made to the lord, either in the manorial court, or into the hands of other tenants of the manor.

tenement: property held in tenure (*MED*); literally, a holding, often, but not always, implying the inclusion of a dwelling.

testament: the section of a will, normally appearing first, dealing with items other than land.

tester (testour): a canopy over a bed, supported on the posts of the bedstead or suspended from the ceiling; formerly (esp. in phrase tester and celure), the vertical part at the head of the bed which ascends to and sometimes supports the canopy.

thirty-day: the thirtieth day after death or burial, similar to **seventh-day** and **anniversary** (*qv*); often called 'month-mind'.

tilthe (161): crop.

tithes: the tenth of a parishioner's produce or wages for the year due to the rector and/or vicar of a parish. The 'great tithes' (crops such as wheat, oats) went to the rector; 'small tithes' (produce regarded as minor such as lamb, chicken, eggs) went to the rector. In most wills 'tithes forgotten' were reckoned in monetary terms.

title: the right to ownership of property.

torch: the largest of the **lights** of a church, used for illuminating the church and at funerals.

tow: 1) fibre of flax; 2) the number two.

towel: a towel can be an altar-cloth.

trental: set of 30 masses, which could be celebrated over a period of time or all on one day; in a **trental of St Gregory**, the masses had to be celebrated at certain specified festivals. (*See* Duffy, pp.293-4.)

trestle: wooden support, used in pairs, for table-top.

'tripod' of iron (in English) (26): a three-legged vessel; a pot or cauldron resting on three legs (*OED*). (first mentioned 1370, then not again until *c*.1611)

trough(s) (trooves): wooden box-like tub, for kneading, brewing, salting, etc.

tunic: body-garment or coat, over which a loose mantle or cloak was worn.

tunicle (tunycle) (168): an ecclesiastical vestment, with a slit on each side of the skirt, and wide sleeves (*OED*, under 'dalmatic', which a tunicle resembled).

underwoods: low shrubs, undergrowth; cuttings, brushwood (*MED*); the product of periodic coppicing in woodland.

use: purpose, end; benefit, profit, advantage. (*MED*)

utensils: equipment, especially within the house.

vespers: the evening office, or service, of the church.

vestments: special garments worn by the **priest** when celebrating mass.

vestry: room in or adjoining a church in which the vestments and equipment for divine worship were kept).

vicar: incumbent of a church appropriated to a religious house, etc., and therefore entitled to only part of the income of the benefice, usually including the small tithes.

vill: the local unit of civil administration.

virgate (virgat) (26): here used as a linear measure of cloth of 3 feet, i.e. a yard.

warden: one who has something in safe keeping, e.g. churchwarden, guild warden.

waste: the illegal consumption or using up of material, resources, etc.

way: road or track;.

will: correctly, the part of the 'testament and last will' which was concerned with real estate;

wootes (228): oats

wounds: *see* **five wounds**.

yeoman: a substantial farmer (in the modern sense), capable of producing a considerable marketable surplus over and above the needs of his family, usually regularly employing non-family labour.

Bibliography

British Library

Add MS 6057, the court book of Croxley Manor (compiled in the sixteenth century)

Add MS 5834, the court book of Croxley Manor (a nineteenth century copy)

Add MS 9063, fol. 216r, 'Rickmansworth from Mr Whitfield' (the church tower)

Add MS 9063, fol. 217r, 'The Exterior to Rickmansworth Church' (the tower & lychgate and Church Street)

Add MS 9063, fol. 217r, 'Rickmansworth Church & Mr Whitfields House Herts' (the church and The Bury)

C.18.e.2 (96), The Rickmansworth Indulgence (1522)

HALS

ASA/1AR, Register of Wills (1415–1470)

ASA/2AR, Register of Wills (1471–1536)

ASA/3AR, Register of Wills (1536–1557)

ASA/7/2, Archdeaconry act book (1515–1543), fol. 78r, statement by George Belche, 17 May 1533.

ASA/8/1, Archdeaconry deposition book (1515–1543), fol. 54v, deposition of Thomas Spenser, 29 Nov 1532.

ASA/8/1, Archdeaconry deposition book (1515–1543), f.56r, examination of Thomas A Dene, 18 Jan 1532/3.

DE/X976/17/126, List of Rickmansworth incumbents compiled (before 1911) by H. R. Wilton Hall, sub librarian of St Albans Cathedral Library.

DSA4/80/1, Rickmansworth tithe award (1839).

DSA4/80/2, Rickmansworth parish tithe map of 1839

DZ/119/2/202A, Rickmansworth church, by H. W. Bursch (dated 1835 but the old church)

DZ/119/2/202E, 'Rickmersworth church', drawn by Thomas Hearne, engraved by John Pye, c.1815.

DZ/120/7/4/44213, plan of 'Freehold Estate called Woodwick', dated 30 April 1760

London Metropolitan Archives

ACC/0312/106 and 107, two documents concerning an agreement about lands in Harefield between John Ashby and John Newdigate, dated 24 and 25 April 1499

The National Archives

C1/15/344, Revell v Skerne (undated, c.1455–1456)

C1/28/511, Thorp v Bourgchier (undated, 1460–1465)

C1/41/268, Revell v Skerne (undated, 1467–1472)

C1/44/70, Revell v Gower (undated, 1467–1472)

C1/44/235, Richard Whitman v. William Creke (undated, 1433–1443)

C1/222/70, Rokeley v Manery (executor of James Cawood) (undated, 1493–1500)

C1/233/71, Willoughby v Milbourn & Manory (executor of Cawood) (undated, 1493–1500)

C1/593/49–50, Henry Wedon, Henry Evelyn, and Richard Foderley, late churchwardens of Rickmansworth v. Thomas Carter, Gereham Richardson and John Wryght (undated, 1518–1529)

DL29/53/1018, manor of Moor, Rickmansworth, bailiff's accounts, 1474–1476

E179/120/114, 1524 Lay Subsidy returns

E315/497, fol. 7, 1307 Lay Subsidy returns

PROB 11/11/666, will of John Ashby (undated, granted probate 1 July 1499)

PROB 11/18/196, will of George Asshby (made 13 March 1514/15, granted probate 18 September 1515)

Printed primary sources

Appleton, S., and Macdonald, M., eds., *Stratford-upon-Avon Wills 1348-1701: vol. 1, 1348-1647; vol. 2, 1648-1701* (Dugdale Society, vol. 52, 2020).

Bell, P., ed., *Bedfordshire Wills, 1480-1519* (Bedfordshire Historical Record Society, vol. 45, 1966).

Buller, P. & B., eds., *Pots, Platters & Ploughs: Sarratt Wills & Inventories 1435–1832* (Sarratt, 1982).

Calendar of Entries in the Papal Registers relating to Great Britain and Ireland, Papal Letters, 1471–1484, vol. XIII, part II (London, 1955).

Cirket, A. F., ed., *English Wills, 1498–1526* (Bedfordshire Historical Record Society, vol. 37, 1957).

Dymond, D., ed., *The Churchwardens' Book of Bassingbourn, Cambridgeshire, 1496–c.1540* (Cambridgeshire Records Society, vol. 17, 2004).

Flood, S., ed., *St Albans Wills, 1471–1500* (HRS, vol. IX, 1993).

Foxe, J., *Actes and monuments of these latter and perillous dayes touching matters of the Church, wherein ar described the great persecutions ... practised by the Romishe prelates* (1st edition, London, 1563; enlarged and reissued in 1570, 1583 and 1587).

Horrox, R. and Hammond, P. W., eds., *British Library Harleian Manuscript 433*, 3 vols (Stroud, 1979–82).

Keene, D. and Harding, V., eds., *A Survey of Documentary Sources for Property Holding in London before the Great Fire* (London Record Society, vol. 22, 1985).

McGregor, M., *Bedfordshire Wills proved in the PCC, 1383–1548* (Bedfordshire Historical Record Society, vol. 58, 1979).

Morris, J., ed., *Domesday Book: Hertfordshire* (Chichester, 1976).

Munby, L., ed., *Life & Death in Kings Langley 1498–1659* (Kings Langley, 1981).

Munby, L., Parker, M. et al., eds., *All My Worldly Goods, I, An Insight into Family Life from Wills and Inventories 1447–1742* (Bricket Wood, 1991)

Northeast, P., ed., *Wills of the Archdeaconry of Sudbury, 1439–1474: Wills from the Register 'Baldwyne', Part I: 1439–1461* (Suffolk Records Society, vol. 44, 2001).

Northeast, P. and Falvey, H., eds., *Wills of the Archdeaconry of Sudbury, 1439–1474: Wills from the Register 'Baldwyne', Part II: 1461–1474* (Suffolk Records Society, vol. 53, 2010).

Palmer, A., ed., *Tudor Churchwardens' Accounts* (HRS, vol. I, 1985).

Parker, M., ed., *All My Worldly Goods, II, Wills and Probate Inventories of St Stephen's Parish, St Albans, 1418–1700* (Bricket Wood, 2004).

Riley, H. T., ed., *Annales Monasterii S. Albani a Johanne Amundesham, monacho, ut videtur, conscripti (A.D. 1421–1440)*, vols. 1 & 2 (London, 1870–1).

Riley, H. T., ed., *Registra quorundam abbatum monasterii S. Albani: qui sæculo XVmo. floruere*, vol II, *Registra Johannis Whethamstede, Willelmi Albon et Willelmi Walingforde* (London, 1873).

Tymms, S., *Wills and Inventories from the Registers of the Commissary of Bury St Edmunds and the Archdeacon of Sudbury* (Camden Society, xlix, 1850).

Weever, J., *Ancient funerall monuments within the united monarchie of Great Britaine, Ireland, and the islands adiacent* (London, 1631).

Printed secondary sources

Amor, N., *From Wool to Cloth: The triumph of the Suffolk clothier* (Bungay, 2016), chapter 3, 'Wool and the wool trade'.

Aston, M., 'Iconoclasm at Rickmansworth, 1522: troubles of churchwardens', *Journal of Ecclesiastical History*, 40 (1989), pp.524–552.

Bailey, M., 'Introduction', in J. Brooker and S. Flood, eds., *Hertfordshire Lay Subsidy Rolls, 1307 and 1334* (HRS, vol. XIV, 1998).

Bailey, M., *After the Black Death: Economy, society and the law in fourteenth-century England* (Oxford, 2021).

Bennet, R. and Wright, J. E., *Church of the Holy Rood, Watford: a history and description of the church* (Watford, 1989).

Bucklow, S., Marks, R. and Wrapson, L., eds., *The Art and Science of the Church Screen in medieval Europe: Making, meaning, preserving* (Woodbridge, 2017).

Burgess, C., *The Right Ordering of Souls: The parish of All Saints' Bristol on the eve of the Reformation* (Woodbridge, 2018).

Campbell, B. et al., *A Medieval Capital and its Grain Supply: Agrarian production and distribution in the London region c.1300* (London, 1993),

Cheney, C. R., *Handbook of Dates for Students of English History* (London, 1991)

Cornwall, G., 'In parenthesis', *The Rickmansworth Historian*, 34 (Spring 1978), pp.843-847.

Cox, J. and Cox, N., 'Probate 1500-1800: a system in transition', in T. Arkell, N. Evans and N. Goose, eds., *When Death Do Us Part: Understanding and interpreting the probate records of early modern England* (Oxford, 2000), pp.14-37,

Cox, N. and Cox, J., 'Probate inventories: the legal background: part 1', *The Local Historian*, 16 (1984), pp.133-145.

Crawley, B., ed., *Wills at Hertford, 1415–1858* (British Record Society, London, 2007).

Cussans, J. E., *The History of Hertfordshire*, vol. III, *The Hundred of Cashio* (London, 1881).

Dade, R. C. T., *The Church of St Mary the Virgin, Rickmansworth* (Gloucester, c.1941)

Doran, S. and Durston, C., *Princes, Pastors and People: The Church and religion in England, 1500-1700* (2nd edition, London, 2003).

Duffy, E., *The Stripping of the Altars: Traditional Religion in England 1400-1580* (New Haven and London, 1992).

Falvey, H., 'The More: Archbishop George Neville's palace in Rickmansworth, Hertfordshire', *The Ricardian*, vol. IX, no. 118 (September 1992), pp.290-302.

Falvey, H., 'The More: Rickmansworth's lost palace', *Hertfordshire's Past*, 34 (Spring 1993), pp.2-16

Falvey, H., 'William Flete: More than just a castle builder', *The Ricardian*, vol. X, no. 124 (March 1994), pp.2-15.

Falvey, H., 'The More revisited', *The Ricardian*, vol. XVIII (2008), pp. 92-99.

Falvey, H., 'Some members of the household of George Neville, Archbishop of York', *The Ricardian*, vol. XXII (2012), pp.55-58.

Flood, S., 'Introduction' in B. Crawley ed., *Wills at Hertford, 1415–1858* (London, 2007), pp.viii-xv.

Goose, N. and Evans, N., 'Wills as an historical source', in T. Arkell, N. Evans and N. Goose, eds., *When Death Do Us Part: Understanding and interpreting the probate records of early modern England* (Oxford, 2000), pp.38–71.

Goose, N. and Hinde, A., 'Estimating local population sizes at fixed points in time: Part II – specific sources', *Local Population Studies*, 78 (2007) pp.74–88.

Gover, J. E. B., Mawer, A. and Stenton, F. M., eds., *The Place-Names of Hertfordshire* (Cambridge, 1938).

Jacques, A., 'Woodwick – a knight's fee manor', *Rickmansworth Historical Society Newsletter*, 90 (December 2010) pp.3–15.

Jacques, A. and C., *Rickmansworth: A pictorial history* (Chichester, 1996).

Laynesmith, J. L., *Cecily Duchess of York* (London, 2017)

Levett, A. E., *Studies in Manorial History* (Oxford, 1938; reprinted 1963).

Martin, G. D., 'St. Mary the Virgin, Rickmansworth: the Church Plate', part 1 & part 2, *Rickmansworth Historical Review*, 18 (June 2019), pp.22–32 and 19 (October 2019) pp.8–17.

Myers, A. R., *The Household of Edward IV* (Manchester, 1959).

Otway-Ruthven, J., *The King's Secretary and the Signet Office in the XV century* (Cambridge, 1939).

Owen, A. E. B., 'A scrivener's notebook from Bury St Edmunds', *Archives*, xiv, (1979), pp.16–22.

Page, W., ed., *The Victoria History of the Counties of England, A History of Hertfordshire*, 4 vols (London, 1902–1914)

Peters, R., *Oculus Episcopi: administration in the Archdeaconry of St Albans, 1580–1625* (Manchester, 1963).

Purvis, J. S., *Dictionary of Ecclesiastical Terms* (London, 1962).

Reyerson, K. L., 'Wills of spouses in Montpellier before 1350: a case study of gender in testamentary practice', in J, Rollo-Koster and K. L Reyerson, eds., *"For the salvation of my soul": women and wills in medieval and early modern France* (St Andrews, 2012), pp.44–60.

Richardson, J., *The Local Historian's Encyclopedia*, (2nd edn, New Barnet, 1986).

Roberts, E., *The Hill of the Martyr: an architectural history of St Albans Abbey* (Dunstable, 1993).

Sapoznik, A., 'Bees in the medieval economy: Religious observance and the production, trade, and consumption of wax in England, c.1300–1555', *Economic History Review*, 72 (2019), pp.1152–1174.

Sheehan, M. M., 'English wills and the records of ecclesiastical and civil jurisdictions', *Journal of Medieval History*, 14 (1988), pp.3–12.

Sutton, A., 'Mercery through four centuries 1130s–c.1500', *Nottingham Medieval Studies*, 41 (1997), pp.100–125.

Thomson, B., 'Rickmansworth parish – beating the bounds (a bluffer's guide)', (in 3 parts) *Rickmansworth Historical Review*, 9 (June 2016), pp.10–16; 10 (October 2016), pp.11–17; 11 (February 2017), pp.11–17.

Thomson, B., *The lost manor of Snells Hall and Cassiobridge House and its people* (Rickmansworth, 2018).

Trice Martin, C., compiler, *The Record Interpreter* (2nd edn. 1910, reprinted Chichester, 1982).

VCH Buckinghamshire, vol. 3, Chalfont St Peter, pp.193–198 (accessed via British History Online)

VCH Cambridgeshire, vol. 10, Isleham manors, pp.427–437 (as above)

VCH Middlesex, vol. 3, Harefield manors, pp. 240–46 (as above)

Woodward, D., 'The determination of wage rates in the early modem north of England', *Economic History Review*, 2nd ser. XLVII (1994), pp.22–43.

Wrightson, K., *Earthly Necessities: Economic lives in early modern Britain* (New Haven and London, 2000).

Unpublished sources

Falvey, H., 'Rickmansworth and Croxley: a community in south-west Hertfordshire during the mid-sixteenth century' (unpub. Advanced Certificate in English Local History dissertation, UCICE, 1996).

Samman, N., 'The Henrician Court during Cardinal Wolsey's ascendancy, c.1514–1529' (unpub. PhD thesis, University of Wales, 1989).

Index of People

Testators and the page number of their will are in bold; if there is another person of the same name on that page, the page number also appears in normal font.

No surname

Agnes, 43, 67, 82

Alianor, 82

Alice, 15, 16, 27, 36, 45

Edward, 45, 167

Elyn, 152, 152n

George, 90

Henry, 3, 56, 78

James, 167

Joan (Johan), 32, 143

John, 28, 45, 89, 130, 166

Joyse, 152

Julian, 44

Katherine, 15, 16, 38

Lettice, 4, 45

Marg', 18

Paul, 23

Peter, 25

Richard, 164, 165

Thomas, 18, 20, 21, 56, 166

Walter, 15, 16

William, 15, 17, 24, 43, 165

Yele, 49

A Dale, John, 119, 123, 126, 128, 132, 137, 139, 152, 164; Robert, 139

A Dene (Adene), Anne, 126; Alice, 146; Emme, 126; George, 146; Harry 96; Joan (Jone), 126; **John**, xxxiv, xlviii, 96, 100, 101, 109, 112, 116, 117, 118, 119, 120, 123, 125, 131, 137, **145**, 163; **Margaret**, lxiii, **95**; Thomas, xxiv, 145, 146, 164

A Lane, Robert, 165

Abelle, Alice, 45

Adall, Robert, 88

Adam, Alice, 47, 48; Julian, 47, 48; **Roger**, xlii, xliii, xliv, lvii, 28, 33, 40, **47**, **48**, 49

Aignel, John, 162

Albon, John, archdeacon, 116, 117, 118, 119, 120, 170; William, archdeacon, 23, 26n, 170

Ald(e)wyn (Aldewen), Ann, 81; Cecily, 111; Edmund, 147, 167; Robert, 81; Roger, 81; **Thomas, 81**, **111**; William, 81

Alen (Alyn), Joan, 153; **John**, lv, 121, 146, **153**, 166

Alexander (Alisaunder), John, 138

Alme, Ralph, 161

Alnewyke, William, archdeacon, lii, 4, 5, 6, 7, 170

Ampthyll, Henry, commissary, 130, 171

Andytor, *see* Audytor

Arnewy, William, 26, 27

Arnolde, John, 9

Arstock, Peter, xxxviii, xliv, **52**

Ashby (Assh(e)by), **Anne**, xxii, xxiii, xxv, 101, 101n, 103, 104, **125**, 126; George, xlv, lxiv, 101, 103, 104, 126; **John**, xxii, xlv, liii, liv, lvii, lviii, lxi, lxiv, lxvi, 86n, 92, **101**, **102**, 125n; Thomas, lxiv; William, 126

Asshele, Robert de, 162

Asshley, [*no name; ?place*], 154

Astwode, sir Richard, 8

ate Crouch, John, 161

ate Delle, William, 162

atte Dene, Henry, 161; Margaret, 61; Walter, 61

ate Fern, William, 161

Martok, *see* Mertok

Martyn (Marten, Martin), Alice, 154;
Isabel, 60; John, 167; Katherine, 60;
Richard, 110, 153, 167; Thomas, 167;
William, 60

Maskell, John, 82

May, William, 97

Maynard, John, archdeacon, 120, 121,
170

Mees, Thomas, xxx, 26

Mels(h)am, Alice, 150; John, 76;
Thomas, 150

Mendance, Robert, xxxvi

Merchaunt, Robert, 28

Mertok (Martok), Agnes, 69; Alice, 70;
George, 70; Hugh, 70; **John**, xxxi, xliv,
xlviii, lxv, 56, 62, 66, 67, **69**, 69;
Margaret, xlviii, 66, 67, 70

Meryweder, **Agnes, 57**; John, 5

Metca(l)f(e), Cecily, 118; **Edward**, xxii,
xxiii, 92, 113, 116, **118**; Jone (Joan),
118; Richard, 118

Michaell (Michel(l)), Joan, 117; **Roger**,
109, 114, **117**

Mikelfeld, Thomas de, 162

Miller (Myller), Joan, 44; Richard, 134;
William, 80, 164

Milward (Mylward), John, xxv, 117, 123,
146, 147, 163

Mole, Johan (Joan), 114

Monant, Robert, xxxvi

Monke, John, 148

Morden, James, xxix

More, Agnes, 100; **Christian, 100**;
Margaret, 100; Roger, 63 (*see also* ate
More)

Morel, Alan, 161

Moyer, John, 165

Musterd, William, 79

Myles, William, 46

Mylsham, Reygnold, 163; Thomas, 118,
164

Myller, *see* Miller

Mylward, *see* Milward

Neville, Cecily, xliv; George, Archbishop,
xl, xliii, xliv, 47, 47n, 48

Nevyle (Nevile, Nevyll, Nevill, Nevell),
Marion, 89; **Richard**, 56, 59, 79, 85, **89**

Newbury, John, 67; Richard, 66

Newdigate, John, 102n

Newell, Elizabeth, xxxviii, lii, liv, lvii, **91**;
John, xxxviii, lii, liv, lvii, **91**

Newlond(e), Thomas, archdeacon, 75, 92,
93, 170

Newman, Robert, 80

Newnham, master Thomas, 149, 171

Newton, Ann, lviii, **81**; William, 81

Norbury, Master Robert, 160, 160n

Nores (Norrys), John, 150, 167

Norton, William, 138

Of the felde, Thomas, 14

Offa, king, xxxiii

Osborne, (Osbern(e)), Anne, xlvi, xlvii;
Emma, 105; George, 105; Johan, 125;
Robert, xlvi

Osemund, John, 162

Over (Ovir) Lettice, xli, 83; **Richard**, xli,
83; Robert, 83, 93, 115; William, xli, 83

Palmer, Robert, 125

Paltok(e), Henry, 113; Roger, 87;
Thomas, 167

Panter, Cecily, 23; Elyn, 124; George,
124; **Henry (Herry),** xxv, xxxi n, **23**,
124; Margaret, 124

Parmer, John, 157, 158

Parsun, William, 161

Paterson, Cutberd, 96; Jone, 99

Pecoke, John, 86

Penner, Richard, 109

Peper, Elisabeth, 149; Sibill, 149

Index of places

Places within Rickmansworth parish are listed first, then places outside the parish.

Index of places

Index of subjects

Subjects organised under these topics: Animals; Arms & armour; Buildings, property &
rooms; Church services & activities; Clothing; Courts; Crafts, trades & goods; Crops &
produce; Farming, lands, manorial matters & tenants; Household items: beds & bedding;
Household items: furniture & other items; Jewellery & coins; Probate, other documents &
legal matters; Status or occupation: churchmen etc; Status or occupation: other; St Mary's.

Jewellery & coins